KU-786-641

Olivia Manning: A Life

OLIVIA MANNING:
A LIFE

NEVILLE AND JUNE
BRAYBROOKE

Chatto & Windus
LONDON

Published by Chatto & Windus 2004

2 4 6 8 10 9 7 5 3 1

Copyright © Victoria Orr-Ewing 2004

Victoria Orr-Ewing has asserted her right under the Copyright, Designs
and Patents Act 1988 to be identified as the author of this work

This book is sold subject to the condition that it shall not,
by way of trade or otherwise, be lent, resold, hired out,
or otherwise circulated without the publisher's prior
consent in any form of binding or cover other than that
in which it is published and without a similar condition
including this condition being imposed on the
subsequent purchaser

First published in Great Britain in 2004 by
Chatto & Windus
Random House, 20 Vauxhall Bridge Road,
London SW1V 2SA

Random House Australia (Pty) Limited
20 Alfred Street, Milsons Point, Sydney,
New South Wales 2061, Australia

Random House New Zealand Limited
18 Poland Road, Glenfield,
Auckland 10, New Zealand

Random House (Pty) Limited
Endulini, 5A Jubilee Road, Parktown 2193, South Africa

The Random House Group Limited Reg. No. 954009
www.randomhouse.co.uk

A CIP catalogue record for this book
is available from the British Library

ISBN 0 7011 7749 7

Papers used by Random House are natural,
recyclable products made from wood grown in sustainable forests;
the manufacturing processes conform to the environmental
regulations of the country of origin

Printed and bound in Great Britain by
Clays Ltd, St Ives PLC

90300000

634642

823.914
MANN

Contents

List of Illustrations

26. Ivy Compton-Burnett at the same party, 1960. © *Keystone Press Agency Ltd*
27. Jerry Slattery, Christmas 1968, talking to June and Neville Braybrooke.
28. Olivia and Reggie.

Francis King, Victoria Orr-Ewing and the publishers are very grateful to Diana Hogarth for her help in tracking down illustrations.

The publishers have made every effort to trace holders of copyright. Should there be inadvertent omissions or errors, these can be corrected in future editions.

Halloo your name to the reverberate hills
And make the babbling gossip of the air
Cry out 'Olivia'.

Twelfth Night Act I, Scene 5

To Michael and Parvin Laurence
with undiminished love

Publications by Olivia Manning

Fiction

The Wind Changes	1937
Growing Up	1948
Artist Among the Missing	1949
School for Love	1951
A Different Face	1953
The Doves of Venus	1955

The Balkan Trilogy

The Great Fortune	1960
The Spoilt City	1962
Friends and Heroes	1965
A Romantic Hero and other stories	1967
The Play Room	1969
The Rain Forest	1974

The Levant Trilogy

The Danger Tree	1977
The Battle Lost and Won	1978
The Sum of Things	1980

Non-Fiction

The Remarkable Expedition	1947
The Dreaming Shore	1950
My Husband Cartwright	1956
Extraordinary Cats	1967

Editor's Note

Wordsworth's phrase about 'the heart that watches and receives' has always seemed to me to be a perfect summation of the lives of June and Neville Braybrooke. For them, observation and reflection all too often took precedence over day-to-day doing. The consequence was a spiritual enrichment, apparent to all those who knew them well. But any significant financial enrichment always eluded them. They were extraordinarily generous with their time whenever any friend or acquaintance, however undeserving, faced a problem, a disappointment or a disaster. But to their work they brought little of the same sense of urgency.

Under the pseudonym Isobel English, June produced some highly distinguished short stories and novels. But regrettably the intervals between their production became longer and longer. As J. R. Ackerley's literary editor, I was delighted when Neville proposed that he should edit the Ackerley letters. But both the commissioning publisher, my cousin Colin Haycraft of Duckworth, and I became increasingly impatient as year succeeded year. In a moment of exasperation I protested, 'But, Neville, you're not *writing* the letters!' However, when the book was at long last delivered, Haycraft and I agreed that no one could have performed the task better.

It was a similar story with this biography. More than a decade has passed since Carmen Callil first commissioned it for Chatto & Windus. Deadlines were repeatedly reset and then overrun. Finally, when Neville was approaching the conclusion of his task, he began to suffer symptoms that I at once recognised as similar to those that, many years ago, had led to the diagnosis that I was suffering from cancer. I begged Neville to have his condition investigated as speedily as possible, but he told me that he was determined to finish the book first. Whether he would still be alive if he had not made that decision it is impossible to say.

Not long before his death he asked me if I would be prepared to get the book into final shape if he were not able to do so himself. I immediately agreed. After his death I found that he had finished all the writing but had clearly not had either the time or, in his ailing state, the energy to make a final revision. There were numerous repetitions, paragraphs clearly misplaced, hiatuses where a name, a date, a quotation or the title of a book had been omitted, and some roughnesses of writing. He had not lived long enough to provide any notes of sources.

In attempting to remedy all but the last of these things – no indication of sources, other than in the text itself, have so far come to light – I am most grateful to have had the invaluable assistance of June's daughter (Neville's stepdaughter) Victoria Orr-Ewing and of Victoria's former husband Brian Rooney, a publisher and editor. Sadly, Brian died while working on the text.

I should like to express my gratitude for her help to Dr Eve Patten of the School of English, Trinity College, Dublin, an expert on Olivia Manning's work.

I am grateful to all those who are quoted in these pages. Any inadvertent errors or omissions may be corrected in future editions, should the holders of the copyright contact the publishers.

Francis King,
London, 2004.

Preface

On the last Monday of March 1994 my wife June, who wrote under the name of Isobel English, and I had worked as usual on this biography. But the next morning, when mysterious black spots suddenly began to appear on June's tongue and her cheeks, I called our doctor. He decided that she should have an immediate blood test at the local hospital in the Isle of Wight. When she returned, she was so weak that she had to be carried upstairs to her room. Later, the doctor rang to say that tests had revealed, beyond almost all doubt, that she had leukaemia and that the hospital had arranged for an urgent blood transfusion for the next morning. Over the Easter Bank Holiday there were further medical consultations, after which Parvin and Michael Laurence agreed to drive her up to London to see a specialist. The Laurences were our devoted friends and Michael was a well-known orthopaedic surgeon.

June then started treatment at the Royal Free Hospital in Hampstead. For the first month of her stay there our hopes – and, it seemed, also those of the staff – ran high. Soon, we were assured, she would be sent home for the weekend, or possibly longer. 'Then I shall be able to see all my friends again,' she said. Sadly, that was not to be. June died on 30 May of that year.

Our method when we were writing this book was that I should provide a rough draft in the morning, which we would read through together after lunch. June would then often alter words and sentences and add new paragraphs. In the evening I would type out the day's work. We did not always work chronologically, because of an incident in March 1993 when I went up to London for a day. At Waterloo Station all passengers had to go through a security check, after information, later revealed as a hoax, had been received that the IRA had planted a bomb. When I got back and told June of this occurrence she said, 'Suppose a bomb had exploded and you had been killed? What would have happened to the book?' We then decided that we must jump forward to the last chapter and write it there and then. As June said, 'We have so much information about what happened after Olivia's death that we must set it down for posterity. Fewer than half a dozen people know all the real facts – and Reggie is dead.' R. D. Smith, known as Reggie, was Olivia's husband. The chapter ran to 10,000 words and took six months to write.

It was in 1956 that we had first met Olivia. Subsequently we received over 300 letters from her. When we were living in London, hardly a week went by when Olivia and June did not have lunch together. With her and Reggie, we spent holidays at Fowey, Venice and Cowes. When Olivia died in 1980, Virago Press approached Reggie about reprinting some of her novels and he then chose June to write the introductions to them. The novels were *The Wind Changes, The Doves of Venus* and *The Play Room*. June was also to write the entry for Olivia Manning in the *Oxford Companion to Twentieth-Century Literature in English* (1996).

After Reggie's death in 1985, Jim Hepburn was invited to discuss with Carmen Callil of Chatto & Windus a possible biography of his mother, the poet Anna Wickham, a selection of whose writings Reggie had edited in 1984. In the course of conversation Jim had said, 'I know the very people you should approach if you want a biography of Olivia Manning.' Francis King – whom Olivia had appointed, along with Reggie and myself, as one of her three literary executors – welcomed the idea with enthusiasm and the three of us then had a meeting with Carmen Callil. That was how the book came into being.

June took with her into the Royal Free Hospital a copy of the paperback edition of Olivia's *A Romantic Hero and Other Stories*, which had been first published in 1967. Sometimes she would read out brief passages to doctors and nursing staff, when they could pause for a moment or two from their duties. 'What a writer your friend was!' a registrar, with a passion for books, exclaimed when June had read to him from 'The Children':

> The pebbles on the beach were shaped like gulls' eggs. Most of them were white. Those that were chipped showed the inner flint like glass.

Even when my wife had begun to sink, I remained optimistic. On her last morning, at four – I was then spending the nights in the hospital – she awoke to ask me to read her some poems from a volume by Herrick that she had chosen for my birthday present. She died peacefully that afternoon.

For the rest of that year, and for the first half of 1995, I was able to write little more than an odd article or book review, and a poem about her death. Then in July I began to think about our biography and opened the cardboard box in which our manuscript lay. I read it through and felt that the time had come to start work on it once more.

Before our marriage – and about a year after my wife's first novel, *The Key that Rusts*, appeared – June had once said to me at the entrance to the lifts at Hampstead Underground station, 'A writer should say every morning – Let the Light shine through me.' We tried to keep to that precept.

While bringing this book to its completion, I have never felt that I was working alone. Sometimes I have found myself looking up and waving. The veil between this world and the next is thinner than is often supposed and I believe that our book continued to be a joint venture. I set this down for the record.

Neville Braybrooke,
Cowes,
2001.

Chapter 1

A Literary Kick-Off

On 2 March 1935, Olivia Manning was walking along the Cromwell Road in South Kensington, London with her friend Celia Jordan. At the time both girls were working in the furniture restoration department of Peter Jones, which they nicknamed 'the faking factory'. At Peter Jones they learnt the art of how to transform undecorated furniture into Regency chairs or tables, or whatever other style a customer might require. Olivia Manning described the process of 'antiquing' in her novel *The Doves of Venus*. What she does not mention, but something which she also taught herself, was the art of touching up a picture and (if necessary) adding a signature to it. 'Would you like me to paint in Boudin's signature?' she once asked June Braybrooke, who had just bought a nineteenth-century seascape in an antique shop in Cowes. 'I could easily have made my fortune as a forger if I hadn't wanted to be a writer.' She made a similar offer to Francis King when he showed her a small picture that he had recently bought – 'It could be a Constable. Shall I sign it for you?'

During that particular walk along the Cromwell Road, Olivia had suddenly turned to Celia and announced, 'Do you know, I am twenty-one today.' She was in fact twenty-seven. In January 1935 she had written an autobiographical sketch of a visit to a dentist in which she remarked, 'And she was getting old: every second older, older.' The story was entitled 'A Change of Mood' and appeared under the name of Olivia Manning in the April–May issue of *New Stories*. When Olivia received her three complimentary copies, she proudly presented one to Celia, saying, 'Here is my first published story.'

This was not true either, because another story of hers, 'A Scantling of Foxes', had been published in the same magazine in the previous year. There had, too, been several other stories and serials, about which she was to keep quiet until well into her fifties. These serials had come out under the name of Jacob Morrow and had been published in her late twenties. She kept tucked away in a drawer until the end of her life a letter of acceptance from the London Agency, offering her a generous fee of twenty-five guineas* in 1929. It was addressed to Jacob Morrow Esq. Morrow was her mother's maiden name and the Jacob came from a recent reading of *Jacob's Room* by Virginia Woolf.

Olivia's parents never owned any other house than 134 Laburnum Grove, at North End in Portsmouth. It was their first home and they both died there. In Olivia Manning's novel *The Play Room*, Laburnum Grove appears as 'Rowantree Avenue' and is described as being 'the dreariest and longest road in Camperlea'. 'Camperlea' is the author's name for North End. Laburnum Grove, which was conveniently near the Royal Dockyard, came to be occupied mainly by the families of petty officers and was referred to locally as 'Brass Button Alley'.

Both children of the Mannings were born at home: Olivia in 1908 and her brother Oliver in 1913. On each occasion a fire was lit in the upstairs bedroom. It was a cold and draughty house – according to Olivia. The doctor attending Mrs Manning at each birth was Dr Weston – the model for Dr Watson in the Sherlock Holmes stories by Conan Doyle. 'You might say I had a literary kick-off,' was Olivia's comment when she learnt this many years later.

The Play Room was published in 1969, when Olivia already had a dozen books behind her. In spite of this, when the *Observer* ran a profile by Ruth Inglis, it was headed 'WHO IS OLIVIA MANNING?' Early in the course of her piece Ruth Inglis recorded a fairly common reaction: 'The name rings a bell, but I haven't read her.' When Olivia relayed this to her novelist mentor, friend and possible lover William Gerhardie, he sympathised with her and confided, 'I wanted my publishers to put on my Collected Edition some words by E. M. Forster: "I have not read him, but I am told he is very good."'

Olivia had high expectations for *The Play Room* and believed that it might become a best-seller. A film of it was three-quarters made by Ken Annakin, but then the money ran out and no further backers could be found. Olivia was disappointed but stoical: 'At least it got me on *Desert*

---

* About £1,125 in today's currency.

Island Discs.' But, despite that publicity, the sale of her novel was no greater than that of any other of her past books – causing her to write to Francis King, 'I had hopes that *The Play Room* might be a selling book, but it was much as the others, so I might as well stop trying to sell.' Ten years later she suggested adapting it for television, but no one showed much interest in the project.

After *The Play Room* there followed *The Rain Forest* in 1974 – her most imaginative novel and also a prophetic one with its forecast of AIDS. She was saddened to find it placed only second in the *Sunday Times* column devoted to fiction and wrote for commiseration to Anthony Powell, who was always supportive of her. She began to think of leaving Heinemann, with whom she had been since 1946 – and in the end she did so. What rankled with her was that she never got a solo review in a Sunday paper. Sadly, it was to be the same story when she moved to Weidenfeld & Nicolson. Until her last novel, which appeared posthumously, no solo reviews came her way in the Sunday papers. Nor was she ever awarded a major literary prize such as the Booker or Whitbread, or even shortlisted for one.

During her career she did several stints of reviewing novels for the *Observer*, the *Spectator* and the *Sunday Times*. In 1978, two years before her death, she had high hopes that she might be taken on by the *Sunday Telegraph*, for which she had written the occasional non-fiction review. The final verdict went against her and a young woman reviewer was appointed: 'I seem constantly challenged by sixth formers,' she said bitterly.

Olivia did not react lightly to any adverse criticism, so that she felt doubly attacked when she learnt that a hostile review in the *Daily Telegraph* by Martyn Goff had been syndicated to an Australian paper. She never forgot Maurice Capitanchik's 1969 multiple review of novels in the *Spectator*, placing her bottom of his column. It had begun, 'Last but by all means least . . .'

Friends rallied round. Anthony Burgess said to her, 'You are the most considerable of our women novelists – and that's a "quote", if you want it.' (Heinemann were to use it regularly for ten years.) Neville Braybrooke passed on to her how T. S. Eliot had told him in 1951 that the book he was proudest of having published at Faber was Djuna Barnes's novel *Nightwood* – then had added, 'Do you know it was never even mentioned by the Sunday papers?' Francis King reminded Olivia that J. R. Ackerley's novel *We Think the World of You*, which won the W. H. Smith Prize in 1961, had originally been placed fourth by Kingsley Amis in the *Observer* fiction column.

But, understandably, Olivia would repeat, 'I don't want fame when I am dead. I want it *now*.'

Chapter 2

The Sailor Father

Olivia's father, who was in the Royal Navy, was called Oliver, after Cromwell. He was born in Clerkenwell on 21 April 1859, the last child of a family of eleven boys. Their father was a house painter by trade; but when he was drunk he would bang his fists on the table and claim to be the bastard son of the Earl of Warwick. Olivia inherited this gift of fantasy: 'I was always in trouble at school for making romantic claims.' He was fifty years old when Olivia was born and seemed to her to be more like a grandfather than a father. As she explained in an article about him in *The Times* in 1975, 'He did not merely belong to another generation, he belonged to history.'

Oliver had been in his teens when his great hero Henry Morton Stanley died and was still a youngish man when Queen Victoria celebrated her Golden Jubilee in 1887. He had seen the head of his best friend cut off, during a sabre charge at the battle of Tel-el-Kebir in which he had taken part in 1892. He had served for a period on the royal yacht *Britannia* and once been mistaken for the King. When Olivia recounted this to Kay Dick in 1963, she said that the King in question was Edward VII; but when she came to repeat the story a decade later in *The Times*, she insisted that it was George V. Always reluctant to reveal her true age, she was worried that people might think that she had been born during the Edwardian era. In each account she describes her father as 'a very handsome, bearded man'.

On 13 May 1960, when the *Radio Times* carried a photograph of Augustus John on the cover, a cousin of Olivia's in Ulster cut out the picture and sent it to her, writing across the bottom 'So like your dear Father'. This was found in Olivia's desk after her death.

Olivia, who kept several photographs of her father, kept none of her mother. 'She was a strange woman, not a happy one,' she confided to Kay Dick.

When Oliver Manning had married Olivia's mother he was a widower. His ship had called in at Belfast and he had fallen for her at a dance. She was lively and had dark good looks. Within less than a month their marriage took place at the Presbyterian church in Bangor on 28 December 1904.

In his twenties he had been married to a red-haired girl called Phoebe, but after a year of happy marriage she had died in childbirth and so had the baby. Some quarter of a century was to pass before he married again. During these years he was known as 'The Merry Widower' by his shipmates. He was a man of ready charm and a skilful dancer: he knew by heart all the leading roles in the Gilbert and Sullivan operas, and had played most of them in amateur productions at home or overseas.

When Oliver had been ten years old, his eldest brother George arranged for him to have an audition at a Clerkenwell theatre. George was convinced that his brother could make a fortune on the halls. However, when the day arrived, Oliver was paralysed with fright and another profession had to be found for him. This turned out to be the Royal Navy.

Olivia never remembered her father's hair being anything but white. In China, in 1900, the Boxers, abetted by the Empress Dowager, had decided to rid the country of foreigners. The German Minister was murdered and missionaries were executed without trial or mercy. The Royal Navy then sent in a raiding party, some of whom reached Peking, a hundred miles inland. The raiding party, led by Olivia's father, was at one period trapped in a cellar and it was here (he maintained many years later) that he contracted the typhoid fever that nearly cost him his life. His ship, HMS *Venus,* had to sail home without him. Nursed back to health by the nuns at a local convent, he found that his hair had turned white during his illness. After the Boxers had been defeated, the Western Powers exacted heavy penalties from their enemy. 'And correctly so,' was the Commander's reaction. He believed implicitly in the Empire and that British foreign policy was always right. He was 'a terrible old Tory', Olivia used to say, and a royalist through and through.

Oliver had never been to school and had spent most of his early years running errands around Clerkenwell, for which he earned a halfpenny a time. He taught himself to read by studying the music hall posters pasted up on hoardings and walls. His mother had died of consumption when he was four. His only memory of her was of one Guy Fawkes Night when she had been lifted out of bed and helped to the window to watch her sons dancing round the bonfire in the garden below. 'A face at the window' was how he recalled the scene: often he came up with such a literary turn of phrase. After her death, the family had split up and Oliver had gone to live with George. By the end of the century all his brothers had died of consumption.

Training ships on the Thames for the Royal Navy resembled, in some respects, the prison hulks described by Dickens in *Great Expectations*. To escape from them was impossible. If they were moored alongside the river embankment, there was a sentry posted to prevent any trainee from making a run for it. But to the street boys – like Oliver – the ship represented a haven of security: it offered food, warmth and clothes as well as rudimentary lessons in seamanship. Often it was a case of learning the hard way. Oliver could remember being chased up the rigging with a knotted rope on dark winter mornings. Frequently frost glistened on the rungs. Once, when some of the boys had been sent up the mast to dress the ship overall for a royal visit and the visitors had stayed an unexpectedly long time, two of his shipmates had fainted and plummeted to their deaths on the deck below.

Later, when Oliver was promoted to the rank of First Class Boy, he was sent on HMS *Impregnable* to the West Indies. The appointment was for seven years, but this was extended to fourteen. Oliver did not return to England until the 1880s. In those days the rise from rating to commissioned officer was a slow one. Oliver Manning was promoted to Gunner in 1892, aged thirty-three; to Chief Gunner in 1911, aged fifty-two; and early in 1914, aged fifty-five, he retired as lieutenant.

When war was declared in August 1914, he volunteered to serve again and was given a job, on patrol boats, in inland waters. By the time he retired finally and for the second time in 1924, he had become a lieutenant-commander.

He served on many ships, starting with HMS *Impregnable* (one of the first 'ironclads'), *Venus, Diadem, Imperieuse, Andromache, Northampton* and *Powerful*. Once he challenged Olivia to compose a poem containing all these names. 'Kipling could have done it,' he told her and a moment later he came out with a string of further ones: *Squirrel, Lerwick, Swift, Bustard* and *Pembroke*.

On the dresser in the dining room at his home there was a collection of

pewter mugs and silver cups. In the middle of the last century his family
had had connections with a pewter factory in Clerkenwell and the owner
of the factory had had Oliver's name engraved on a pewter mug to
celebrate his twenty-first birthday.* Sadly, Olivia was to lose her father's
twenty-first birthday mug when she moved from a flat in Baker Street to
a house in St John's Wood in 1954. But the silver cup that he had won, for
being the best shot on HMS *Diamond* from 1881 to 1884, she managed to
hang on to. She also possessed a silver napkin ring with the names
engraved on it of some of the ships on which he had served. Shortly before
his death, when he was over ninety, Olivia asked him if he could
remember the names of the other ships on which he had served. She then
had these added. The napkin ring had originally been a present to him
from a close friend, who had had inscribed on it 'To a Jolly Good Fellow'.

Surviving neighbours at Laburnum Grove in Portsmouth reminisced to
the Braybrookes about the Commander. He was a womaniser, they all
recorded. 'He was always a very dapper man,' said Doreen Buston, 'with
a well-cut suit and smart trilby.' Another neighbour said, 'He was rather
short when you stood next to him, but at a distance he gave an impression
of height. He could be very amusing.' Mrs Long, who lived on the
opposite side of the street, remembers his affection for little dogs, of which
he owned several over the years. 'It was one way of making friends with
the ladies. Quite often he would let them off the lead – if he spied a pretty
face coming towards him.'

   During the General Strike of 1926, over 3000 volunteers came forward
in Portsmouth to run the local services. Among them was Commander
Manning, who had hurried down to the Town Hall to find out of what
assistance he could be. He was asked, 'Can you take a boat across the
harbour?' He replied, 'Yes, or round the world if you like.'

   Olivia and her younger brother doted on their father. 'When you saw
them all out together,' said Mrs Parkinson, a retired schoolteacher who
lived close by, 'they always seemed to be laughing.' Olivia herself, recalling

---

* 'Pewter' was to become a favourite word of Olivia's when she wished to describe
stretches of grey water, or an overcast sky. In her first novel, *The Wind Changes*, the
countryside is said to be covered with 'pewter-grey ice'; in the second volume of the
Balkan Trilogy, a lake is said to be 'pewter-dark'; and in *A Different Face* there is a
reference to 'the last pewter bleakness of the dusk above Coldmouth' (alias
Portsmouth).

those far-off days when they had enjoyed visits to the Royal Dockyard Museum or picnics on Portsmouth Hill, described the three of them as 'happy children'. But they were children whose life at home was often marred by a nagging mother: 'My father had a tremendous sense of humour and my mother had absolutely none.'

Chapter 3

Her Mother

Olivia's mother, who was always a pretty woman, never lost her County Down accent. She had been born in 1873 in Bangor, a predominantly Protestant seaside town a few miles from Belfast. She was fourteen years younger than her husband. When their first child was born in 1908 in Portsmouth she was thirty-five years old.

Her name was Olivia. For some unknown reason Oliver and Olivia, as parents, called their two children Olivia and Oliver.

Mrs Manning is remembered by Christine Davis, a young friend of Olivia's at Portsmouth, as a high-spirited woman, who wore long dangling earrings. 'When I was at school I was fascinated by them and wanted to own some like them.' Kathleen, another school friend of Olivia's, can recall how at one of Olivia's birthday parties she carelessly spilt a glass of lemonade over her frock, and Olivia's mother rushed her upstairs to wash it and dry it out: 'She was a very practical and kind-hearted lady.'

Most of the neighbours, though, agreed that Mrs Manning was a bossy woman, who dominated her family and henpecked her husband. Her daughter was to point out that there was a duality in her nature: 'My mother regarded men as superior beings, but insisted that it was a woman's duty to rule them.' She was, it appears, a person riddled with prejudices. When she referred to her husband's first wife Phoebe, whom she had never seen, she would remark critically, 'You know she had all this red hair' – red hair in her book being an indication of being a bad lot.

Olivia's mother was one of ten children who had been brought up as strict Presbyterians. When she married she was totally opposed to keeping alcohol in the house – except at Christmas or for medicinal purposes. But occasionally, on a red-letter day such as a birthday or an anniversary, she would give in and drink a glass of sherry. Her face would then grow bright pink and she would say, 'That wine has taken my head.' Nor was Mrs Manning an enthusiast for card games, as her husband was. She would grudgingly admit, 'I suppose you can say that at least they do no harm.'

Her father, David Morrow, had been a successful publican. When he died in November 1910, all the shops in Bangor put up their shutters and closed down for the day. Mrs Manning had disagreeable memories of drunken men staggering from the family pub and throwing up in the gutter. David Morrow was something of an authoritarian bully, especially in his relationship with his wife, Mazoura MacShane. In a codicil, which was later attached to his will, he wrote that he was reducing Mazoura's inheritance because of 'very unsatisfactory behaviour' known only to himself. Some people speculated that this might refer to sexual mis-demeanours. The truth was that she was always prepared to stand up to her husband and tell him off if he was in the wrong – which was something he found intolerable.

Mazoura was an American by birth. Her father had been a prosperous slave owner, living on the banks of the Mississippi. He had called her Mazoura after the river. At the age of sixteen she had married David Morrow, who was only a few years older than herself and who had travelled steerage to the New World to try to make his fortune. He was described by his friends as a very powerful-looking man, with more than a streak of adventurer in him. Shortly after he and Mazoura were married in America, he took her back to his home in Northern Ireland – a place in which she always felt an exile, according to her granddaughter Olivia. This is perhaps not surprising, since Mazoura believed that she had sunk in the world: the one-time daughter of a rich slave owner, she was now merely the wife of a jumped-up peasant. Olivia's mother would not have disagreed with this verdict, for the picture that remained uppermost in Olivia's mind of her grandmother was of 'an old peasant woman, crouched over a peat fire, smoking a clay-pipe'.

Among her papers, Olivia's mother kept a joint letter that her father, in his best copperplate handwriting, had sent her and her husband, shortly before Gunner Manning embarked on a period of service in Australia in 1910. In this letter he wished his son-in-law 'every success in his career in the Antipodes', and expressed the hope that on his return home he would find his wife in good health and his baby daughter Olivia 'a well-mannered little maid'.

In a paragraph specially intended for the baby's mother he offered her two bits of advice: 'first that it would not come amiss if she sang this lullaby to her child:

> Dance to your Mammy, my bonny babe,
> Dance to your Mammy, my bonny wean,
> For a good ship will come from England's shore
> To bring your Daddy home again.'

Secondly, he admonished her to heed the proverb 'If trouble comes, slam the door in its face'.

At the Old House and Home, the pub which he owned and ran in Ballymagee Street, he had the reputation of being a bit of a philosopher landlord. The *County Down Spectator* in its obituary noted that for a short time he had been a schoolteacher in Dundonald and later an enthusiastic member of the local Masonic Order. He did not believe in Sunday opening. He was sixty-five when he died.

When Mazoura used to come and stay with her daughter in Portsmouth, she enjoyed visiting the salesrooms and auction houses. Nor was she nervous about making bids. On one occasion she boasted of how she had bought a sewing machine for practically nothing, but discovered too late that its needle was broken. This would have been unimportant had it not been that it was of German origin and Britain was then at war with Germany. After the Armistice, Mazoura tried to trace the manufacturers, only to discover that they had gone out of business. So the Commander pushed the machine under the stairs. In the late 1920s, during one of his periodic clear-outs, he presented the machine to the local Conservative Association, of which he was an active member. Their Ladies Branch tried to purchase a needle that would fit the machine – but were unsuccessful. Eventually it was sent to a museum, where it was exhibited under a label which read 'An Early Middle Period Example of a Sewing-Machine'.

When Oliver Manning and his wife moved into 134 Laburnum Grove, they were the first occupants of the house, which was gaslit. In the entrance hall there were plaster cherubs decorating the cornices and acanthus leaves round the central light. 'I got rid of the lot,' said Peter McKenna, who bought the house after Mrs Manning's death in 1954. 'They were absolute dust traps.' June Braybrooke asked if he had made any alterations to the house since moving in. 'Well, I put in a bathroom on the first floor and I scrapped the outside lavatory. There was no heating of course upstairs in those early days, except for open fires in the bedrooms if one was ill.' June remembered how Olivia had told her that when she was young and went upstairs in the winter to write she used to wear mittens.

'When we first saw this house', said McKenna, 'we were informed by the agent that the last owner – Mrs Manning – had been a lady who collected a great many ornaments.' This was something that Olivia remembered about her home: 'You weren't allowed to move a single ornament in the house, everything had to remain in the same place. If my mother told me to do the dusting, and I moved an object by so much as half an inch, she replaced it exactly where it had been.' Olivia could remember the quarrel that once blew up when her father removed a pair of silver-mounted emu's eggs from the sideboard in the dining room and put there two Chinese vases of no great value, which he had bought at a sale. 'My father adored auctions, but my mother was terrified about what he might bring home next. Once it was four dozen gym shoes. He was an inveterate bargain hunter. And so am I.'

Another of her mother's habits, which infuriated Olivia as a child, was that whenever she was playing out in the garden she would be severely ticked off when she came in: 'You look like a tinker's brat. Go upstairs at once and tidy yourself.' In spite of this Olivia was the apple of her mother's eye. She was spoiled and cosseted by both her parents, and quite often encouraged by them to entertain their friends by singing a song or dancing a hornpipe. Sometimes, in the back garden, Olivia would put on little plays, which she made up for the benefit of her father. If he dropped off while she was acting them she always forgave him. On many occasions Olivia's mother would call out to her cheerfully, 'Come into the kitchen and talk to me while I do the washing up' – and Olivia would run gladly into the house to be with her mother.

Yet later, in both her writings and conversations, these happy scenes were usually forgotten and Olivia became highly critical towards her mother. In 1981, in a radio programme devoted to Olivia Manning a year after her death, Olivia's husband Reggie Smith recalled how he had said to her when Mrs Manning was very ill, 'Your mother is an old woman now. Try to forgive and forget.' Olivia had snapped back, 'You don't know my mother. She has a mind as rigid as cast-iron.' Another time

Olivia was to say of her mother that there was no give and take in her: 'She would never let a grievance slip by. She might forgive someone for a misdeed, but she never forgot it.'

At times when Olivia was going on about her mother, Reggie felt that she might have been speaking about herself: 'The two ladies were both very Ulster. That's the key to their two characters.'

Her mother's sourness, resentment and rigid propriety were things which Olivia found difficult for many years to write about, but which she was prepared to examine with Kay Dick in the first of the two interviews that she gave in 1963. They concerned the birth of her brother, Oliver, when she was five, and her father's long stream of infidelities.*

Olivia's brother once said to her, 'The first thing I remember is falling downstairs. You pushed me. I had to climb up further than you so you couldn't push me again.' Olivia used his comment verbatim to open her short story 'A Visit', which she completed in 1935 and set in Belfast. Olivia told June Braybrooke, 'When Oliver was tiny and we were in Portsmouth, I had a go at trying to bump him off on the stairs.'

Oliver was christened, like Olivia, at St Mark's church in North End in 1913. Two Olivers and two Olivias in the same household frequently caused confusion – though Mrs Manning always pronounced her daughter's name 'Ollov'. Olivia had been an adored only child. With the birth of Oliver, everything was to change. She was shunted to second place in her mother's affections – though not in her father's. But, because of the war, he saw much less of his children than did their mother.

Oliver was a delicate child with a weak chest – and this in particular made him the centre of his mother's attention, which could, over matters of health, be obsessive. Olivia remembered, when she was tiny, having her chest wrapped up in Thermagen wool – used in those days to protect children from getting pneumonia. She detested it and yelled about it. She

---

* It is worth noting here that in her first book of interviews, with Stevie Smith and Ivy Compton-Burnett, Kay Dick had already shown a remarkable talent for eliciting previously withheld confidences and probing hitherto unplumbed depths. It was the same in her subsequent volume *Friends and Friendship*, which included the interviews with Olivia Manning. Both Stevie Smith and Olivia told June Braybrooke that they regarded these interviews granted to Kay as rewarding legacies for her, long after they themselves were dead. Obituary writers and biographers have drawn heavily on Kay Dick's tape recordings.

said that it felt like being wrapped up in a harness. Her brother, always far more docile, kept quiet.

Once when her brother was still in long clothes, Olivia put a thermos flask on the stairs, with the idea that when her mother came down she would trip and drop the baby. Her aggression towards her brother, when young, was quite marked. That he should so often be given preferential treatment merely because he was a boy struck her as grossly unfair. When the two of them had been playing on the beach in Bangor during the war, their mother would constantly remark, 'It's all right for a boy to look a mess, but you do expect a girl to take some pride in her appearance. Girls should keep clear of mud and rocks.'

Olivia and her brother spent a long time with their mother both north and south of the Irish border, when between 1916 and 1917 their father was serving on the inland waterways in Britain and later at Haslar Camp near Gosport. By then Olivia had long since ceased to be the centre of her mother's attention. She never forgot the day when Mrs Manning told her, 'You're a terrible disappointment to me – and that's a fact. You were a real charmer, you amused everyone in Laburnum Grove and you danced and sang beautifully. Now look at you – a wretched sulk-pot and so disagreeable.'

The effect of such harsh criticism, which grew more frequent, was to make Olivia withdraw more and more into herself and to develop feelings of deep inferiority. Before the family left for Bangor she attended a Dame's School in Laburnum Grove. There, in fury, she would throw her lesson books on the floor and scream her head off. 'She was a bit of a bully as far as her brother Oliver was concerned,' said a pupil at the same school.

Yet, as time went by, Olivia began to recognise her brother as an ally in the home. When he made jokes about her large nose, she was able to accept it in good part. In Ireland too there were many times on the beach when they would play happily together. In a rock pool, at low tide, they found a crab which they adopted and called 'Congo'. They would pick him gently out of the water and offer him crumbs which they had brought specially from the house.

In Ulster they would sometimes cross the border to stay with relatives and friends in County Clare or Galway Town. On sandbanks by the sea they would sit and gaze out across the water towards the huge rocks and small islands in the distance. Local people would talk about the Islands of the Blest – and the children thought the islands in front of them could well be them. They would imagine how one day they would row out to them and perhaps camp out for the night and light a fire. Olivia had an adventurous spirit and, since she was the elder of the two, was always the leader. Back in Portsmouth after these long stays in Ireland, the children were to find another Island of the Blest, less than half an hour away. This was the Isle of Wight, with its chines, secret coves, tropical vegetation and coloured sands. One of the watercolour paints in Olivia's first box had been called 'Solomon's Gold' and this was a name she was never to forget. She uses it in *The Play Room* to describe one of the layers of coloured sand to be found at Alum Bay. In 1970 she wrote of a trip which she and June Braybrooke had made there, 'I often think of that wonderful afternoon we had there with the very delicate mist hanging over everything and the foghorn going and our trip round the Needles. All the summers of one's life add up to a few days like this.'

One of Olivia's favourite books as a child had been *The Water Babies*, which her mother read aloud to her. Until her death Olivia was able to recite long sections from it by heart. The Reverend Charles Kingsley, who had a parish in Hampshire, had many fond memories of visits to the Isle of Wight, which in his book served partly as the model for St Brandan's (*sic*) fairy tale island. The island was the imaginary place, beyond the Blaskets, to which the saint with five other hermits had sailed after they failed to convert the people of Kerry to Christianity. Kingsley writes of the Kerry people, who remained unconverted, that 'they were changed into gorillas, and gorillas they are until this day'. Some critics have thought the book anti-Irish in tone. But this never struck Olivia. 'After all,' she would argue, 'gorillas are God's creatures, too.' She never had any sympathy with the anti-Darwinian prejudice of fundamentalist Christianity.

Kingsley, despite his dog collar, was an author to whom she was much drawn. Of a swarm of bees he had once written, 'How do we *know* they have no souls?' When he was Rector at Eversleigh, he had made friends with a pair of sand wasps, one of which he had rescued from drowning in a handbasin. The wasps' home was a large crack in the window frame of his dressing room, which he refused to have mended. 'Absolutely right,' was Olivia's comment.

Olivia inherited her love of animals from both her parents; but though she readily acknowledged this in the case of her father, she was much less willing to do so in that of her mother. In *The Play Room* there is a scene where the mother, Mrs Fletcher, rounds on her husband: 'If you want your tea, you'll put that cat down and come to the table.' Commander Fletcher, a retired and improvident naval man with an eye for the ladies, is forced to put the cat on the floor. As he does so he whispers to the animal, 'Poor old Sugarpuss! Poor old fellow!'

The first part of the book, describing a week's holiday that the Fletchers' two teenage children have spent on the Isle of Wight as paying guests, ends with the words 'Tomorrow they must face again the emotional confusion of home'. Many of such scenes in the book are taken straight from life. When brother and sister tell their mother they are determined at all costs to go on an Isle of Wight holiday, Mrs Fletcher chides them, 'Go, then, go. If you want to leave your poor mother, who has given her life to looking after you, go . . . go . . . go . . .' This was the kind of emotional blackmail to which Olivia and her brother were to become accustomed. Sometimes when they came in from a walk, or back from school together, they would stop outside the front door so as to be forewarned if their parents were rowing with each other.

After Mrs Manning was widowed in late 1949, Olivia gradually became more attached to her. Having by now resigned herself to being married to a compulsive philanderer, Olivia could sympathise with her mother, who had endured the same situation. Neither mother nor daughter ever contemplated divorce or even a separation – Mrs Manning on religious grounds, Olivia on what she later defined as 'moral principles'.

When Olivia completed her 1951 Irish travel book *The Dreaming Shore*, she decided to dedicate it to her mother. 'You owe it to her,' Reggie said. Mrs Manning was so much delighted with the dedication that she went round showing it to everyone with the boast 'Ollov at least knows Ireland like the back of her hand'. Her daughter, with four books behind her, was fast becoming a celebrity.

Some twenty years previously, Mrs Manning had announced to her neighbours that Ollov was about to have a long story published. This story, entitled *Rose of Rubies*, set in Paris and appearing under the pseudonym 'Jacob Morrow', was serialised by the *Evening News* of Portsmouth. Mrs Manning was beside herself with pride and could hardly wait for the first instalment to appear. When it did, she said to Alison Galpin, who lived a few doors away, 'Do you know, my Ollov has never been to Paris? She worked out every detail from a street map, which she bought here in Portsmouth and took up to her little bedroom.'

In 1954 Mrs Manning died after a short illness. Twelve years later, in 1966, Olivia wrote to June Braybrooke whose mother had just died, 'It is always the same when one's mother dies: however much one has done, one is consumed with guilt at not having done more.' She summed up, 'There is really nothing to be done about it – it is in the nature of things.'

Chapter 4

Schooldays

Olivia was secretive about her schooling. In *Who's Who* she stated that she was 'privately educated', and on *Desert Island Discs,* in 1969, she smudged over the issue by telling Roy Plomley that she had spent a large part of her childhood in Ireland. To be precise she had spent just over three years there, two of which had been during the First World War.

In Portsmouth she had started out by attending a Dame's School, a few doors away from her home. In Bangor, during the war, she went to the Presbyterian School in Main Street for several terms. Between 1914 and 1918, except for this Irish interval, Olivia was a pupil at Lynton House School in Kingston Crescent, in the Buckland area of Portsmouth. Some of the experiences that she underwent there are touched on in *The Play Room,* where Lynton House School is called Buckland House School.

Miss Thorpe, who was the headmistress of Lynton House School, was keen on amateur theatricals. One contemporary of Olivia's at school was Thelma Lott, who remembered that at the end of one term Olivia took part in a sketch in which she played the role of a postmaster. 'Yes,' insisted Thelma Lott, 'a postmaster. Olivia liked dressing up as a man and was good at it.'

Olivia lacked stage presence. Nor did P. H. Newby, in 1950, believe that she would be an ideal broadcaster: 'Her voice is too thin in my opinion,' he wrote to a BBC colleague. The original tape of *Desert Island Discs* is full of 'ums' and 'ers', which had to be cut. She was invited to appear only once on Melvyn Bragg's television series *Paperback Writer,* her choice of book being James Joyce's *Dubliners,* which she admired greatly. 'I think these stories are the best thing Joyce ever did.' But when it came to elaborating on this before the camera she seemed to dry up. 'I get a knotted-up feeling inside, like waiting to be executed,' she told

Auriol Stevens of the *Guardian* in 1969. All the same, she never lost her love of the performing arts, and when she was in London hardly a week passed by when she did not go to a theatre or was 'dragged to the suburbs of Outer Mongolia by Reggie* to see some tuppenny actress as Rosalind'. She was a loyal supporter of the Hampstead Theatre at Swiss Cottage.

At Lynton House School Olivia acquired the reputation of being a determined, but rather a shy child. 'She could be quite friendly to you – and yet you always had to be the first to make a move,' said Hilda Lucas. 'She needed to be drawn out.'

During the summer each year there would be an excursion to Hayling Island, where the children would sit on the sands having a picnic. On the way to the beach, they would be expected to walk in crocodile ranks, two by two. Olivia objected to this and showed her protest by kicking angrily at stones or by lying down on the pathway. 'Let her cool off' was the attitude of the mistress in charge – and Olivia usually did just this. She could never understand why she and her friends were not allowed in the water to paddle or swim. 'School rules are school rules,' she was told. 'Why can't they be changed?' was her constant reply.

After Lynton House School, Olivia went to Portsmouth Grammar School with her brother Oliver. Later, at the age of fourteen, he was sent as a day boy to St John's in Southsea – a Roman Catholic college. Commander Manning and his wife had little sympathy for Catholicism as such, but chose the school because it had the best educational record in the area. Like his father, the young Oliver inherited a love of theatricals.

In the playground of the Grammar School, Oliver and Olivia were often ragged by the others because of their absences in Ireland: they were known consequently as the 'half foreigners'. Both had very dark hair and olive complexions. The Irish part of their family in Bangor liked to claim direct descent from the Spanish grandees who had sailed with the Armada in 1588 and been shipwrecked off the west coast of Ireland.

At Portsmouth Grammar School Olivia and her brother were fascinated by the maps hanging on the classroom wall, which revealed just how much of the world belonged to Great Britain. At home the Commander would stress that this was due to Britain's supremacy at sea.

---

* Reggie Smith, her husband.

One of his favourite sayings was 'The Navy is not like the Army. It cleans up after itself.'

These sentiments found their way into Olivia's Irish travel book, *The Dreaming Shore*, which starts off with a description of her arrival in Cork by boat in 1949. A century before this, when Queen Victoria had visited the port, it had been renamed Queenstown in her honour. But the name had not lasted long and it soon reverted back to Cork. Commander Manning would say proudly to his daughter, 'In 1938, when the Royal Navy pulled out of Ireland, everything was left shipshape.' What a contrast, he maintained, to the way the British Army had left Ireland when the troubles ended in the 1920s.

Olivia thought similarly. In her view the British Army were 'amateur', 'dirty', 'wasteful' and 'left things like a sluttish housewife'. For her, as for the Commander, the Navy with its cleanliness and professionalism always remained the Senior Service in every sense.

As well as maps of the British Empire in the classroom at the Grammar School, there were maps of the Holy Land and of Great Britain and Ireland. She wrote in her Irish book after a visit to Glengarriff, 'Here we were well into that wild broken corner of Ireland that flies on the schoolroom atlas like a wind-tattered flag.' Donegal, in the same book, was compared to 'a vast cape that has been blown aslant and torn to ribbons by the wind'. These were images that had struck her as a girl – and she retained them. 'You have a definite talent,' said one of Olivia's teachers, handing back an essay about 'A Trip to Ireland'. In the case of the Holy Land maps, Olivia was fascinated by the small insets of biblical scenes. 'I loved the details, not the important figures like the Kings, but the sheep on the hills or the camels in the distance.'

Camels were animals that she specially liked drawing as she grew up: 'Early on, I was able to identify with them as beasts of burden.' In the Christmas story she noticed how the camels knelt on the ground to be unburdened of their gifts, an appropriate act, she thought, for beasts bringing gold, frankincense and myrrh to a child born to be a King.

Olivia was brought up in a home where poetry played an important part, especially for her father. When he had been away at sea, and on watch at night, he had learnt by heart complete scenes of Shakespeare, and passages from Tennyson, Longfellow and Thomas Hood. How exciting he had made these poets sound to his daughter. But when she took them down from the shelf and examined their collected poems she had found the double columns of heavy grey print off-putting. How much more rewarding it was, she concluded, to hear her father reciting *Hiawatha* than to read it to herself.

Once, when he had turned up at the door with a pianola in a van, her mother took one look at it and refused to let it be put in any of the rooms. Instead, it had to be pushed under the stairs, along with the abandoned sewing machine.

The 'Selections from Sullivan' that had come with the pianola were never played, since it turned out that it was in need of repair. The Commander was therefore obliged to hum his own favourite numbers. Eventually, in the 1920s, he persuaded his wife to give her own rosewood piano, as well as the pianola, to a local dealer in exchange for an upright piano. To her next-door neighbour Mrs Manning referred to the exchange as one of her many trials and martyrdoms, for the Commander, she confided sourly, soon lost all interest in the new piano. For several years, as was the custom at the time, Olivia was forced to have piano lessons. They were absolutely useless. 'I have no musical gifts,' she told Roy Plomley on *Desert Island Discs*.

By the time she was four years old she had learnt to read. Tucked up in her bed on a summer's night, she enjoyed reading fairy stories to herself. She liked to lie on her mother's bed and imagine fairies playing on the pampas grass in a vase, which she had been told by her mother was real 'fairy grass'. She told June Braybrooke in a letter in 1966, 'The memory of my imagined fairies is still vivid in my mind.'

At the age of seven, Olivia began to think of herself as the Ugly Duckling in Hans Andersen. But she knew that the duckling finally turned into a white swan. In her teens she used to have dreams in which Vanessa Bell and her sister Virginia came floating towards her like beautiful swans. It was about this time that she borrowed *Jacob's Room* by Virginia Woolf from the public library.

At the far end of Laburnum Grove was the public library – a narrow red-brick building, with the name 'Carnegie' embossed on a scroll of yellow cement. After school, the children who lived nearby would line up outside the library, the taller ones pushing the little ones to the back of the queue. Only two books could be taken out at a time by each child – 'a novel or a story book and a book of an improving nature'. At a talk that Olivia gave in 1970 she commented, 'Fiction in my youth was not taken seriously by my local library. The staff were dedicated to the principle of *educating* the working classes.'*

Once, having visited the public library near her home when she was ten, Olivia thought that she had got away with two novels, instead of one novel and a volume of an improving nature. For several weeks she had been trying to borrow a book with the promisingly romantic title (so she misremembered from the library catalogue) *The Princess Orchid*. Always, it was out on loan. Then, one day, she struck lucky. But when she picked up the volume to take home with her she was disappointed to find that its real title was *The Priceless Orchid* and that it was nothing more exciting than a botanical study of a new variety of orchid.

At home in Laburnum Grove, most of the books on the shelves were poetry, although there were a few novels, including complete sets of Dickens and Thackeray. There was also a copy of George Eliot's *Adam Bede*, which Olivia's mother had reprovingly confiscated from her when she was fifteen on the grounds that it was 'not a nice book for a young lady to read', although it was her father who had given it to his daughter to stop her from mooching around the house.

Mrs Manning and the Commander did not see eye to eye about their daughter's literary tastes or her artistic gifts. When she was little her father had been only too happy to smuggle back from the naval stationery store on Whale Island large account books with marbled edges in which his daughter could both write and draw to her heart's content. Nor, at the time, had her mother objected to this. But once Olivia was in her teens, it was a different matter. There was her future to be thought of, and a career. In 1923, the same year in which Olivia's mother had confiscated *Adam Bede*, she had come across her daughter reading a copy of the *Times Literary Supplement*. She had scolded her, 'Young men do not like young ladies who read papers like that.' Olivia was convinced that her mother had never even looked inside the *Times Literary Supplement*. Mrs Manning repeatedly made it clear to both her children that she stayed on in Portsmouth only in the hope of seeing them safely settled and married.

---

* In Cowes public library, Olivia was introduced by June to a local butcher, who had been brought up on the Carnegie principle. Fred White, as he was called, would inform his more literary customers that he had read all Balzac's and E. M. Forster's novels. From this Olivia decided that, having been forced to read improving books when he was young, he had in later years, like herself, turned into a compulsive reader of fiction.

Over the years Olivia and her brother had become accustomed to their parents' quarrels and, when he was fourteen, Oliver had coined the phrases 'universal uproar' and 'sullen sulks' to describe the emotional climate of

One three four
Bryn-y-moor.

'Bryn-y-moor', meaning 'the hill above the sea', was the name Mrs Manning had given their home when she first moved into Laburnum Grove in 1905.

Whenever Olivia heard her parents beginning a quarrel, she would rush upstairs to her room. There, she could retreat into annuals such as *Chatterbox* and *Little Folks*. The children in *Chatterbox*, she noticed, did not have parents who quarrelled. She also observed that these children were socially several cuts above her own family. In *The Play Room* there is an autobiographical scene in which Laura is mocked about her snobberies by one of the girls at Buckland House School. 'Oh boo-hoo-ho! Look at me! My daddy's a naval officer, my daddy is. Ever so brave, he is! We're a cut above common shop-keeping people, we are!'

At Lynton House School Olivia had indulged in making up stories about her background: 'I told them I had a nurse and a nursery, and that I would soon be going to boarding school.' The truth was that Olivia was going to Bangor with her mother, because her father had been called up and a war was on. The more she boasted, the more she acquired the reputation of being a show-off, and the more she was cold-shouldered by her companions. So, to compensate herself for this, Olivia began to make lists of books that she would like to read, including all Angela Brazil's. For Christmas and birthdays she picked out books with titles such as *The Prettiest Girl in the School* or *The Luckiest Girl in the World*. Yet neither of these enviable states was hers.

After her twelfth birthday her interest in schoolgirl stories came to a sudden end. But her love of fairy stories, and especially Charles Kingsley's *The Water Babies*, never left her. What had occurred between her twelfth and fourteenth birthdays was that she had discovered what she was later to refer to as her 'first grown-up novel – and what's more three books in one'. This was Rider Haggard's Zulu trilogy. So exciting did she find Rider Haggard that she was thought by her mother to be running a temperature:

'You must stay in bed for at least today and tomorrow.'

The local library had only a limited selection. There was, though, in the centre of Portsmouth, a large bookshop with a collected edition of Rider Haggard's works, with thick buff pages and grey-green covers, which cost two shillings a volume. By carefully saving up her pocket money, Olivia was able to buy one a fortnight, and between the ages of twelve and fourteen she claimed that she had read everything that he had written.

One evening at Laburnum Grove, when the family were drinking their supper milk before going up to bed, Olivia made the statement that she was an authority on Zulu history. 'Would you like to test me out?' she asked. Her father was mildly amused and kept quiet. But her mother, who prided herself on her practicality, came quickly to the point: 'Reading and wanting to write or paint are all very well as hobbies, Ollov, but what about learning to type? A secretary has always been a pearl of great price.'

Chapter 5

The Art Student

By the time Olivia was sixteen she had left school and become a trained typist. 'I can use *all* my fingers on the keyboard,' she told her parents proudly. In the evenings from then onwards, and for the next four years, she was a student at the Portsmouth Municipal School of Art. But when her American grandmother Mazoura died of a sudden brain haemorrhage early in 1924, she had to interrupt her studies and go over to Northern Ireland with her mother and stay there for some time. The local paper printed an obituary of her grandmother, which Olivia cut out and kept.

Olivia had loved Mazoura and always remembered her with affection, for she was a witty and entertaining woman who liked to encourage the young in their ambitions. Many years later Olivia quoted one of her bons mots, when she was commissioned to write a piece about hunting for the *Observer*. Olivia used her grandmother's words to describe a group of Old Etonians who had barracked during an RSPCA meeting, with the result that those who spoke against blood sports had been unable to make themselves heard. 'If they consider themselves the crème de la crème,' Mazoura had commented, 'then heaven help the skimmed milk.'

When Olivia returned from Bangor there arose the question of how she was to earn a living. Since leaving school she had had several typing jobs – one with a solicitor's firm and another in an architect's office – and even worked as a junior at a beauty salon. But she stuck at none of them. 'I could not take them seriously,' she later told her husband Reggie. 'I felt my future lay elsewhere.' The 'elsewhere' to which she referred was the world of art – painting or writing. 'I was good at both, so I really did have to choose,' was her comment to June Braybrooke.

Throughout her early years she had painted pictures and written stories. She kept her easel in the hall. She filled pages of notebooks with 'scribble,

scribble, scribble' – like Mr Gibbon. Then, when she got tired of writing poems and stories, she picked up her paintbrush. Many of Grimm's fairy stories she tried to rewrite and illustrate.

'Look at what I am reading,' she had announced rather boastfully one day at Lynton House School to Beryl Williams, who was sitting next to her. This was a story entitled 'The Glass Coffin' by the Brothers Grimm.

Her friend glanced at it and replied, 'My mother does not allow me to read stories like that.'

'Fancy allowing your mother to dictate,' replied Olivia crushingly.

Portsmouth Municipal School of Art was situated on the top floor of a building in Park Road, which stood at the back of the Town Hall (now the Guildhall); the same building housed the Portsmouth Municipal College and the Portsmouth Training College for Teachers. One day an instructor from the latter, meeting Olivia by chance in the hall and thinking that she looked both a lonely and artistic type of girl, lent her some copies of *John O'London's Weekly*. This was to prove a turning point. In 1975 she was to recall,

> My journey out of literary darkness reads like one of those post-Wellesian novels written in the '30s: lower middle class hero, unlettered but aspirant, comes across a copy of *John O'London's Weekly* and never looks back. A whole new area of life is revealed to him – an area where books are Important.

Notice her use of the word 'hero'. Olivia's view in the 1920s was that heroines tended to come from the upper classes. At the beginning of her career she was also convinced that male writers received more serious attention in the press than did women writers. Even after she had dropped the Jacob Morrow pseudonym in 1931, when she was twenty-three, there were still four more years to go before she was prepared to reveal to her readers that she was a woman. In the interim period she used the name O. M. Manning when submitting manuscripts to editors.

The instructor at the Training College for Teachers who had intro-duced her to *John O'London's Weekly* – but whose name she could never remember – asked her on another occasion if she had read any of Bernard Shaw's plays. Olivia was puzzled for a moment – did one actually *read* plays? Occasionally she had *seen* one at the local Theatre Royal, where seats were not cheap unless one sat in the gallery and the crowd could be unruly. 'No girl should go there on her own,' was the Commander's opinion.

Having collected a full set of Rider Haggard, Olivia now set about collecting a set of Shaw's plays. Some that she bought were first editions. 'I told myself that he had put paid to God – meaning the petty social tyrants of provincial life who would, I felt, if they could, hold me down . . .' She was greatly inspired by the Shavian challenge to bourgeois conventions, prejudices and snobberies. What a beguiling title she thought *Plays Pleasant and Unpleasant.* 'It's full of gunpowder,' was her reaction after reading it.

As she progressed from Rider Haggard to Bernard Shaw, so she moved to the section in the Public Central Library called 'Modern Literature'. By the late 1920s she was beginning to admit to herself that Shaw was not quite modern enough for her: plays like *Mrs Warren's Profession* (1902) and *John Bull's Other Island* (1904) already had a dated feel. 'But his *Saint Joan* will probably last for ever,' she informed her father.

Sometimes on her way to evening art classes she would drop in at the Central Library. The range here was far greater than at the North End branch and there was a fine reference department as well. Nearby was Victoria Park, which had aviaries filled with many exotic birds, including peacocks. To the accompaniment of the high-pitched screams of these noisy creatures, Olivia read her way through most of D. H. Lawrence, Wyndham Lewis, Aldous Huxley, John Middleton Murry and the early William Gerhardi (who was later to add an 'e' to his surname). Gerhardi was a genius, Olivia thought, but sometimes also a silly ass.

Middleton Murry, with his enthusiasm for Russian literature, led Olivia straight to Dostoevsky and then on to Tolstoy, Turgenev and Chekhov. Women writers did not attract her in the same way – with two exceptions: Katherine Mansfield and Virginia Woolf. When not attending evening classes, she would hurry home to her room and try to compose sketches and stories worthy of them. She read none of the classical novelists such as Jane Austen or the Brontës and dipped cursorily into Dickens. The sinister illustrations in her copy of *Adam Bede*, which her mother confiscated from her, put her off wanting to finish George Eliot's novel for several years to come.

During one summer holiday from the art school she brought back to the house Jung's *Psychology of the Unconscious* and was immediately bowled over by it. Her father found it in her room and picked it up to look at it: he had heard of Freud, but not of Jung. After several minutes he put the book down and told Olivia, when he later saw her that evening, that he did not think it suitable for a girl. Apart from this one instance, he never attempted to censor her reading, as did her mother. He did, though, have reservations about James Joyce's *Ulysses*: 'All right for a sailor to read, but then I've knocked about a bit. Certainly not a book for the ladies.'

By the time Olivia had finished her art course in 1927, she had collected a reasonably sized portfolio of pen-and-ink sketches and paintings, but few of this period have survived. One set of drawings that has done so is an exercise book of botany notes that contains a number of pencil sketches of flowers (buttercups, roses and irises) and of leaves (horse-chestnut, oak and sycamore). Inside the cover is written the date 1926 and below it,

> Hic liber ad me pertinet
> Si quis furetur,
> Per collum suo pendetur,
> In hoc modo

Illustrating this Latin text, Olivia has drawn beneath it a man in a large bucket who is being threatened with being ducked. A loose sheet, dated June 1927, has also been added. This contains another sketch, serious in intention, to illustrate the way in which plants assimilate carbon.

In the Central Reference Library Olivia was known among the staff as 'the girl with the bright pink toenails'. She had good legs and long thin feet: 'I take a triple A in shoes,' she told Louis MacNeice when she first met him in 1939.*

---

* In 1961, out of the blue, Olivia was to receive a letter that would bring back memories of these far-off days. The writer was a Mrs K. M. Saunders, a Portsmouth housewife, who had once worked in the reference department of the Central Library. She had in her living room, she told Olivia, an unfinished watercolour sketch by Roberta Waudby, which showed Olivia sitting on a kitchen chair, dressed in a grey coat and skirt, with three green stripes round the neckline of her jumper and an enormous red flower pinned in the lapel of the jacket. Roberta Waudby, who had encouraged Olivia at the art school in Portsmouth, had later gone on to make a reputation painting Nativity scenes for Christmas cards issued by Mowbrays. Mrs Saunders reminded Olivia of the occasion when the professional life model had failed to turn up and Olivia had volunteered to replace her. There was in Olivia a mixture of daring and timidity.

Kenneth Holmes, who was at the same School of Art, remembers Olivia as 'a long thin Modigliani figure'. Two pen-and-ink drawings which he made of her – one at the time and one from memory in 1986 – show her wearing a cardigan over an artist's smock and a long bead necklace. Her dark hair is bobbed short with a fringe. Holmes was to observe, 'She didn't conform. Her appearance always differed in some way from the rest.' Looking back over the years, he writes, 'I can see that young Olivia was intellectually brighter and more aware of Life than we were who were confined to smaller horizons.' He notes too that, unlike the remainder of the students, she did not appear to have any particular feelings for the opposite sex and suggests that this added to her individuality. His final word for her is 'aloof'. Other students of that time found her 'uppity' and 'supercilious'. Even her brother used to say she was a 'snooty' girl: but then 'snooty' was a favourite term of his, which he applied to most of the female sex under twenty-one.

The students with whom Olivia shared her class were a mixed bunch. Greta Burton's father was a labourer, Patricia Beroley's an Army colonel and Vera Brockman's a prosperous gents' outfitter in the town. (Portsmouth did not become a city until 1927.) Some reappear as background figures in the school scenes of *The Play Room*. The male students included Albert Bindwell, the son of a policeman; Prince Naht Bhodiprassarta of Siam, who sported a different and exquisite silk suit every day; and the aptly named Pratt, who once nailed a bloater inside his desk, which produced a stench that was to puzzle the authorities for several days. Kenneth Holmes's father had risen to be a commander in the Royal Navy, like Olivia's. In the years ahead Holmes was to rise to be Assistant Chief Inspector of Public Health in the City of Portsmouth.

During his period at the School of Art, Holmes maintains that there was 'no moral laxity' and such bohemianism as existed went no further than breaking the rule which stated that no one should leave the classroom once a lecture or lesson had begun. In spite of this, students were delegated by other students to sneak out of class, cross the Guildhall Square and return with 'provender'. Provender included cream buns, bought for a penny-halfpenny each. The young Holmes held the record of eating twelve in a go, drinking fifteen glasses of water afterwards and then giving an exhibition of animal noises, while rolling wildly about on one of the benches. Such behaviour was not to Olivia's taste. 'I am definitely not amused,' she would say haughtily.

At the time when Olivia was living at home as an art student, the most she ever earned as a copy typist was fifteen shillings a week, of which she had to give her mother ten. Her hours were nine to six and sometimes included all Saturday. Her parents were anxious to keep her at home. Whenever she mentioned that she would like to go to London, her mother grew fractious: London was a dangerous place, especially for young girls on their own. During her late teens Olivia shifted from job to job, the most rewarding of which was her short spell at the beauty salon: 'I learnt how to make up. One tarty girl taught me how to look seductive by rougeing my knees. But the boys weren't up to much. I longed for London boys.'

A year after leaving the School of Art, Olivia had her first lucky break. In April 1928, when she was twenty, a painting of hers was chosen for the annual art exhibition held every May on the South Parade Pier at Southsea. The late Peter F. Anson, who exhibited that year but was considerably older than Olivia, told Neville Braybrooke when they met in 1966, 'Olivia Manning was a striking girl. There was something about her work which made you want to look more than once.'

That first exhibition in May 1928 must have seemed like a dream come true. Not only was her painting singled out by the local paper, but it started a controversy in the correspondence columns. A reader wrote in under the initials L. C. W.,

> I was one of a small party which collected round No. 157, 'A Study in Tempera', in the Exhibition of the Art Society on the South Parade Pier. Although we were quite unknown to each other, the work aroused sufficient interest to develop a lengthy discussion, in which opinions sharply divided. Our only point of agreement was that the painting required some extra explanatory title. The choice of colour, design, and the symbolic figures are surely meant to convey some thought or meaning. Would it be asking too much of the artist to give us some enlightenment? Does it stand for 'the Annunciation'?

On 18 May, Olivia Mary Manning, as she signed herself, replied to the question. Her 'Letter to the Editor' was given pride of place and was the first letter of hers ever to have appeared in print.

Sir, – I feel that your correspondent is justified in requesting some interpretation of my picture now on exhibition at the South Parade Pier (No. 157 'A Study in Tempera').

The title conveys little for two reasons: (i) my intense dislike of sentimental or 'every-picture-tells-a-story' titles that attract attention to the picture more for their own sake than for the merit of the work; (ii) the difficulty in finding a title that would adequately convey the meaning of the picture.

Although I would prefer the study to be judged merely as a decorative composition, as it has mystified many I will attempt to give some interpretation of it. The symbolic figures are as follows:- The red-haired Man holding a white cross is Jesus Christ; He is clad in blue, the colour of all those forsaken hopes and lost causes He has taken upon Himself. The woman is obviously the Virgin Mary (virtue); the lilies symbolise purity, her sombre dress austerity. The central triple-faced figure (around which the controversy appears to be) is Humanity . . .

Olivia now began to think that she was well on the way to becoming a professional artist. She was even asked for her autograph on one occasion when she visited the exhibition. Moreover, a second exhibition – but this time a one-woman show – was to follow swiftly.

Olivia was not musical and could not sing in tune. She saw sounds in terms of colour and read with great attention Rimbaud's *Alchimie du Verbe*, in which he provides a key to the vowels, with A standing for black, E for white, I for red, O for blue and U for green. In her pocket notebook she devised her own colour key to the vowels, with A for white, E for green, I for blue-mauve, O for yellow and U for orange. On *Desert Island Discs* in 1969 the record that she chose out of the eight to take to the 'Island' was Sibelius's 'The Swan of Tuonela'. She saw it as silver.

The comments made by those visiting her exhibition at the Regent Cinema varied from praise to mystification. But her brother, with a simple brother's pride, said later that his sister had anticipated Walt Disney's *Fantasia* of 1936. She herself, though, never again returned to this 'kind of paper patchwork art'.

For Olivia there remained the problem of exactly what kind of artist she should be. Painting materials were expensive and after she had paid her mother ten shillings a week for her keep there was not much left over. She longed for Christmas and birthday presents, and hoped that they would come in the form of cash. Until she was nineteen, she was certain that she wanted above all to be a painter. Now, aged twenty, she was less sure. There was her other calling, which was to be a writer. She would give it a chance, she decided, and started a novel. It would be about 'a journey which was an adventure', with Paris as the setting. It would open on the French train:

> 'Are we past Amiens?' asked the woman in the corner as she awoke with a start and instinctively raised her hands to adjust her hat . . .

Olivia felt that the time had come to see her bank manager and optimistically told him that she might be paying in some cheques in future in the name of Jacob Morrow.

Chapter 6

The Rose of Rubies

Like the subsequent Jacob Morrow novels – *Here is Murder* and *The Black Scarab* – *Rose of Rubies* is in serial form. It ran to nineteen instalments and included illustrations by an artist on the staff of the *Portsmouth News*. One illustration shows the heroine travelling on the Calais–Paris train in a seat next to a Frenchman with a panama hat and wide cummerbund. Above the drawing is printed in capital letters – A GREAT MYSTERY TOLD BY A NEW AUTHOR.

Why was Olivia so secretive about this first novel and the two serials that followed it? Each book was sold for an outright sum of £25 and with the first fee she bought herself a typewriter. She was twenty-one when the *Portsmouth News* started to run the serial in October 1929. Later, it became clear that she did not wish people to know that she had been a published writer before the Second World War.* It was not until after her death that her husband, Reggie Smith, discovered that she was older than himself. 'It was quite a shock when I learnt the truth,' he told Margaret Drabble when she was preparing the entry for Olivia in her *Oxford Companion to English Literature*.

Rose of Rubies concerns a young girl (Helen Massey) who takes a job as an English governess in Paris and then becomes involved in a search for a rose made entirely of finely wrought gold decorated with rubies. It once belonged to a religious sect said to have been founded in the seventh

---

* In *Bookmarks* (1975), an anthology sponsored by the Writers Action Group (founded by Brigid Brophy and Maureen Duffy), Olivia contributed an autobiographical piece, in which she went so far as to claim that, when she heard on the wireless of D. H. Lawrence's death on 2 March 1930, she wept all the way to school. She was in fact twenty-two.

century. The members of the sect believe that this precious jewel possesses certain alchemical qualities, which will be revealed when it finally becomes the property of its rightful owner. The chosen person will have the power to transmute base metals into gold, and there will follow a perfect age during which there will cease to be 'envy and calumny and hate and pain'. Running parallel with this mystical aspect of the story is a tale of deception, murder and kidnap.

There are passing references to the translation of Messahalah's *De Orbe*, *The Visions of Elizabeth von Schonaw* and the *Liber Dicinorum Operum Simplicis Hominus*. Helen Massey, on her first night in Paris, notices that in her bedroom there is a good reproduction of a Crivelli and an interesting shelf of books: 'She scanned the covers – Voltaire, Rameau, Rousseau and the de Goncourts.' Helen Massey, along with Olivia at this stage in her life, likes to air her superior knowledge. Referring to Anatole France's novel *La Rôtisserie de la Reine Pédauque*, she tells her employer that she will be 'quite happy and occupied staying at home to decipher Monsieur France's excellent French'.

Olivia had done her research carefully in the reference department of the Central Library in Portsmouth and consulted books on alchemy, endaemonism, iconography and gemmology. In a long speech about the psychic power of precious stones, Helen's employer speaks of the melodeus, which was supposed to utter a cry 'when touched by a thieving hand' and of 'the aspilateses, which, so writes Democritus, is a sure protection against fire'. Neither 'aspilates' nor 'melodeus' are words which appear in ordinary dictionaries.

The young Olivia had a weakness for long and obscure words, but would make fun of others who used them. In the year following the publication of her first serial, when a friend referred to someone 'sitting assiduously under the mistletoe', Olivia remarked sharply, 'Is "assiduously" the longest word you know?'

'Don't become an intellectual snob,' warned the Commander at home.

There was little reaction to Olivia's novel when it came out, except pride by her family and words of encouragement from friends. Even her brother's friends, who thought her a bit of a show-off, conceded that she was cleverer than most of the girls whom they knew. But no London publishers wrote to her to make enquiries about future Jacob Morrow works. Olivia could not help comparing her lot with those literary newcomers who had made overnight successes in the same year, such as Evelyn Waugh with *Vile Bodies*.

She put *Rose of Rubies* and the following two Jacob Morrow serials away in a drawer, but not before she had corrected a number of printing errors in the first of that trio.

Chapter 7

'Olivia Manning is a Beautiful Name'

In December 1929 Jacob Morrow won the fourth prize with 'The Sunwaite Ghost' in a Christmas short story competition sponsored by the *Hampshire Telegraph*. The following December another ghost story appeared in the same paper, entitled 'Quinces' – though this time it was signed O. M. Manning. Olivia felt that she had built up sufficient confidence to publish under her own name. Besides, there were advantages to be considered. For one thing, she wanted to be known among her friends as a published writer. 'It gave me the kudos I needed,' she was to admit many years later.

These two ghost stories are the only ones that she ever wrote. Yet all her life she was drawn to tales of the supernatural. Sometimes she would punctuate the course of an interview with a direct question to the interviewer – 'What do you feel about ghosts?' 'Are you concerned with reincarnation?' This could be disconcerting, as Ruth Inglis found when she had interviewed her for the *Observer* on 6 April 1969: 'Did I believe in life after death? I floundered. No, I don't think so, I said lamely . . .'

Reggie used to keep his eye open for any items in the press of a 'spooky nature' that he thought might interest his wife. In the margins of an article that was published on 24 October 1974 in the *Listener* about ghosts, subtitled 'A case for Reincarnation', he pencilled, 'Olivia – I think you might write a short story touching on these capers. Love, R.' The 'capers' included an account by a man who had witnessed his own hanging.

In Portsmouth Olivia had irritated her brother's friends by asking them if they believed in reincarnation, or an afterlife. Usually they would stare blankly at her, or on some occasions challenge her. 'Oll,' they would begin, 'how *can* you believe in life after death?'

She would silence them with, 'What is more extraordinary than being alive?' She always loathed it when they called her 'Oll'. Her father was much more sympathetically disposed towards her in these matters: he would put a tick by items about haunted houses, psychic happenings and people who claimed that they had come back from the grave – then leave them in her room upstairs. She was to amass quite a collection of such pieces from the *Portsmouth News* and the *Daily Telegraph*.

However, Olivia seldom kept her files in any order, or arranged them chronologically. To anyone going through her papers, the impression is of a writer who haphazardly collected items on any subject that interested her and put them in the nearest folder to hand. Thus a folder might contain articles on Hispano-Suizas from the *Autocar*, travel pieces on the Greek islands from *The Lady*, or accounts of flying saucers sent to her by fans in America. Guests, when asked to pour the drinks, would find pages of manuscript, royalty statements and electricity bills loose upon the tray. She also kept some of her make-up there. You could easily trip over a saucer of cream for a cat. Her kitchen, too, had its chaotic side. The novelist J. G. Farrell, to whose memory she dedicated her last book, once found a bottle of skin tonic in the refrigerator beside a tin of tomato puree. At home in Portsmouth her mother had been obsessively tidy and Olivia had never been allowed to leave her books or papers in the sitting room. Her easel, which her mother allowed her to keep in the hall, had always to be neatly folded up and stacked against the wall.

As her brother grew older, he was full of pride in his sister's achievements as a painter and a writer. But his friends remained unimpressed. Stanley King, who lived near them, wrote to the Braybrookes in 1986, 'Olivia in those days purported to be a writer, but we knew she had no talent for it.' He then added, 'But how mistaken we were!' Among themselves, Oliver's friends would quietly smirk at his sister when, attempting to play the lady-writer, she would lean back on a chaise longue and listen disdainfully to their conversation while smoking a cigarette from a long holder. Nor did she approve of their high jinks, although she would occasionally tag along with them to a pub. She was quick to disassociate herself when they unscrewed the second 'I' from LADIES TOILET, leaving it to read LADIES TO LET. What a contrast to that occasion many years later when she herself changed a chalked-up notice in a Hampstead gay pub, the William IV, from MENU UPSTAIRS to MEN UPSTAIRS. This was in the last year of her life.

*

At the beginning of her career Olivia found it more difficult to write about women than men. In 'Growing Up', the longest short story that she ever wrote and chosen in 1948 as the overall title for her first book of short stories, she has a scene, set in the 1930s, where an aspiring young writer called Anna is invited by a publisher to his office in Great Russell Street to discuss a collection of short stories by her. The publisher, Lewis Mitchell, is based on Hamish Miles, who worked at Jonathan Cape. Anna confides in Lewis,

> At first I couldn't write about more than two people at a time. I couldn't . . . I couldn't handle three or four or a crowd. I couldn't somehow get the grouping of them. But now it's easier. And I used to find women difficult. I used to identify myself with one of the men.

Numerically there are far more male than female characters in Olivia Manning's fiction. With heroines, unless they are modelled on herself, she always had problems.

Between 1929 and 1935 Olivia wrote some twenty short stories. One of them, 'A Change of Mood', was chosen by Edward O'Brien in 1935 for his annual anthology of *The Best British Stories*. It is not included in either of Olivia Manning's collections of stories of 1948 or 1967. Most of her early stories were sent out several times – Olivia was persistent in this respect – but many returned like homing pigeons. Finally, after the Second World War, she put them away in a cardboard box labelled 'Dead Stones'. She said to Reggie, 'I may resurrect some of them. You know how I hate wasting anything.'

To go through this box is to be reminded of Olivia's early interest in Freud. For instance, 'Gerald and Eva' is a psychological tale of a house-maid who becomes a mother substitute for a young boy whose own mother has deserted both him and his father – described as 'a dark spider of a man'. Olivia's early reading of Russian folk tales colours her story 'The Uncertain Feeling', about the Tartars and a prince who, after many thrilling adventures, asks for the hand of the youngest daughter of a princess.

In 1933 Olivia wrote in expectation of help and advice to Geoffrey West, who reviewed books widely. 'I am still trying to write,' she began. 'I live amongst people who have no interest in literature and who only laugh at

anything I write . . .' Another story of hers at this period was 'The Way
Things End' which, though rejected, shows a helping hand at work –
perhaps West's – since, for example, 'earnt' is crossed out in it and
replaced with 'earned'. In it, an apprentice optician terrifies his girlfriend
by telling her that he has been treating a woman for gonorrhoeal
ophthalmia but had not washed his hands before leaving the clinic.
Portsmouth, like most naval towns, had its red light district. Petty officers
would warn their men to give a wide berth to any girl the whites of whose
eyes were yellow, since this was a sign that she was probably suffering from
gonorrhoeal ophthalmia. One of Olivia's brother's friends, whose father
was a dentist, had passed this information on to her.

In February 1929, just before her twenty-first birthday, Olivia had begun
to keep a pocket notebook in which she made literary notes and entered
quotations that appealed to her. Halfway through, one note reads, 'A
poem called "Syphilis" was written in Latin by Fracastorius, pub: 1530.'
There is also a reference to 'the seductive indecency of Laclos and
Crebillon fils'. Another, which she copied out in green ink, is a passage
taken from Odo of Cluny of the tenth century.

> If men could see beneath the skin . . . the very sign of a woman
> would be disgusting to them. Consider what is hidden in
> women's nostrils, in their throats, in their stomachs . . . And
> we, who would not touch with our fingertips vomit or dung
> – how can we long to clasp in our arms a mere bag of
> excrement?

A passage from St Bernard is about the decay of the body in the grave,
and another from a fourteenth-century historian is about the tortures to
which John de Leyden and his followers were subjected before they were
burned to death by red-hot pokers, by the order of the local bishop. From
W. B. Yeats, who was to write of how

> Love has pitched his mansion in
> The place of excrement

she was to quote freely.
     This pocket book of hers is like a commonplace book in miniature and

draws on texts and sayings by Pascal, Havelock Ellis, Petronius, C. E. M. Joad, Leopardi, Herbert Read, Milton, Robert Graves, Tolstoy, George Moore, Walter Pater, Frank Rutter, Adler and Bertrand Russell. The only women quoted are Clothilde de Vaux and Katherine Mansfield. There are also short passages, copied out from encyclopaedias of music, about Palestrina and Schumann, and from scientific works about electrons and the speed at which light travels. Several items are initialled O. M. or O. M. M. and come direct from the author herself. Two typical entries are,

We may look backwards but we must always go forward. O. M.

Hamlet, Prince of Denmark – that classic God of dreamers. O.M.

Or, here she is haltingly struggling with words to set down what Pascal means to her:

Reading the Pensées I sometimes sensed an inexpressible, a pain inexorable, so deep sounding one knew they echoed down a mighty chasm such as is agony to plunge. I felt that I too had glimpsed, if only for a fast fleeting instant, something of its depth. O. M. M.

During the first half of the 1930s, Olivia was to strike lucky three times with the same magazine. *New Stories* was the English counterpart of the American *Story* and both magazines, in retrospect, appear to have had a left-wing slant. Launched in 1934, *New Stories* had six editors: H. E. Bates, then regarded in England as the great white hope of the short story; Edward J. O'Brien, an early pioneer in short stories; Arthur Calder-Marshall, who was at the outset of a successful literary career; Hamish Miles, who was Edward Garnett's close colleague at Jonathan Cape; L. A. Pavey, whose brainchild was *New Stories*; and Geoffrey West, biographer and critic. When Olivia saw the list, her first reaction was 'All the editors are men. I have a feeling I shall be successful!' But when she made this comment to a member of the Literary Society in Portsmouth, she had as yet met none of them. She had told the same society at a meeting in 1933 that in the writing stakes there were good writers, less good writers and charlatans. 'Naturally we all belong to the first two,' she proclaimed. 'Religions and political affiliations are of no concern,' she added. In 1966 she drew the same conclusions in an interview that she had with Kathleen

Anscomb, published in *John O'London's*. She added privately on that occasion, 'No male novelist has the supreme artistry of Jane Austen, and no female novelist has the scope, word-power and humour of Dickens.' In the 1930s Olivia had not read Jane Austen and only glanced at Dickens.

Although *New Stories* did not pay for contributions, Olivia was greatly encouraged by being among such distinguished rising stars as Stephen Spender, Dylan Thomas and Pamela Hansford Johnson. As soon as her first story, 'A Scantling of Foxes', had been published she became more convinced than ever that she must move to London and find a job. After day excursions, she even went so far as to say to her parents that she loved the smell of the Tube – something that in fact she always detested.

In the first part of the 1930s Olivia completed two novels of her own and sent them out under the name of O. M. Manning.* The first 'was written on Dostoevskian lines, immensely long and immensely expensive to post'. One rejection note – from Cape – had this typed on it: 'Let me remind you of the words of a great writer: "Look into your heart and write . . ."' The great writer was Sir Philip Sydney. Whoever sent the note had forgotten to sign it.

The result was that Olivia immediately began work on a second novel. It was about the misery of living in a provincial town and of a hero who escapes to a Paris garret only to die of consumption. The fact that ten of her father's brothers had died of consumption had given her a special interest in the disease.**

When Edward Garnett looked at the second manuscript he told his assistant at Cape to send a note of encouragement. The assistant was Hamish Miles, who added the invitation that, if she was ever in London, she might come in to see him at his office. Edward Garnett had sent Hamish a note about Olivia to say that not since the manuscript of D. H. Lawrence's *The White Peacock* had arrived on his desk in 1911 had he 'been

---

* No manuscript of either of these two novels has survived because, much against Reggie's advice, she decided to destroy both of them when, after her mother's death in 1954, she went down to Portsmouth to prepare to sell the house in Laburnum Grove. 'She had a great bonfire in the garden,' Reggie said sadly.
** When the manuscript came back regularly with a heavy thud on the mat, her father would say, 'Poor little Ollov.' This was sympathy that Olivia could do without. 'I will not let Dumps pity me in this way,' she wrote in a diary. 'Dumps' was her special name for her father. 'One day Dumps will be proud of me,' she told her brother.

so sure he was recommending a writer of a similar order'. Hamish later copied this out and gave it to her.

Her first meeting with Hamish was something that she was never to forget. At it he had asked her why she wrote under the name of O. M. Manning. When she replied that she thought literature was a man's world and she wanted to be thought of as a man, he looked her straight in the eyes and said, 'Olivia Manning is a beautiful name. It is a half-hexameter.' From that moment on she decided she would publish under no other name. She knew instinctively, too, that with this man, who had offered her this new identity, she would become inextricably involved – sooner or later.

Chapter 8

First Love

Hamish Miles was in his late thirties when Olivia first went to see him at Jonathan Cape. He had been with the firm since 1929, and for a short time in 1934 had also taken over the editorship of *Life and Letters* from Desmond MacCarthy. Edward Garnett, whom he regarded rather more as the 'boss' at Cape's than he did Jonathan Cape himself, had great faith in Hamish's unfaltering editorial eye. Malcolm Lowry* and Stevie Smith were among Hamish's discoveries.

Hamish was both an editor and a translator. André Maurois's books were among those he translated and he was the first person to conceive the idea of a Translators' Guild. His lifelong, though never fulfilled, ambition was to translate Flaubert's complete works. It was characteristic of him that whenever he found a book worth translating, he would quickly pass it on to someone else instead of taking on the task himself.

It was generally accepted that Hamish Miles knew everyone worth knowing in the literary world – a view endorsed more than once by Rupert

---

* Olivia always thought of Lowry as belonging to the generation before her own: but he was in fact a year younger than she was. In the 1960s she often smuggled out from the public library in Swiss Cottage his *Under the Volcano* in the hope of gaining converts for him. She would say to friends, 'It must be read very slowly, without the pressure of an expiry date. You can keep it as long as you like, so long as you eventually return it to me.' In her borrowing from public libraries, Olivia was a law unto herself.

William Gerhardie was another writer whose novels – especially *The Polyglots* and *Of Mortal Love* – had a very special place for her. In her second Jacob Morrow serial, entitled *Here's Murder*, Gerhardie's books are on the shelf of the room which the hero rents off Fleet Street. On several occasions she suggested to Hamish Miles that he should invite Gerhardie to join the Cape list. Nothing came of this.

Hart-Davis. But Hamish was cautious when it came to introducing literary friends to each other. However, he was willing enough to give Olivia proof copies of the firm's new books. One of these was Monk Gibbon's *The Seals* (1935), to which Olivia, with her love of animals, responded with enthusiasm.*

There is no doubt that Olivia's meeting with Hamish Miles determined her to come to London. In retrospect, she was to say, 'It seemed to me I did not start living until I came to London.' Of the time before she met Hamish she said, 'I existed in a limbo of loneliness, longing for someone I had yet to meet.' London, Olivia was convinced, would provide the solution to everything. But, to her parents, the capital represented danger – especially for young girls living in digs on their own. In spite of all their warnings, Olivia carefully read through the 'Situations Vacant' column in *The Times* each day, answering any advertisement that struck her as a possibility. For several months she drew a blank. Then, early one morning in a fit of desperation, she impulsively caught the bus to Victoria and took a portfolio of her drawings and paintings round the art galleries and agencies. Nobody showed much interest.

At long last, when she was just about to give up reading the 'Situations Vacant' column, an advertiser from Threadneedle Street to whom she had written over a month previously rang up to arrange an interview. The interview was fixed for 10.30 a.m., but on her arrival at the office she found a dozen girls ahead of her in the queue applying for the same job and she had to wait for more than an hour. After an abortive interview she rang Hamish Miles. 'Come immediately,' he said. As she put the receiver back, she felt convinced that 'a great occasion was at hand'.

Hamish Miles was slightly built and not very tall. He was full of confidence and very much at home in the world of letters. His manner was that of an Oxford don. Balliol had been his college. Beside him in his office was a chair stacked with copies of the right-wing paper *Action Française*. As he discussed Olivia's literary ambitions with her, he

---

* In a chapter on 'The Hills of Donegal' in her Irish travel book *The Dreaming Shore* she writes of how, in 1949, she tried to visit Monk Gibbon at his Donegal home – only to find that he was away in London. 'I would have been glad to tell him how, years ago, newly come to London, I had read his book *The Seals*, and his writing had recreated for me this Donegal shore so completely that I went about for days in a dream.' Despite Olivia's enthusiasm for the book, Hamish never introduced her to Monk Gibbon on the Irishman's visits to London.

nervously moved around the pens and pencils on his desk. Olivia found him sympathetic to talk to and confided in him how she had failed in her interview earlier that day. 'But you have not failed at this interview,' he reassured her. When she told him how London intoxicated her, he smiled benevolently.

On her way back to Portsmouth that evening she wrote in her diary, 'Hamish has a hedonist's mouth.' She noted, too, in the same entry, that Hamish had said, 'When you come back to London and have a job, we must have dinner together to celebrate.'

A few weeks later, through the help of a retired naval friend of her father's, she found a job in London.

On the day that she left Portsmouth her mother repeated her warnings about the dreadful things that could befall girls in the big city on their own. 'I won't describe them,' she went on. Then she added sarcastically, 'If her ladyship cannot keep herself in London, she can of course return home. Don't get the idea we can send you money to live off.' It was Mrs Manning's personal view that her daughter would not last a fortnight in the capital.

Olivia's job in London consisted principally of typing out lists and addresses for the van drivers at Peter Jones in Sloane Square. She had to clock in at 8 a.m. and, when the vans began their rounds an hour later, she was left in charge of the telephone in the delivery department. Customers would frequently be extremely rude to her if their orders did not turn up on time. 'They would vent their rage on me – not the drivers,' she would later reminisce. 'The drivers were men. It was my misfortune to be a woman.' Her wages, as she referred to them, were thirty-five shillings a week. 'Had I been a Londoner, they would have been £2 a week.' On the back of an envelope she was to make this note: 'In the provinces you have "wages", in London a "salary".' When she rang Hamish and told him what she was being paid he said, 'Monstrous! Simply monstrous!' But he did not volunteer to help her find another job.

During her first week in London she had lodged at the Girls' Friendly Society near Euston Station. In her dormitory two bossy women, who had been residents for nearly a year, used to talk non-stop and allow no one to sleep until they themselves were ready. This was hard on Olivia, because she had to be up at 6.30 to reach Peter Jones by 8 a.m. However, within a week of coming to London she found herself a large bedsitter in

Margaretta Terrace in Chelsea, only ten minutes' brisk walk from Peter
Jones. Hamish was appalled when he saw the place. 'My dear child, you
can't possibly stay here. Look around for something better. Let's go out to
dinner meanwhile and talk things over.'

Olivia had never been out to eat in a London restaurant before.
Hamish's car with its shabby cloth hood surprised her. She had expected
something more sophisticated – perhaps a drophead Sunbeam Talbot,
such as her brother Oliver now owned.

The Soho restaurant, which Hamish chose, was Au Jardin des
Gourmets. The knowledge of how wicked her mother would think her
for eating French food at a French restaurant offered an extra excitement. When Hamish admitted that he was a married man with two
children, she had visions of her mother assuming that she was well on
the road to perdition. How on earth, Olivia wondered, would her
mother have reacted if she had known that, in addition to all this, her
daughter's companion had actually translated a book about the wicked
Lord Byron – written by André Maurois and brought out to acclaim by
Cape in 1927? While working on his translation Hamish had spent
several days at Newstead in Nottinghamshire, where Byron had once
lived, checking the names of places that Maurois had from time to time
capriciously rendered into French. There was one such name that
completely foxed him – *La Voie Nuptiale*. Then, on the last morning of
his stay, it dawned on him that it meant 'bridle path'. What a contrast
between Hamish's romantic gallantry and the treatment that she
received at home, where everything she did brought forth criticism and
grumbles! She had grown weary of her mother complaining that her
daughter was too clever by half and that cleverness was best left to boys,
and of advising her that she should stop looking down her nose with
such obvious disdain at her brother's friends since 'You might still find
yourself a husband among them'.

Olivia proved herself to be an appreciative dinner guest that evening
and Hamish a charming host. Many years later she was to tell Francis King
that that was the first occasion when she realised that she could fascinate
a man. Hamish told her that an important future lay ahead of her as a
novelist. When she mentioned the novel that she was planning about the
Irish 'Troubles', he at once encouraged her. She then naïvely promised to
include him as one of the central characters.

*

At first Hamish and Olivia only met once a week and, not wishing to cause scandal or gossip, he chose a different restaurant each time. They argued intensely about literature, particularly when she claimed sweepingly that the Russian novelists were by far the greatest. Hamish countered by declaring that the greatest novel in any language was *Madame Bovary*. 'One day I shall translate it as it really should be done. It's a task that I am reserving for old age.' During her next lunch hour Olivia went out and found a second-hand copy translated by Eleanor Marx-Aveling.

As time went on, their evenings together became more frequent and the mentor-pupil relationship began to alter. He still entertained her with literary gossip and stories of how Augustus John would keep cabs ticking up outside the Café Royal while he had yet another *fine*, and of how *Action Française* once referred to a French prime minister as '*cette giraffe bisexuelle*'. 'How restricting are our own libel laws!' he said with a sigh. But into their conversation there was now creeping a more serious and personal note. One evening he told her that his wife lived in the country and that, since they were Roman Catholics, their marriage was an indissoluble one. His wife, he told Olivia, was a partial invalid 'who could no longer tolerate sex'. He himself had fallen in love with a neighbour – a woman whom he mysteriously referred to as 'V'. They had had a tempestuous affair and, although it was over now, they remained friends.

Hamish never attempted to lie to Olivia. He knew that she came from a home in which her father had deceived her mother. At Sylvia Beach's bookshop in Paris he had bought a copy of James Joyce's *Ulysses* and this he now presented to Olivia. In it he inscribed 'From Ulysses, the Wanderer and Deceiver'.

One night after she and Hamish had dined together, they went back to her new room in Oakley Street and, while she waited for the water for the coffee to boil on the gas ring, he sat close beside her on the floor. Then, suddenly, he swept her up and carried her over to the bed. She wrote afterwards,

> Like Madame Bovary, I could say 'I have a lover', and transported by the experience, I told him: 'The first time I saw you, I knew it would end like this.'
>
> He agreed: 'Yes. When you came into my office, there was a little flash. Like lightning. I felt afraid.'
>
> 'Afraid? Why afraid?'

'Oh! My dear, you must realise how complicated my life is.
I was afraid of making things worse.'

Halfway through 1937 Hamish was offered the editorship of the *Times Literary Supplement.* Olivia too had improved her job at Peter Jones. She was no longer typing lists for the van drivers, but working in the reproduction studio, where a number of young artists decorated furniture. She had first become aware in the canteen of this privileged group known as 'the artists' and longed to join them. She took her portfolio to a buyer, who was well disposed towards her, and he in turn showed it to the head of the studio. Mistakenly, the head thought that Olivia Manning was Ruth Manning Saunders – an up-and-coming artist. The confusion was to result in 'one of the happiest seasons' of Olivia's youth. She called it a season because it did not last long. Unfortunately, there sprang up a rivalry between Olivia's friend, who was only a buyer, and the head of the studio, and she became the victim of it.

In an article commissioned in 1970 by the *Sunday Times* (but never published) Olivia wrote of herself in 1937 as a girl barely out of her teens, with a lover in his forties. 'Sex for both of them', she wrote, 'was the motivating charm of life.' Olivia, in fact, was about to be twenty-nine and her idyllic first love was soon to be shattered.

Olivia and Hamish met one evening outside the Ritz, went to Kew Gardens and afterwards watched a Marx Brothers film which they had already seen twice. Back in his flat in Bloomsbury, he tried to make light of things. But he already knew from what the doctor had told him earlier in the day that he was a seriously ill, perhaps even dying, man. The next morning he had a luncheon appointment. When he went off for it, Olivia walked with him as far as the Underground. After they had said their goodbyes, she stood on the pavement and watched him as he disappeared into the station. The thought then suddenly came to her that, if she were never going to see him again, she would remember this moment for the rest of her life. She was to write years later, 'I have never again stopped to look back when someone I love is leaving.'

At a party given at Cape the following week, Olivia arrived hopefully imagining that, as usual, Hamish would be there. She had now become a Cape author with the publication in April of her first novel, *The Wind*

Changes. Cape had advertised the book widely, which had pleased her. But Hamish was nowhere to be seen. Unwilling to draw attention to herself and nervous that, if she asked any of the staff where he was, they might put two and two together, she decided to approach John Hayward. There were two reasons for opting for him. First, he was always helpful to young girls. Second, the fact that he was in a wheelchair meant that, if one began a conversation with him, he could not easily escape.

'Why isn't Hamish here?'

'Ah! Poor Hamish,' he replied. 'How sad! Does anyone know exactly what is wrong with him?'

Olivia did not wish to press him for more information or let on how little she knew. But she left the party feeling distinctly rattled.

In the week that followed she began to try to piece together the events of the past ten days. After the last occasion on which she had seen him, he had rung the next day to say that his wife had had a collapse and that he had many things to sort out. Olivia had waited patiently to hear again – but, as fate would have it, it was on the one night when she had gone to a film with Stevie Smith that, she later learnt, he had rung to tell her that he was far from well. As the days dragged by and turned into weeks, and she could still get no news about him, she decided to visit his flat. All the caretaker would say was that Mr Miles's belongings were still there and that it would be more than his life was worth to let anyone in. 'Mr Miles is a very private kind of gentleman,' he concluded.

As Hamish had kept their love affair utterly secret Olivia felt that she had no right to insist. There was, however, one person who knew both Hamish and herself, and who might be able to help. This was the popular and worldly novelist Mrs Marie Belloc Lowndes, sister of Hilaire Belloc. She had once invited Olivia to dine with her at the Ivy, and she had been both generous with praise and supportive when *The Wind Changes* had come out. Learning that Olivia's advance from Cape had been £25, Mrs Belloc Lowndes had urged her to insist on a better one from Knopf in America. She had also put in a good word for Olivia at Heinemann, in the hope that they might offer her secretarial work. Mrs Belloc Lowndes now agreed to ring Cape and make enquiries. When she did so, she learned that Hamish had been admitted to an Edinburgh hospital, where his father was a surgeon: Hamish had developed a brain tumour. 'But surely they can operate,' Olivia said when she heard the news. 'They *must* operate.' The desperate tone betrayed everything to Mrs Belloc Lowndes, who said briskly, 'I am sure they will do everything they can.' The two women never spoke again.*

The tumour might be inoperable, Olivia thought, but sometimes tumours regressed. Having been repeatedly told at school that faith could move mountains, she began to bargain with God: 'I offered unlimited faith in exchange for a miracle.' Nothing happened. Even the London church bells mocked her on Sunday and brought back memories of her excruciating boredom at religious services in her youth. To make matters worse still, she now had no job. After the head of the studio had manoeuvred her out, Peter Jones had offered her back her old job in the delivery department, but she had refused to accept this and her refusal was reported by the firm to the unemployment office. Consequently she was rejected for unemployment benefit.

Then her fortunes turned – at least temporarily. The Medici Society offered her a job at £4 a week – her highest salary to date. 'Prosperous for the first time in my life, I rented a flat in Bloomsbury near to Hamish's.' But her prosperity was to be short-lived. Having learnt that she had published a novel and was writing a second, the manager of the firm summoned her to his office and informed her that, if she had the time to write novels, she could not be giving her full attention to her work. She replied that she only wrote at the weekends and late at night. That simply was not good enough, he said, since he expected his staff to conserve all their energies for their work. He then threatened to sack her unless she would swear on the Bible to give up novel writing. When she refused to do this she received a week's notice. The manager was a Quaker. Since during the war Hamish had served with an ambulance unit run by the Quakers, Olivia thought that the story would amuse him. Some curious scruple, however, had in the past prevented her from writing to him care of his father and it did so once again now. In her heart of hearts she was still hopeful of a miracle that would enable Hamish to return to London to take up his post as editor of the *Times Literary Supplement* and once more to be with her.

Meanwhile she was again out of a job – and too proud to tell her

---

* When told this story, Francis King suggested that perhaps Mrs Belloc Lowndes and Hamish might have previously had a love affair. Might she not even have been the 'V' of which he had spoken? For a moment Olivia looked stunned. Clearly the idea had never occurred to her. Then she said, 'Well, it's certainly a possibility.'

parents. She began to exist on what she called 'a starvation diet' – tea and toast. One evening, walking back to her room in Oakley Street, she had the impression of being three feet above the pavement. Then next day she fainted in Southampton Row. A kindly passer-by then took her to Charing Cross Hospital. A doctor, finding that she weighed less than seven stone, lectured her on 'banting' (as dieting to lose weight was then often called): 'You modern girls are all the same. Go home and buy yourself a steak.'

Soon afterwards Olivia found employment – this time with Edward O'Brien, the American who had been one of the editors of *New Stories* and who had included a contribution of hers in his *Best English Stories* of 1935. He had been given the task of organising readers for Metro-Goldwyn Meyer and was said to employ half of literary London for this purpose. This was an exaggeration, but Olivia found a number of her friends working for him. He was a generous and thoughtful employer. His team of readers had to provide synopses of new novels and then assess their possibilities for the cinema. 'I read so much', said Olivia, 'that I temporarily lost all pleasure in reading. But it was a livelihood and it kept me from starving.'

Meanwhile, she screwed up her courage and wrote to Hamish's father to find out what progress his son was making in hospital. By November she had saved sufficient money to pay the fare to Edinburgh. But when she wrote to tell Hamish's father of her impending visit he replied, 'Poor Hamish does not recognise anyone now.' She then gave up.

In consequence Christmas 1938 was 'Hell – absolute Hell'. There was no one in Olivia's family in whom she wished to confide. She was glad when the three-day holiday was over and she could get back to work. Before the end of the year she learnt that Hamish had died. *The Times* carried an obituary, which Edward Garnett marked and tactfully left for Olivia in his library which she was cataloguing. She read it through – then twice more: 'Over those days I gave myself to private grief that can only be suffered once in a lifetime.' Outwardly she had to remain the soul of discretion. Here is part of a note pencilled in January 1938, which she left among her papers:

> The sound of his voice is fading even now in my mind and each day the lines on his face require more effort to recall. Yet

still, and I know it will be ever so, I would give all the fifty years before me to live again the last one of my knowing him.

A little later, in 1938, Olivia found herself in Edinburgh on a cold, wet afternoon and went to visit the Cathedral Cemetery there. As she did so, she recalled, she saw in her mind's eye Hamish raise his shoulder and put his head on one side and laugh at her, as he used to do. He had done precisely this when they had first met in his office and she had told him how London intoxicated her. Now, on this bleak afternoon in Edinburgh, it had seemed to her as if the sky had brightened for a few moments.

Hamish Miles had been her first publisher. She had been at once swept up by his gallantry and good looks. He reminded her of Leslie Howard, the film actor. Hamish had always told her that a girl as pretty as herself would have no difficulty in finding a husband. 'Maybe,' she had replied. 'But will I ever find anyone another who can criticise my work and help me as you have? I have not forgotten that afternoon when you made me go through a story and questioned me about the use of every adjective.'

In fact, Olivia had already seen such a person – although she had yet to meet him. One evening in 1936, having had dinner in a restaurant in Coventry Street, she and Hamish had watched a rowdy procession of marchers crossing from Piccadilly to Leicester Square. They were shouting, 'We want arms for Spain.' The police had charged to keep order and one police horse had mounted the pavement close to where Olivia was standing. The rider had apologised.

Hamish had turned to Olivia and, speaking as the right-wing Catholic that he was, had observed, 'These people simply do not know what is going on in Spain. Only Franco can save the country and preserve the Spanish way of life.'

By the summer of 1939 Olivia was to think differently. For in that noisy procession had been her future husband, Reginald Donald Smith, a paid-up member of the Communist Party and one of the most vociferous among those who had been chanting 'We want arms for Spain'.

Chapter 9

Introducing Reggie

Reginald Donald Smith, or Reggie as he was generally known, attended the first Marxist classes to be held in Birmingham in 1932. These were at the university, where he was soon to form a Socialist Club, inviting E. M. Forster and Naomi Mitchison, among others, to speak to his fellow students. During a short visit to Cambridge in the 1930s, Reggie met Anthony Blunt – and commented many years afterwards, 'I think I presented A. B. with a conundrum: was I rough trade, or was I a gent slumming? I think that it went through his mind that I might make good spy material.' Others, at times, have suggested that Reggie could have been either a Soviet agent or a double agent for the British government. But this seems unlikely, since he was both patriotic and unable to keep a secret. His Marxism presented the paradox of being totally genuine and oddly ingenuous for someone so clever.

Louis MacNeice, who taught classics at Birmingham University, coached Reggie in Latin and became his lifelong friend. He remarks in his autobiography *The Strings are False* that, though Reggie was the son of a master toolmaker from Aston, he could not have been less like those middle-class students who pretended to be 'working-class proles' at Oxford and Cambridge. 'There's no point in deliberately dropping your aitches,' Reggie once told his friend Walter Allen, who was three years his senior. Both Reggie and Walter Allen had been to the King Edward Grammar School at Aston, along with the poet Henry Reed and George D. Painter, the future biographer of Marcel Proust. Reggie himself was an early Proust enthusiast.

He was born on 31 July 1914 and from the age of twelve, after reading *David Copperfield*, decided that he wanted to become 'a teacher to share the wonder of such books with others'. But in the classroom he was often called a dunce because he could not read what was written on the blackboard. The truth was that he had very short sight and did not wish to involve his parents, who were badly off, with the expense of buying him a pair of spectacles. His mother used to go out 'charring', since her husband suffered from poor health and had frequently to take off days from the factory where he worked.

In 1938 Reggie applied to join the recently founded British Council and was interviewed by Lord Lloyd, a high Tory and former pro-consul in Egypt. One of the questions that he asked was, 'Is your French good enough to take a Duchess to dinner?' Reggie answered boldly, 'Yes – and good enough to entertain her for the rest of the evening.' His curriculum vitae had included: temporary actor in Herbert Marshall's Touring Company; post office sorter at Christmas; part-time summer archaeologist for Sir Mortimer Wheeler; English teacher at two private schools; editor of *Mermaid*, the Birmingham University journal; and a passionate enthusiast for rugby, cricket and chess. He kept quiet about his love of betting on the horses at which, in most years, he came out even. Lord Lloyd had never before seen such an application. He noticed, too, that the candidate's hair was well cut and that he was smartly turned out. The application was successful.

Little did Lord Lloyd know of the terrific stage management that had gone on earlier. Reggie had come up to London for the interview from Dudley, where he was teaching. John Waterhouse, then music critic on the *Birmingham Post*, had lent him a suit for the occasion. Several fly buttons were missing, so Reggie extemporised with a safety pin. Then, just before he left Walter Allen's flat in Bloomsbury, Walter had rushed round to his local dentist and borrowed an umbrella and an Anthony Eden hat. Reggie was a tall man, well over six feet. The hat that Walter had borrowed was a size five. But carrying all before him, as Reggie so often did, he swept out through the front door and called back, 'I'll not wear the hat. I'll just hold it in my right hand. If it rains I'll use the brolly-ho.'

After Reggie had spent seven years – which included those of the war – abroad with the British Council, he joined the BBC, first in the Features Department, then in radio drama. During this time he produced the complete canon of the Shakespeare plays, and was instrumental in helping Harold Pinter and Richard Burton in their early broadcasting days. Later, in the 1970s and 1980s, he became a university lecturer – first in Northern Ireland, next at Guildford in Surrey. He wrote a long article on Arthur

Koestler for *Orion* in 1945, at the suggestion of its editors, C. Day Lewis and Rosamond Lehmann, and in 1984, a year before his death, he published a book. It was entitled *The Writings of Anna Wickham* and subtitled 'Free Woman and Poet'.

Reggie was a great lover of women. In a synopsis for an autobiography that he prepared for Weidenfeld a few months before he died, he gives one section the heading 'Women, Sex, Love'. Underneath this heading he states that these three things have made him a feminist which, he adds, is 'exceptional in my class, which is fiercely macho and sexist'.

At a party given by the Braybrookes in 1966, when Olivia happened to be away, Reggie made amorous advances towards four of the women present. All were married – a mother, her daughter and goddaughter, and an older friend in her mid-forties called Virginia Moody. All of them rejected him, but were entertained by the originality of his approach, which was, 'Are you interested in extramarital fun?' Fun was the operative word, since he never had any intention of breaking up his own or other people's marriages.

Virginia Moody was a friend of Auden's, as Reggie had discovered at the party. Auden had dedicated *The Dog Beneath the Skin* to Robert Moody, her second husband. Reggie was also a friend of her first husband, Frederick Laws, who for many years had been the literary editor of the *News Chronicle*. One week after the party, Reggie turned up unexpectedly at Virginia's flat in Hampstead, only to find a group of stuffed-shirt neighbours there. They had come to discuss what attitude to adopt to the landlord of the block, who planned to levy a steep increase in the service charges. It was obvious from the start that they did not take to Reggie – or his humour. At one point, having already drunk several pints before coming, he started to sing,

> We the upper *chemises farcies*
> Simply hate the landlord classes
> We would like to see their arses
> Tightly packed with broken glasses.

It became increasingly clear to him that Virginia's neighbours would be relieved when he left. Sensing this, he turned to them on the point of his departure and announced cheerfully, 'I am so glad I have annoyed you all.' Then, within earshot of everyone, he said to his hostess, 'The next time we meet, Virginia, we'll have a bloody good fuck.'

Reggie took the attitude that the pretentious should be cut down to size. However, he did not hold it against the women who refused his advances. After his death, the wife of one of his friends summed up his attitude in the *Guardian* in this way: 'He believed that if you made passes, then at least twenty per cent of the time you would succeed.'

Reggie, like Commander Manning, was a charmer. At Birmingham University it was said that he was as much at ease drinking pints with the factory hands where his father worked as with his fellow students. Helen Gardner – the future Eliot scholar, who taught at Birmingham for a while – remembered Reggie as having perfect manners. Once, when she had asked a schoolgirl to tell her what she had most enjoyed about a particular poem, the girl had rebuked her, 'Poetry isn't to be enjoyed. It is to be evaluated.' Reggie's view was that, on the contrary, poetry must be enjoyed before it can be evaluated. By the end of his life there was little English poetry that he did not know by heart. In 1974, during the twenty-minute car journey from Cowes to Billingham Manor, he learnt a hundred-line poem by Kipling. As a student at Birmingham he was word perfect in the name part (some 750 lines long) of *Othello* within three days. At a celebration dinner for Wynford Vaughan Thomas, when the BBC commentator's memory failed him while reciting a poem that he had written as a young man, Reggie, who had only once seen the poem, took over and was word perfect. When rehearsing plays he soon knew all the parts.

Early on in his teens Reggie had met Auden, MacNeice and Malcolm Lowry at the home of the Case brothers, who lived nearby in Birmingham, and whose parents had always kept a place for him at their dinner table when he was a schoolboy and a student. The Case boys, Robert and Martin, had medical and scientific ambitions, and through their family Reggie was introduced to J. B. S. Haldane and Lancelot Hogben – both with a talent for writing popular books about science and medicine. Through the Cases he was also able to meet Maurice Wilkes, famous later for his pioneering work on EDSAC (the Electric Delay Storage Automatic Calculator). Reggie told Neville Braybrooke proudly in 1989, 'You see I was brought up in the Athens of the Midlands.'

When Olivia was first introduced to Reggie by Walter Allen outside Peter's bar in Southampton Row in July 1939, she had gone through 'a sad eighteen months'. During this period she had sweated away for Metro-Goldwyn Meyer and scarcely ever eaten a meal without having a book propped up in front of her. In a good week, she later said, she could read six books. The fee for a report of some five hundred words was half a guinea.

Reggie, who was on leave from his first British Council post in Romania, had prepared himself for this meeting with Olivia. He had read *The Wind Changes* and thought it showed 'signs of genius'. He had, moreover, discussed both it and her with Walter Allen. When he saw her it was love at first sight. He felt protective towards her from the start. 'I want to nurture her talent,' he told Walter.

She was less sure of Reggie and at the beginning kept asking Walter what he thought of him. He told her that he regarded Reggie as the most remarkable of his friends and that he was a man who did not give a damn for anyone's opinion. Walter entertained Olivia with stories of how Reggie had subsidised his fees at Birmingham University by playing Contract Bridge with Egyptian students – and always winning. He also told her of Reggie's talent for making up calypsos and creating joke characters like Madame Alexandra Pushover, the Russian Ballerina, or E. Chuda Titsoff, the author of *Her Polish Lover*. Walter could be free in his talk – but then so could Olivia in hers. The first time that she had invited Walter round to her flat in Woburn Square she had asked him to bring half a bottle of Gordon's gin because she had a bad period coming on. Although Walter was never in love with her he would say, 'I admired her greatly.' In his autobiography of 1981, *As I Walked Down New Grub Street*, he writes, 'She had a wit that was devastating and was as formidable a young woman as any in London.' Olivia liked and admired Walter.

Eventually, although she continued to question Walter about his friend, Olivia knew that she had fallen in love with Reggie. Unlike plain, stunted Walter, Reggie was tall and romantic-looking, with dark curly hair. He was dashing, classless, full of kindness and with an ability to inspire others. Hamish had told her that she was going to be an important writer. Reggie told her that she was going to be a great writer.

In bed one day, Reggie proposed marriage. In the course of their whirlwind relationship Olivia had repeatedly asked Walter, 'Is he serious about me? Is he serious?' She now felt that he was serious.

So it was, on 18 August 1939, that Reggie Smith and Olivia Manning were married at Marylebone Registrar's Office. Among the witnesses were Stevie Smith* and Walter Allen. The Registrar, a woman, invited the best

---

* Reggie always referred to Stevie as their 'bridesmaid'.

man, who was Louis MacNeice, to produce the wedding ring. 'Is a ring obligatory?' asked Reggie.

The Registrar was taken aback: 'Well, not obligatory, but certainly customary.'

Reggie replied firmly, 'In that case we'll dispense with it.'*

War was growing more and more likely, and, nine days after the marriage, Reggie was ordered to return to Bucharest within thirty-six hours. So Olivia travelled on her maiden passport, since there was no time to get a new one. As Reggie remarked a few months before his death, 'Olivia was a sailor's daughter and she said to me, "I'm going to Bucharest with you, come hell or high water." And once she had made up her mind, nothing would make her change it.'

Among those who came to see them off at Victoria Station were Walter Allen and Stevie Smith. They each had noticed on the certificate at the Registrar's that Louis MacNeice's Christian name had been written as 'Louise' – but said nothing. 'One day a biographer will find it out,' Stevie whispered to Walter. Olivia's date of birth was recorded as '2 March 1911'; no one present knew that she had advanced it by three years.

---

* Reggie was often to give Olivia rings – many of them very beautiful – but he never gave her a wedding ring.

Chapter 10

Stevie Smith

Olivia met Stevie Smith for the first time in 1937.

Olivia's first novel, *The Wind Changes*, had been published in April of that year and been well received. Storm Jameson, then at the height of her fame as a novelist and critic, had provided a 'puff', which had been used in a *Sunday Times* advertisement: 'A really accomplished piece of work. She can create living men and women and allow them to develop by the logic of their own natures, which is the gift of a real writer.' The anonymous reviewer in the *Times Literary Supplement* drew attention to her 'novelist's eye for disciplined detail' and ended, 'This novel shows unusual promise.' The book, however, enjoyed nothing like the overnight literary success of Stevie Smith's *Novel on Yellow Paper* published (also by Cape) the previous September. 'And quite rightly,' Olivia had generously told Hamish Miles.

Hamish had refused to introduce Olivia to Virginia Woolf on the grounds that Woolf would 'tear her to pieces'. Nor was he any too anxious that she should meet Stevie, when Olivia proposed it. One evening, however, when Hamish had taken Olivia out to dinner at L'Escargot in Soho, Stevie had come in with some friends and he had then been left with no choice but to introduce the women to each other. There was an immediate rapport – though Olivia admitted to feeling in awe of Stevie on account of her having achieved so much fame at such a comparatively early age. Stevie was then thirty-five years old. Olivia, who was just on thirty, characteristically told Stevie that she was in her mid-twenties.

Literary fame, Stevie used to tell Olivia blithely, was totally un-important. She held the view that the more people went after it, the less likely they were to achieve it. Money, on the other hand, was a different matter. Stevie never earned much from her writings. 'I make far more out of reciting my poems than writing them,' she used to say in the 1960s. Towards the end of her life she tried to raise money by selling her manuscripts through a Kensington bookshop. She was disappointed when no offer followed. Her sister Molly was seriously ill in hospital in Devon and she wanted to help her financially.

Before she got married, Olivia had lived in bedsitters, the first of which, as has already been recorded, was in Margaretta Terrace in Chelsea. The rent was fifteen shillings a week. It was a room on the second floor, overlooking the street and had a gas ring to cook on. The furniture consisted of a double bed, an armchair and a chest whose empty drawers, when pulled out, she found to be thick with dead fleas. Olivia came to the conclusion that it would be unwise to mention the dead fleas to the landlady, who anyway spent most of her time in the basement of the house with a man friend. The man friend wore a patch over one eye, had a grand manner and was not above slitting open the letters on the hall table if he thought they might contain postal orders. Other lodgers warned Olivia that he snooped about the rooms when they were out and would pocket any loose change that he saw lying around. Above the bed Olivia hung a copy of Douanier Rousseau's *Snake Charmer*. She had to hide this away whenever Stevie came round, because of her terror of snakes.

Olivia was always pleased to be asked out to Sunday lunch by Stevie, at her aunt's in Palmers Green. She used to ring Stevie from a call box at Sloane Square Underground station or, if it was raining, ask the landlady's permission to use the phone in the house – if it had not been cut off, which it frequently was for non-payment of the quarterly bill. Stevie, on the other hand, had a phone of her own and would sometimes make a joke about the Palmers Green exchange. 'When in doubt, dial a PAL,' she would say to Olivia.

Architecturally, Avondale Road in Palmers Green and Laburnum Grove in Portsmouth were not so unalike, both being terraces of single-fronted houses, built around the turn of the century. But, as far as Olivia was concerned, there was one enormous difference. Stevie might write poems about Palmers Green being one of the outer suburbs, but at least it was part of London. Olivia had grown to dislike her home town of Portsmouth and to be ashamed of it.*

Olivia admired Stevie's aunt, Margaret Annie Spear, known to her friends as Madge but to all readers of Stevie Smith as the 'Lion Aunt', 'Auntie Lion' or 'the Lion of Hull'. She was a very hospitable, rather bossy woman, who was on the stout side. She believed in fair play at every level of life. When she cut up bacon rind for the birds and put it out in the back garden, she would stand watching at the kitchen window and tap briskly on the glass if she thought a thrush or blackbird was taking too much and so robbing the sparrows of their share. If the ginger tom came prowling along the walls, Stevie – or Olivia or whoever was there – would be told to shoo him off.

Stevie's friends were always pleased to be invited over to meals when Aunt was at home. The Lion of Hull never lost her Yorkshire accent. Up until her late fifties she did all the cooking for Stevie and herself, and for any visitors that they might have. Stevie, who had a good deal of nervous energy, but who was never very robust, tired easily and was entirely dependent on Aunt. Once when Aunt had broken her leg and was confined to the bedroom upstairs, Stevie rang George Stonier, who worked for the *New Statesman*, and asked him how to boil an egg.

In several books about Stevie it has been noted that Aunt was a daily reader of the legal reports in *The Times*, but Frances Spalding is the only biographer who draws attention to the fact that this was one of the few ways open to women to learn about the seamier aspects of life. Aunt had a slightly racy side to her character and she read much else besides *The Times*. Books about India and Indian dialects fascinated her and, as Olivia discovered, they both shared a passion for the lives of heroic soldiers. General Gordon was one of these.

'What a remarkable person your aunt is,' Olivia told Stevie in 1946, wishing she had such an eccentric relation.

---

* In her novel *A Different Face* she renamed Portsmouth 'Coldmouth'. In the Balkan Trilogy Portsmouth is never named, but referred to as 'the hated city'. After her friends Michael and Parvin Laurence bought Billingham Manor on the Isle of Wight in 1977, they used often to invite Olivia and Reggie for the weekend and drive them down from London passing through Portsmouth. On the way to the ferry they would actually pass the end of Laburnum Grove. Never once did Olivia let on that she had been born and brought up there. Nor, out of loyalty, did Reggie ever mention it either.

'We're both lucky,' replied Stevie. 'I have Aunt, but you have the amazing Reggie to inspire you.'

Stevie saw Reggie as Olivia's provider, if not a very spectacular one. He was, of course, also to become the inspiration and central character of many of Olivia's novels. When Olivia told Stevie at a party in January 1953 that she had a novel, *A Different Face*, coming out, Stevie enquired mischievously, 'Is Reggie in it again?' Stevie was not backward in asking Reggie – whom she first met in 1939 – to listen to her poems. Once, when she was intoning to him her poem 'Le Singe qui Swing' to the tune of 'Greensleeves', his eyes drooped and she suddenly stopped in the middle. 'Monkeys really do swing,' she insisted.

In *The Doves of Venus* the character of Nancy Claypole is modelled on Stevie Smith – though Olivia made one or two obvious attempts to disguise this. Nancy is portrayed as a tall, plain girl who has been to the Slade, whereas Stevie was small and attractive, and had been trained at a secretarial college. The central character in the novel is Ellie Parsons, aged eighteen, who has come up from Portsmouth to London to try to make her way as an artist. She is a self-portrait of the young Olivia.

In the following passage Olivia describes Stevie's feelings about sex and men in general:

> I'm bored with men [Nancy tells Ellie]. I was thinking only tonight how much nicer it would be to have a woman friend. Don't you think we have much more fun together, enjoying things, saying what we think, being free, instead of each trailing around pandering to the vanity of some stupid man who expects you to be grateful because he buys you sardines on toast?

In one of her poems Stevie described her home at Avondale Road as a 'house of female habitation'. At one time her mother, sister, great-aunt and aunt were all living there under the same roof. Her father, who was in the Royal Navy, rarely came back on leave and, when he did, he was not exactly welcome. Once, in an attempt to win Stevie's affection, he brought her a parrot from West Africa and walked into the hall with the bird perched on his shoulder.

Stevie was sixteen when her mother died and twenty-two when her great-aunt died. In her late teens and early twenties she had had one or two romps with chaps, as she put it to June Braybrooke's first husband, Ronald Orr-Ewing, but these were more in the nature of larky wrestling matches than sexual encounters. There is no truth whatsoever in the story that she was the woman whom George Orwell seduced one afternoon in Hyde Park – although she certainly enjoyed his company and used him in her novel *The Holiday*, where he is partly Bernard and partly Tom. At one point Bernard declares categorically that women who wear scanty underclothes seldom settle down to family life. Although Stevie was not robustly sexual, she enjoyed the titillation of slightly risqué conversation. Years later, when she was in her fifties, she used to enjoy talking about sex, usually with men who were gay. 'One feels so much safer with queers,' she confided to Barbara Jones. Her emotional interests centred on women and she had a number of crushes in her life, including one on Olivia.

As a writer Olivia often sailed close to the wind and was twice threatened with a libel action: once in 1966 and again in 1977. But in her portrait of Nancy Claypole in *The Doves of Venus* she probably wanted Stevie to recognise herself. The reference to 'sardines on toast' was one clue. There were other sharp asides in the book, for the relationship between the two writers was always one of kiss and scratch.

Oddly enough, both were later commissioned to write books about cats. In 1959 Batsford commissioned Stevie to provide the captions – which Olivia thought fey and soppy – for a collection of photographs of *Cats in Colour*, and eight years later Olivia herself agreed to write for Michael Joseph a book, *Extraordinary Cats*, which proved, in effect, to be chiefly about her Burmese cat Miou and several Siamese that she had owned. Privately Stevie thought Olivia's cat 'memoir' lacking in imagination and her review of it in the *Sunday Times* did not exactly please Olivia, who remarked of it to Reggie, 'It's a give and take affair.' One passage runs,

> Miss Manning has a particular affection for Siamese and Burmese cats and she has many loving and studious things to say about these elegant animals. Just a little perhaps she is inclined to use them as a stick to beat about with. But probably she is in fun when, instancing such distinguished cat-lovers as Lord and Lady Snow, she dismisses dog-lovers as a low lot. Always, on controversial subjects, Miss Manning is

apt to be more agitated than original. But who wants to be original about vivisection and catnapping?

Her book is beautifully written . . .

Reading no further for the moment, Olivia summoned Reggie from next door. 'What's the old bitch up to now? Stevie's getting a bit long in the tooth. I'm glad I don't have to see her. She's a snake.' Then, as an afterthought, she added, 'Always has been.'

Reggie tried to pacify his wife: 'She may have only made that criticism because she felt she ought to say something unflattering. The Sunday editors like that. H. E. Bates was told to make his reviews bite.'

But Olivia could not be mollified. 'No. No! Let's face it. Stevie's lethal about me. Consider our friendship at a total end. I'm spelling the word out – E N D – so that you now know.'

Reggie fell back on a line of argument that he often used when danger lay ahead. 'Well, at least Stevie's put you top of the column.'

'I know,' Olivia replied. 'But what the hell does she mean by saying I am "agitated"?'

'Your book will sell,' he consoled her. 'Hatchards are going to put it all over their window.'

In *The Doves of Venus* Nancy and Ellie, when they are alone together, talk about chaps. Nancy asks Ellie if she has ever gone 'the whole hog' with one. Ellie turns scarlet with embarrassment. 'Did you?' she asks.

'Of course. Lots of times,' replies Nancy boastfully. Stevie can hardly have missed the irony of having such words put in her mouth. Nancy also makes some typical Stevie-like comments when she describes how she and her boyfriend take off their spectacles when they sleep together. 'It's terribly funny', says Nancy, 'to see the two pairs cohabiting on the mantelshelf.'

The truth about these spiteful jabs of Olivia's was that she wanted to get her own back on Stevie for a poem about Reggie that she had written during the war when Olivia was abroad. Olivia did not discover this poem until some years after her return to England.

Olivia had discussed with Stevie her possible marriage to Reggie Smith. Within weeks she had married him. During the August of 1939, on the brink of war, no one knew what would happen next. At a time of such flux, people were eager for permanency in their relationships. Figures of marriages at register offices soared and the newspapers carried interviews with engaged couples, revealing an attitude to marriage of 'Now – or never'. Olivia expressed this in vivid language: 'We young people . . . were rather like those gypsies who, facing a German firing squad, fell upon one another and made love.'

When Olivia married Reggie in the third week of August, Stevie felt that she had lost her 'dearest, dearest friend'. On 8 September Olivia wrote to her from Bucharest, 'Stevie darling, do write soon and tell me lots . . . You know how much I want to see you again . . .' The two women kept in touch by letter throughout the war and Stevie did her best, albeit without much success, to try to place some of Olivia's short stories and sketches. The two friends missed each other dreadfully. Gone for ever were the happy times when they had explored the capital together and had wandered freely through the streets of Soho in a way that their mothers would never have dared to do. Most Saturdays they would plan outings to museums – the Victoria and Albert was a favourite haunt – and in the late afternoon would then drop into a Classic cinema to see a French film. 'What will become of us?' was a question they often asked each other. They believed that the whole world lay ahead of them and that they would achieve great things. Pliny's 'Never a day without a line' became Olivia's maxim in 1936. 'I'll go along with that too,' said Stevie.

The more Stevie brooded about Olivia's marriage, the more resentment grew in her. Why had this wretched man barged in and broken up a perfect friendship? In Stevie's third book of poems, *What is Man?*, which came out in 1942 but which she had started to put together at the beginning of the war, a poem entitled 'Murder' contains these lines:

> My hand brought Reggie Smith to this strait bed –
> Well, fare his soul well, fear not I the dead.

When this poem was reprinted after the war, Stevie thought it prudent to alter Reggie Smith to Filmer Smith. But, unfortunately, years later Olivia happened to come on a copy of a new edition. She immediately noticed that, in an illustration of a tombstone accompanying the poem, Reggie's initials – R. D. S. – were still clearly to be seen, unchanged. She was furious.

Up until the publication of Olivia's fifth novel *The Doves of Venus* in 1955, Stevie had always been an admirer of her friend's work and had reviewed her last three books with enthusiasm. In consequence, when she discovered that Olivia's book was among a batch of new novels sent to her for review by Terence Kilmartin, the literary editor of the *Observer*, she could not have been more pleased.

The review, when it appeared on 23 October, had been placed top of the column, above Colette and Edgar Mittelholzer, and began flatteringly enough: '[A] beautiful novel . . . Miss Manning always writes with a poet's care for words.' But the final paragraph was, at least in Olivia's opinion, shot through with malice. In it, Stevie accused Olivia of suffering from 'moral naïveté', and the book of finally lacking 'balance of thought' in its account of middle age and youth. Terence Kilmartin said to Neville Braybrooke at a party given by Muriel Spark, 'As an actor and director, Reggie knew all about the pitch and toss of first nights. But, poor chap, he had to endure Olivia's publication days as well.' He added, 'I heard on the grapevine that she threw a pair of shoes at Reggie in her rage with Stevie.'

Olivia never took kindly to criticism of any sort. As with many writers, praise was an addiction for her and already on the literary horizon there were two up-and-coming novelists who might seriously challenge her position: Doris Lessing and Iris Murdoch, both thirty-six. With considerable anxiety Olivia observed their growing fame, frequently complaining that each was now accorded solo reviews in the Sunday papers – a distinction that she was never to achieve during her lifetime. 'Stevie isn't my friend any more,' Olivia announced to Reggie. 'Why didn't she pass the book on to someone else, if she had all these reservations about it?' June Braybrooke, who remained friends with both, was amazed to hear each pronounce categorically of the other, 'Olivia is a very dangerous woman', 'Stevie is a very dangerous woman'.

The result was that during the latter part of their lives Olivia and Stevie hardly ever saw each other. Yet when they met by chance at a Hampstead party in 1958, they spent the entire evening on a sofa talking together and ignoring everyone around them. On the other rare occasions when they ran into each other, Stevie would press Olivia to come over to Palmers Green for the day. But Olivia would always be full of excuses. It was too long a journey, she had a bad cold, or she could not leave her cat on his own for all that length of time. Only when it was too late did Olivia regret having resisted these attempts at a rapprochement.

In 1962 in the book department of John Lewis, in Oxford Street, Olivia and Stevie shared the same platform for a talk on poetry and literature. As soon as it was over they parted and went their separate ways. 'I accepted the invitation', Olivia explained afterwards, 'because I was hired and needed the money.'

During February 1971 it became known that Stevie was mortally ill and several newspapers rang Olivia about writing an obituary. Her reply to all of them was that she had nothing to say about Stevie. But one evening, being curious to know more details, she telephoned the publisher James MacGibbon, who was Stevie's executor. He told her that Stevie was very frail and there was little chance of recovery. 'Well, if she's really ill,' Olivia said briskly, 'we'll have to let bygones be bygones.'

Stevie smiled when this was reported to her. 'Heigh-ho,' she said to herself softly.

Olivia never really got over Stevie's death. 'She haunts me,' she would say. On 27 April of that year Olivia and Reggie attended a memorial tea party at the Ritz for Stevie, hosted by James MacGibbon and Norah Smallwood. At it, the poet Patric Dickinson made a speech that was, as so often on such occasions, exaggeratedly eulogistic. At one point he described Stevie as a 'fey, child-like character'. 'Like hell she was,' the composer Elizabeth Lutyens muttered under her breath to Olivia.

By then Olivia had decided that someone should record the real truth about Stevie. She and Reggie had no doubt that Stevie was a poet with more than a touch of genius. But, in Olivia's estimation, she was spiteful and malicious in character. At about the same time as Olivia began to think about writing such a memoir of Stevie she was approached by the *Sunday Times* for a contribution about her. Stevie had now been dead for over five years. So Olivia began seriously to consider the idea. But she had reservations. 'Would I be able to be objective enough about Stevie?' she asked. And, 'Stevie is still the rage and people might think I was suffering from jealousy if I criticised her. Young people worship her.'

Olivia began to make notes in the summer of 1975 and eventually wrote fourteen pages, which she then had to put aside in order to get on with some reviewing. When she returned to look for her notes on the sofa, where she had hidden them under a cushion, they were not there. Search as she and Reggie did, they could not find them.

Looking back on the incident, Olivia liked to entertain the idea that the ghost of Stevie had read the notes with disapproval and spirited them away. She particularly enjoyed teasing her rationalist friends with this possibility, while they in turn would come up with all sorts of explanations. Francis King decided that Reggie had tactfully removed the notes. Others variously surmised that he had put them absent-mindedly in his pocket, they had blown out of the window, or Alex the cleaner had thrown them away by mistake. Olivia was not convinced by any of these explanations. To her, their disappearance was a definite sign that Stevie was still around somewhere.

The story of the lost Stevie Smith notes does not end here. Several years after Olivia's death, pages five to fourteen were discovered at her solicitor's, in a tin trunk stuffed with her papers. This, though, still leaves unsolved the mystery of what became of the first four pages.

In the pages that have survived Olivia comes up with the speculation that Stevie's father might have had Indian blood in his veins, since this would have accounted for her rather dark skin and why 'her eyes were brown – that is really, really brown'. Olivia continued, 'Most dark-haired English people have hazel eyes. Her eyes were circles of a pure, deep brown.' Commander Manning had had a repertoire of stories about people with 'a touch of the tar brush', who were unaware of it.

In her notes Olivia then goes on to maintain that Stevie's clothes were made out of 'furnishing fabric'; she also refers to her 'little girl shoes', which Stevie usually had to buy in the children's shoe department. But, more important to Olivia than all this, she offers an explanation for Stevie's 'bitchy review' of *The Doves of Venus*. She draws attention to the passage in the novel where Quentin Bellot, who is a womaniser, says of his ex-wife Petta,

> She is terrified of death. Positively neurotic about it. If she has
> a tooth out, she fights like a tiger under the anaesthetic. That
> shows a deep-rooted fear of extinction.

In her notes Olivia observes,

> Stevie claimed to be in love with death but, when given an
> anaesthetic by a dentist, she fought like a demon and the man
> came rather badly out of it. I put this in a novel of mine called
> *The Doves of Venus*, which displeased Stevie . . .

Such an explanation might have been accepted by the public in general, for they knew nothing about the real relationship between Stevie and

Olivia. 'You may be able to pull the wool over the eyes of the *Sunday Times* readers,' Reggie told Olivia, 'but there will always be those who know the truth.' He was referring to the Nancy Claypole portrait of Stevie in *The Doves of Venus*. He also reminded Olivia of what a cult figure Stevie had become since her death and reported that he had heard on the grapevine that she was soon to be the subject of a BBC feature programme and possibly a play as well. He cautioned Olivia, as he often did, to proceed circumspectly. Reggie had a surprisingly pusillanimous streak. Once, when he was producing at the BBC a script by Stevie about Palmers Green, she had found him very unwilling to correct the famous actress Flora Robson – another Palmers Green girl – on a point of pronunciation of a local place name.

Olivia always listened carefully to what Reggie had to say. She began also to reflect that if she attempted to distort the facts by attributing Stevie's bitchy review to the scene in her novel about the dentist, it would destroy her original intention of writing truthfully and accurately about her one-time close friend. At some future date she would get down to writing an autobiography and then, she decided, she could devote a whole chapter to Stevie. It was this projected autobiography that eventually became the two fictional Trilogies – the Balkan Trilogy and the Levant Trilogy.

There was also another reason for Olivia putting off writing about Stevie. The more she thought about her erstwhile friend's admirers, the more she realised that most of them had never truly known her. To them, she was no more than 'an eccentric, amusing, oddly-dressed little person'. They had not the slightest idea of her true nature: the young woman who had slashed her wrists in the office; the girl who had an absolute terror of snakes – even in pictures or photographs; and finally of 'Stevie the Scorpion, who knew exactly where to strike for her own advantage'. Nor had Olivia any desire to let the public in general know about her squabbles with Stevie and of how she had once been so deeply hurt when she had read that spiteful poem, probably occasioned by jealousy, about Filmer Smith, alias Reggie Smith, entitled 'Murder'. Far better to follow Reggie's advice: 'If the lost pages of notes ever do turn up, that will be the time to think again about Stevie – not now.'

Chapter 11

The Balkan Adventure Begins

On the opening page of the Balkan Trilogy Harriet Pringle, Olivia's alter ego, speculates nervously, 'Anything can happen now.' The trilogy – *The Great Fortune* (1960), *The Spoilt City* (1962), *Friends and Heroes* (1965) – like all Olivia Manning's work, is three-quarters autobiographical for, as she stated in a note that she appended to Walter Allen's essay on her work in *Contemporary Novelists*, 'My subject is simply life as I have experienced it and I am happiest when writing of things I have known.'

When the Smiths arrived in Bucharest on 3 September, Olivia, whose circumstances so far had been comparatively austere, was immediately dazzled by the sort of lifestyle available even to a young British Council teacher and his wife. The capital of Romania had the reputation of having one of the finest cuisines in Europe. Dragomir's, the exclusive grocer's, was as internationally famous as Fortnum & Mason's. Caviar, steak and every conceivable game bird were served in restaurants into the early hours.

The constant presence of beggars outside restaurants like Capsa's or Cina's took some getting used to. Often these beggars showed off wounds, as they pleaded with outstretched hands and the age-old cry of '*Mi-e foame*' ('I am starving'). So it was that Olivia found that she had to adapt not merely to a new luxury, but also to the perplexing, alarming and distressing envy and importunity of all those people to whom even an adequate wage was denied. Adam Watson, *en poste* at the British Legation at the time, has said of her at that period, 'You must remember Olivia was a provincial girl. She had got to London from Portsmouth. But she had not been abroad much – and certainly for no length of time.'

When the telephone rang on their first night in a hotel, Reggie had to remind her that it was a novelty in Bucharest. People rang each other just for the fun of it. Since in some instances these calls were an early form of blind dating, Reggie did an imitation: "Allo cherie! 'Ow are you? Shall we 'ave a little flirt – yes, no?' But Olivia was not amused when a girl rang four times in an hour to speak to Reggie and on each occasion refused to give her name.

Since refrigerators were also a novelty, most housewives went out shopping every day, or else, if they had servants, despatched them to do so. Olivia had to follow this daily routine. At Dragomir's they would cut sirloin off the bone in the English fashion, if so required. They had an English grocery counter near the door, selling Cooper's Oxford Marmalade, Corned Beef and Quaker Oats. But behaviour at Dragomir's was totally different from that at Fortnum & Mason's, where Olivia had occasionally gone to buy delicacies for Hamish and herself when he was coming to supper. Men at Dragomir's were automatically given preference over women. 'Once in the shop the men shove and push like mad,' she wrote to her parents.

Outside in the streets it was a different story. There, the women did the pushing. In the Calea Victoriei, the great shopping street which commemorated the 1878 victory over the Turks and the end of the four hundred years of Ottoman rule, it was possible to buy every kind of luxury: French silks, Italian leather bags and English cashmere sweaters labelled '*pulloverul*' and '*golful*'. Yet, when Olivia went over to look at the shop windows, she would find herself being shoved aside by other women, whom she had soon nicknamed 'the steamrollers'. On these occasions Reggie would take her arm to protect her. Sometimes she would break away from him and decide to walk on her own in the road itself. 'I'm not Romanian,' she would say defiantly. 'I'm an Englishwoman and I shall walk where I please.'

'You are a modern Lady Hester Stanhope,' Reggie would tell her with pride. The comparison always pleased her.

As the phoney war continued the cafés began to sell iced cakes shaped to look like naval mines. Some were called 'Maginots', others 'Siegfrieds'; they could be distinguished by their streaked and coloured icing, which represented the flags of France or Germany. Sometimes, in this neutral country, the waiters would mistake the nationalities of their patrons and then quickly have to switch the cakes around.

Over the months there was to occur a noticeable change at the English

Bar of the Athenée Palace – a hotel largely patronised by the British colony. Until the fall of Paris in June 1940, Olivia was to note that when a dry Martini cocktail was ordered, a dry Martini was served. But once the Germans had reached Paris and their fortunes were in the ascendant, if a dry Martini was ordered the waiter would invariably bring back three Martinis, having mistaken dry for '*drei*'. Though it retained its English name, the bar was becoming increasingly taken over by the Germans. The English, since it was now summer, sat outside in the hotel garden.

Olivia, unlike Reggie, was always prepared to do battle. One evening, when they had gone to dinner at Pavel's, one of the best restaurants in the city, they approached a table and Reggie sat down at it. But, being short-sighted, he had not noticed the reserved sign. Immediately the head waiter stepped forward, pointed to the word *reservat* and shook his head: '*Nu, nu, domnule.*' Literally '*domnule*' means 'lord' but in Romania even the lowliest are often so addressed. The head waiter had then tried to lead them to another table near the orchestra. But Olivia refused to follow. 'The noise will be deafening,' she complained. The waiter next took Reggie aside and a second later he relayed to Olivia what the man had said. 'He says there's a war on and we're fortunate to be offered a table in time of war.'

Olivia snapped back, 'Tell him it's England's war, not Romania's.' In the end she got her way and the head waiter led them to one of the special tables, set apart from the rest. This scene, with one or two modifications, she records in the opening volume of the Balkan Trilogy.

When hurriedly preparing for her departure, Olivia had only been able to get hold of a guidebook dated 1931 from the public library in Marylebone. From it she had learnt that Bucharest was a city composed of many one-storey houses, standing among gardens and orchards, which made it the greenest and most spacious capital in Europe. But what she saw when they arrived was vast areas being cleared as sites for new blocks of flats. The first morning when she looked out of their hotel bedroom window, workmen were demolishing buildings close by. When dusk fell, the men were still there but now they were working by flares. The scaffolding looked far from safe. The diplomatist Ivor Porter, in his book about wartime Romania, *Operation Autonomous* (1989), suggests that in Britain such scaffolding would have been condemned. In 1979, a year before Olivia's death, she was shown recent photographs of Bucharest and thought that the capital had been transformed into 'a kind of downtown Manhattan'. Her memory of it was of 'a confusion of concrete skeletons, of empty spaces and of Royal Palaces partly covered with tarpaulins'.

At first Reggie and Olivia rented a flat, but later moved into one occupied by Adam Watson, their friend at the Legation. They had enjoyed their flat hunting, particularly Olivia, since it gave her a chance to see the inside of many Romanian houses. She noticed how the women, so elegantly turned out in the street, lolled about in their apartments like odalisques, in crumpled dressing gowns, their hair pinned up and their feet sunk into feathered mules. Among themselves, they guzzled Turkish delight and told each other's fortunes with packs of cards. One block was advertised as comprising six flats of *lux nebun*, which Reggie said meant 'insane luxury'.

Café society, which she had never experienced before, thrilled her – though perhaps more in retrospect than at the time. The cafés were centres of wit and gossip – but for Olivia exhausting, too. Reggie was a night owl who loved to talk into the small hours of the morning. 'I'm a rarer kind of bird,' she would say. 'I tire easily.' Often she would leave him holding forth in cafés and slip home. She was fearless and never minded walking through the streets on her own. She had acquired the habit of slipping off to bed when the company became too exuberant, or was likely to stay too long. This was always to be her way. When she had a house in Abbey Gardens, in St John's Wood, she would often jump up and down outside the drawing room and then tell the hard core of guests who remained that they must leave since the people underneath were banging on the ceiling to complain about the noise. Francis King, unobserved by her as he came out of the lavatory, watched her do exactly this.

The talk in the Bucharest cafés centred very much on how the war was going and whether the Romanians' neutrality would hold. The Jews and the peasants were favourite topics. Olivia would confess to her compatriots that she did not trust the peasants an inch; they were lazy and indolent because they were badly fed, and they were badly fed because they were lazy and indolent. In the Balkan Trilogy she puts this argument into the mouth of David Boyd, a character based on Hugh Seton-Watson, the son of R. W. Seton-Watson, whose *History of the Roumanians* (1934) remains essential reading. Boyd in the trilogy says, 'We lost this country . . . through a damn-fool policy of supporting King Carol at no matter what cost to the rest of the community.' This was still Olivia's opinion when, in 1956, she was asked by Sir Basil Liddell Hart to contribute an article on Romania to *A History of the Second World War* of which he was editor-in-chief.

Hugh Seton-Watson recorded that Olivia was not a very forthcoming person and spoke little, but that when she did say something her comments were worth listening to and very much to the point. Once, when Reggie had been making excuses for the Bucharest cab drivers who short-changed foreigners and for the maids who cheated their mistresses, Olivia had cut across with the comment, 'The working classes were not *born* more dishonest than the upper or middle classes.' Hugh noticed that, though Reggie made a waffling response, he could provide no real answer to his wife.

On another occasion when Reggie was in full flood about the merits of Soviet justice and how much better things were organised in Moscow than in London (or in Bucharest), Olivia had silenced him in front of Hugh by saying, 'Darling, you know only four words of Russian and one of them is *Pravda*.' Once in the presence of some Jewish friends in Bucharest, Reggie had put forward the idea that if the Russians invaded Romania, the restrictions on Jews would cease and they would be free to follow whatever profession they wished. His friends had looked from one to another in amazement. They knew of Reggie's courageous visits to see Jews who had been imprisoned in the Vacaristi Jail – and they knew he was a man of high principles. But they regarded him as a total innocent as far as politics were concerned.

When he rambled on about Europe having an outdated economy, they smiled politely. When he said that each member of Romania's workforce supported four non-workers, they wondered from where he had got these statistics. When they asked him precisely how large this workforce was, he replied, 'About a twentieth to a thirtieth of the country's population.' They then pointed out, courteously, that there was a considerable difference between a twentieth and a thirtieth. Colleagues, such as Ivor Porter, thought Reggie 'woolly', while Denis Hills was later to describe him as 'sporting an ingenuous sort of Marxism'. All the same, such people valued his friendship too greatly to allow his political ideas ever to become the cause of a serious rift.

Among themselves they sometimes discussed Mrs Reggie Smith. Where, politically, did she stand? Olivia said her views were those of 'a confessed reactionary moving in left-wing circles'. When questioned further, she said this applied not only to her but also to many of Reggie's friends and of those working for the British Council.

From time to time Olivia would accompany Reggie to the Doi Trandafiri – a café known as a meeting place for intellectuals and reds. Earlier, the Café Napoleon had performed a similar function. Before his marriage and during his first year in the capital in 1938, Reggie had regularly frequented the Napoleon. 'It used to be a meeting place for revolutionaries – painters, musicians and poets,' he explained to Olivia. 'That's why King Carol is having it flattened.' When Reggie spoke of painters, musicians and poets, he took it for granted that they were men of the Left. As a result T. S. Eliot, a poet whom he greatly admired, was always a knotty problem for him. From the moment that she had married him, Olivia had known that on certain issues she would have to argue* with him – but she often included a joke. 'Look,' she had said once as they passed the site of the old Café Napoleon. 'You can still see a strip of the old red wallpaper – in memory of Marx, I don't doubt.'

When they were first married, Olivia believed that she would follow Reggie to the ends of the earth. But there were moments in their early days together in Romania when she did ask herself whether they should stay on in Bucharest. Friends reported that she became panicky as a German invasion seemed more and more likely. On the back of an envelope she wrote, 'Are we, like Nero, playing the fiddle while Romania prepares to burn?' In 1940 there were a number of other European countries in which the British Council was still operating, among them Turkey. This caused Olivia sometimes to wonder whether it would not be wiser for Reggie to ask for a transfer to Ankara or Istanbul. Working for the British Council was a reserved occupation, so there was no chance of his being sent home to serve in the forces. In any case his eyesight was so poor that he would

---

* Olivia was to say of her marriage that she had learnt it meant that she must keep her eyes – and often her mouth – closed. A good example of this occurred in 1979 when the Smiths were staying with their friends Parvin and Michael Laurence at Billingham Manor on the Isle of Wight, and the news came through on the radio that Mountbatten had been killed while out sailing by an IRA bomb hidden on his boat. 'He was a bloody fascist,' Reggie said. Olivia held her peace, as did the rest of those present. No one wanted to argue. Over the years she had become accustomed to such outbursts and had learnt that silence was the best policy. Nor did she react when he weighed in against religion – 'all that sacred mumbo-jumbo,' as he used to call it.

never pass a medical. She also considered a return to home and England. But would he be able to find a worthwhile occupation there? In *The Times* – which always arrived two days late in Bucharest – she discovered that there was a demand for schoolmasters and lecturers in universities. Well, Reggie had been a former teacher. Her mind was full of such possibilities for his future, when suddenly life came to a halt and making a decision was no longer an immediate necessity.

This happened when Reggie had to be rushed to the Royal Clinic for an emergency appendectomy. On 21 September, the day of his operation, Iron Guardists assassinated the Prime Minister Armand Calinescu. That same afternoon, when Olivia visited Reggie, the idea suddenly came to her that, since he was still half anaesthetised, it would be easy for her to have him carried to a waiting ambulance and driven to the Gara du Nord, to be put on to the Orient Express destined for Calais. She was later to write of this episode,

> Something however made me absolutely sure that the right thing was for us to stay on in the capital. Reggie had this great sense of duty and a few days earlier he'd told me that he did not wish to let his colleagues down by leaving the country.

So Reggie and Olivia stayed on in Bucharest and the preposterous plan was never put into action. She did not tell him about it until many years later, when they were back in England. His flattering response was, 'Thank God we remained. If we had left, there would have been no Balkan Trilogy.'

When Reggie came out of the Royal Clinic, Olivia said to him in the taxi home, 'Well, that was the first crisis of our marriage! How am I doing?'

'I've no complaints,' replied Reggie in a businesslike way.

'But I'm not very domestic,' she persisted.

'Domestic enough for me,' he answered, bringing the conversation to a close. Running a household was never something at which Olivia excelled. When still living at home in Portsmouth, she had confided in her brother that she could not bear the idea of 'a suburban and orderly marriage'.

At that time Romania was full of cloak-and-dagger drama. Reggie's salary was £350 a year, which was princely compared with that of Romanian teachers, the worst-paid members of the upper middle class.

'They make up their income by doing a spot of spying,' Olivia was told by
the English wife of a Romanian army officer. 'So don't worry, my dear, if
Reggie is looked upon as a spy.' This was said in October 1939. The words
were prophetic. In less than a year the Gestapo broadcast Reggie's name as
that of a wanted man.

As the months went by, the Smiths became more and more aware that
Hitler's agents were infiltrating this supposedly neutral kingdom. By 1940
the Germans were arranging to buy wheat from the farmers at twice the
usual price, so as to garner favour with the local peasantry. In 1938 King
Carol had officially put down the Iron Guardists, or Legionaries of St
Michael as they were romantically named; but the movement remained
very much alive, despite the execution of its leaders, including Zelea
Corneliu Codreanu, in November of that year. Codreanu's charismatic
character had already turned him into a legend, and he was regarded as a
man who had loved the peasantry and pledged to destroy the Jews and the
Communists. At the time of his death in 1938 there were less than 800
Communists in the country; but by linking the Communists with the
Jews, he had exploited the hatred that his countrymen had sustained for
so long against the Russians. Meanwhile, Hitler saw the Guardists as a
potential Fifth Column, which might be useful for his purposes.

Olivia's letters home recorded the slow shattering of the Romanian
dream for her. She mentions the impact of the German invasions of
Denmark and Norway in April, followed a month later by those of
Holland, Luxembourg and Belgium. All the newsreels shown in Romania
were, she told her parents, now pro-Nazi. She wrote of meatless days and
how taxis were no longer allowed to cruise the streets for fares because of
the petrol shortage. Nor was it long before the Legation required British
subjects to fill in details of birth, address, place of work, next of kin and
religion. When the turn of the Smiths came, the vice-consul pointed out
that Reggie had left blank the space for religion. 'What were you baptised?'
he asked politely.

'I never was baptised,' Reggie replied.

'Well, you must put something. You can't put nothing. Atheist is not
allowed.'

Finally Reggie put 'Congregationalist'. His reason was that he had been
told that Congregationalists in the Army were excused church parades.

On the way home Olivia asked him why he had never been christened.

'I've no idea,' he answered truthfully. 'But you knew I was a rationalist

(*Above*) Olivia's maternal grandmother, Mazoura. American by birth, she was sixteen when she married David Morrow and moved from Mississippi to Northern Ireland.

(*Above right*) Olivia's father, Oliver Manning, known to her as Dumps and to neighbours as the Commander, served from boyhood in the Royal Navy. From the time of his marriage to Olivia Morrow until his death, he and his wife lived in the same house: 134 Laburnum Grove, Portsmouth.

(*Right*) Olivia and her brother Oliver (*below*) – named after their parents.

Self-portrait: Olivia at art school.
She had to decide between a career as a painter or as a writer.

Hamish Miles, the editor at Jonathan Cape who convinced Olivia of her talent as a writer. Her first lover, he died of a brain tumour, a loss from which she never wholly recovered.

Stevie Smith. She and Olivia had enjoyed a close friendship as girls in London before the war, but this soured when Olivia put thinly disguised portraits of Stevie into her novels. In turn Stevie criticised Olivia's work in her reviews.

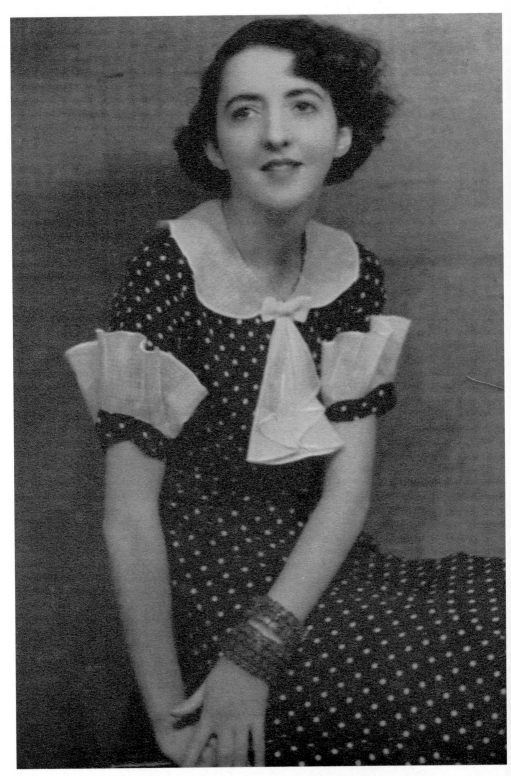

Olivia in the 1930s. Born in 1908, she often lied about her true age, in order to disguise that she had already become a published writer before the war.

Reggie Smith. He married
Olivia in London in August
1939, just before war broke out,
and then took her with him to
Bucharest when he returned to
his British Council job there.

Olivia in Romania, Christmas 1939.
Her wartime experiences in Bucharest
formed the basis for her most successful novels,
The Balkan Trilogy and *The Levant Trilogy*,
in which her fictional characters Harriet and
Guy Pringle are portraits of herself and Reggie.

Olivia

Olivia's brother, Oliver, with his bull-terrier in Portsmouth.

Olivia and Reggie (right of picture) listening to music in Cairo.

David Abercrombie, with whom Olivia and Reggie shared Adam Watson's flat in Cairo. They both admired the breadth of his culture and often sought his advice.

Bernard Spencer, one of the editors of *Personal Landscape*, and a writer whom Olivia admired in Greece and the Middle East. Her character, the poet Castlebar, in the *Levant Trilogy*, is based on him.

The diplomat, Ivor Porter, during his adventurous years in Bucharest. His book, *Operation Autonomous*, contains lively accounts of Reggie and Olivia and their shared life.

when you married me. I didn't want any religious mumbo-jumbo at my wedding.'

Olivia became worried. 'You'll go into Limbo, darling, when you die. That's where the unbaptised go. We won't be together any more.'

Back at home, they had tea. Then, half an hour later, remembering what she had said earlier and finding that the pot was cold, Olivia stood up and poured what was left in it over Reggie's head, saying, 'I baptise thee, Reggie, in the name of the Father, and of the Son and of the Holy Ghost.' Then she stopped. 'I can't remember if there are any more words to the prayer.' She recounts the scene in *The Spoilt City*, the second volume of the Balkan Trilogy.

That book carries the explanation that Reggie's father was an old-fashioned radical, who had brought up his son as a freethinker. Olivia was to say that Reggie had a religious temperament – and certainly he had a habit, when abroad, of going into Catholic churches and lighting candles for friends, and then writing, on picture postcards of them, to tell them that he had done so. Olivia maintained that he believed not in dialectical materialism, but in what amounted to a form of 'Holy Russianism'. She would add, 'Russia for him means people, people, people.' Reggie made vehement excuses for the early Soviet Russian alliance with Hitler. 'Russia knows what she is about,' he announced of the Red Army's attack on Finland at the end of 1939. But in 1956 when he was forty-two and Russia invaded Hungary, he decided finally to resign from the Party. There was a distinction to be made, he believed, between Russian imperialism and Leninist-Marxism.

As the month of June 1940 progressed, news filtered through of the Dunkirk evacuation. The Romanians began to look at their old allies with a mixture of pity and suspicion, for the English now seemed certain to be defeated. New alliances might have to be formed. Russia was out of the question – she was always the predatory bear waiting to seize Bessarabia and Bukovina. But what about Herr Hitler? What might he and his armies do for Romania?

During Dunkirk, Olivia remained very much her father's daughter. One day she proclaimed to those around her at the Athenée Palace, 'Just think of it! The Navy have saved our Army.' Turning to *The Times*, she read out, 'Over 335,000 officers and men have been saved by our strategic retreat.'

A middle-aged member of their party, a woman secretary from the staff of the British Legation, then declared contemptuously, 'A retreat is a retreat, whether it is strategic or not.'

Olivia countered, 'A strategic retreat is only like losing a battle in a war. It is not a surrender. We will win in the end – you wait and see.' She spoke with patriotic confidence. Reggie went along with her – though his main concern at the moment was not the war but his forthcoming production of *Othello*. He himself was to play the leading part, as he had done eight years earlier when he was a student at Birmingham University.

The Anglo-Romanians whom he auditioned for the production included a few of his students. The part of Desdemona, originally reserved for Olivia, he gave to the English wife of a Bucharest lawyer. Reggie's reason was: 'Husbands and wives don't make the best acting teams.'

To that Olivia retorted, 'What about Alfred Lunt and Lynne Fontanne?' This couple almost invariably acted together on the London and New York stages.

'Well,' replied Reggie after a long pause, 'they may act together successfully but off the stage their life is one of hammer and tongs.' The matter was now dropped and Olivia agreed to help him with the costumes and make-up. In one of the Bucharest newspapers, these were highly commended.

Reggie's performance as Othello was judged a towering success by the Bucharest dailies, several of which included photographs of him in the role. According to Olivia, he was 'for a day or two the talk of the British colony'.

'He was so noble,' John Amory, the British Council's director, said to her. But one Romanian schoolgirl remembered the performance for another reason. She and her class had sat in a front row, in the charge of two nuns. During Act V Othello's wig slipped off – and there was a titter among the girls. The nuns tried to shush them. But worse was to follow. Reggie's blacking-up had been less than thorough, so that, when he rolled across the bed, it was quite obvious not merely that he had forgotten to put on pants under his tights but also that he had failed to black up the ample bottom and private parts exposed. The girls tittered once more – even louder. Let Denis Hills finish the story: 'The glaring footlights had turned him into a naked radish.'

Afterwards, in his dressing room, Olivia chided Reggie, 'You shocked those convent girls.'

He took it in good part. 'I had too much to think about. The scene changes weren't as quick as they should have been. Anyway I expect the girls enjoyed it. They've got to grow up some time, and in any case probably know more about sex than we did at their age.'

Before they had left England, Reggie had warned her, 'When you meet young girls in Bucharest, you must remember that they will put on a show of being as innocent as anything. If something slightly improper is said they will look quite blank. The assumed innocence is part of their dowry.' He then went on to tell her a story that was doing the rounds. 'A Romanian and a Hungarian were walking up a main street. The Romanian named the price of every woman they saw. "But aren't there any innocent women?" asked the Hungarian. "Of course," replied the Romanian, "but they are very, very expensive."'

Olivia herself had a taste for risqué stories and limericks, and would occasionally invent her own. Picking up a *leu* note one day, she pointed to the corn on the cob printed on one side. 'A portrait of King Carol in private,' she said mischievously. 'You may not recognise the likeness immediately, but I suspect there are a lot of *jeunes filles* who would.' Reggie told Olivia to keep the joke for the future. She did – and in the Trilogy attributes it to Bella Niculescu, the English wife of an officer in the Romanian Army.

During his first year in Bucharest, Reggie had become friendly with – and perhaps even had an affair with – a half-Jewish girl. He had seriously considered marrying her in February 1938, so as to give her a British passport. On his return to Bucharest with Olivia as his wife, this girl had tried to keep up their former intense relationship. In the opening volume of the Balkan Trilogy there is a scene in which the girl (Sophie) attempts to force Reggie (Guy) to come and see her, and threatens that, if he refuses to do so, she will jump out of the window. In the end Olivia (Harriet) agrees, but only on condition that she goes with him. This incident, like so much else in the Trilogy, actually happened.

Whenever Olivia had a free hour or so in Bucharest, she would return to her writing. At that time her main project was her book about Stanley and his search in equatorial Africa for Emin Pasha. She read widely, borrowing from the British Council shelves not merely books relevant to the work in hand but whatever Reggie recommended. Among other things he introduced her to Romanian poetry. Through him, she met some of the country's leading poets at literary gatherings, where they would read their work aloud. Among them were Zaharia Stancu, who had founded the paper *Azi*, to which Reggie contributed articles on Auden and other left-wing writers, and Mihail Sadoveanu, with whose family Reggie would play tennis when he and Olivia visited them. On these visits Olivia envied the way in which the daughter of the house would slip upstairs to write poems and stories. 'Oh happy state,' she would say with a sigh.

It seemed to Olivia that there were 'two nations' in Romania – the short, stocky, often tricky townspeople and the tall, thin, more democratic peasantry, in whom resided the country's folklore and culture. The dress of the latter had hardly altered over the centuries, whoever their overlords might be – Russians, Turks or Austro-Hungarians. On the full-skirted dresses of the women were embroidered plants and animals – of which she was to be reminded many years later when she and Reggie visited the cave paintings in the Dordogne. 'Nothing changes much,' she wrote to June and Neville Braybrooke on a local picture card.

Romanian music, Reggie explained to her, was mainly gypsy or peasant. Frequently, the peasant music praised the green leaf (*frunza verde*) or celebrated the miraculous moment when spring arrives and the mountain streams suddenly turn into torrents. These songs coincided with the end of the snow and of the *crivat*, the icy wind, that through the winter months blows fiercely from Siberia. When he put his mind to it, Reggie had a talent for foreign languages. Olivia thought that he should set about compiling an anthology of folk songs and poems under the title of 'The Green Leaf'. 'You could do the translations in rough and I could polish them.' He liked the idea and entertained it seriously for some time. But as with so many of his projects, nothing came of it.

A year before her death Olivia said to Neville, 'I don't find it surprising so many Romanian writers came from the villages. Sadoveanu came from a country district in Moldavia and Stancu was born in a village. What they excel at is dealing with village life – returning from fields with scythes. They loved music and dancing and drinking. That was *their* Romania. Ceaucescu wanted to ruin everything. He was a grey man. He once had a cat shot!'

In the summer of 1940 Olivia did a brave and surprising thing: to help out a woman friend, she took over a journalistic assignment from her. This was to visit Julius Maniu, who had once been Prime Minister of Romania and who, it was mistakenly thought in some circles, could return to power and save the country from the seemingly imminent German occupation. Reggie, *Othello* now behind him, was busy with plans for a summer school of English studies, at which he would be chief lecturer. Getting an interview with Maniu would provide Olivia with something positive to do.

'Yes, go . . . It will be good for you. An adventure.' These words are put into the mouth of Alex Linden – Olivia's first attempt to write about Reggie as a character. *Guests at a Marriage*,* which she wrote in Jerusalem between 1943 and early 1944, is, in effect, a blueprint for the first two volumes of the Balkan Trilogy.

Olivia flew part of the way and then took a train. Many years before she had told Hamish Miles that she believed 'a magical immunity protected the journalist'. When she arrived in Cluj, the capital of Transylvania, there was confusion everywhere. The town was bursting with Germans and the hotels were overrun with them. Some people said Maniu had already arrived by train the night before; others that there were hordes of peasants waiting at the station to welcome him. A wife of a Hungarian doctor informed Olivia that Maniu had travelled by car and was now at his home. Olivia decided to take a chance on this. 'It proved a lucky hunch,' she said afterwards.

Maniu, who was sixty-nine but looked much younger, greeted her courteously. But since he did not speak French or English at all fluently, and since Olivia's Romanian was confined to a few words, the interview was little more than a series of elementary sentences, smiles and bows. Olivia left disappointed, feeling how much more could have been achieved if only she had been a linguist or had thought to bring an interpreter with her.

After a long, much-delayed journey back to Bucharest, she met Reggie with the words, 'At least I saw Maniu for a few minutes – even if I didn't get much out of him. He's square, short, elderly and looks like an actor. "Let's wait and see" seems to be his reaction to the crisis.'

In *Guests at a Marriage* Maniu is called 'Manska'. There is, as in real life, a language problem during an all too brief interview. After leaving his house, the Olivia character pauses by the roadside and notes, 'Met

---

* The manuscript runs to 166 pages – though some are missing – and is now held at the Humanities Research Center at the University of Texas. It has never been published – though it might, possibly, interest a university press.

Manska. Pomonia's only honest man. Charming. Shallow.' This meeting is not mentioned in the Balkan Trilogy – though Olivia does give an account of it in her short story 'A Journey', which she included in *Growing Up*, her first collection. There Maniu says, 'We must have patience. Now we can do nothing, but our time will come. I return now to Bucharest to work for our cause.' Olivia thought these were the usual political clichés, and in 'Journey' and in *Guests at a Marriage* she sees him as little more than a gracious, suave actor-politician. In reality he added up to rather more than that. Ivor Porter puts it this way: 'He was one of the least flamboyant heroes any country has ever produced – honest, prudent, often right and completely lacking in the bombast of war.'

The most striking difference between Olivia and her fictional alter ego Harriet is that, whereas Olivia was a professional writer, Harriet remains a housewife with artistic leanings. The description of her in *The Bloomsbury Good Reading Guide* (1988) as 'a genteel 1930s "English Rose"' could not be more ludicrously wide of the mark. Both Harriet and Olivia have strong literary views and each is married to a lecturer. Harriet is twenty-two, whereas Olivia was thirty-one. Harriet's parents have divorced and remarried, and it has been left to an aunt, now dead, to bring her up. Harriet is independent, unconventional and tough. Harriet Pringle, like Olivia Manning, is a half hexameter. In the trilogy Guy Pringle is promoted to Number One at the University in Bucharest, whereas Reggie was in fact Number Two at the British Institute. Number One was Ivor Porter who, after the Second World War, was to become Ambassador to the Geneva Disarmament Conference and subsequently to Senegal. There have been confusions about the role of Porter in the Mannings' lives in Bucharest. As late as 1995, in the course of an otherwise excellent article about King Michael and Romania in the *Sunday Telegraph*, Malcolm Arnold wrote inexplicably that Guy Pringle was 'modelled' on Porter.

Porter describes Olivia in 1940 as 'severe' and says that when she, he and Reggie went to cafés in Bucharest 'she never really joined in'. At home she made 'you feel that, as soon as you had sense enough to leave, she would like to go to bed'. Denis Hills recalls Olivia at the same period as 'a pale, skinny girl with a small, oval face, bright button eyes and thin legs' and remarks that when Reggie came home with noisy chums, who would ransack the kitchen, she would soon retreat to the bedroom. It was a pattern of behaviour that in later years became well known to their intimates.

The Balkan Trilogy follows the course of history. But Olivia had a way of often transferring her own experiences to others. Thus it is not Harriet Pringle who goes to Cluj in 1940, but Prince Yakimov, whose aim is to see his friend Freddi von Flugel, now a gauleiter in Transylvania. Several of the members of the British Institute in the novels are lightly disguised portraits of staff at the British Council. The account of the Pringles sheltering Sasha Drucker, the son of a rich Jewish banker, in their flat, is an invention. But the Smiths knew, or knew of, people who had sheltered Jewish friends or deserters from the Army.

Sometimes those who had read Olivia's accounts of Reggie would ask her about him. After a *Yorkshire Post* luncheon in 1978, at which she had been one of the speakers, a woman had come up to her to find out more. 'Do you write down what he says?' she enquired.

'No, I try and remember. At a restaurant in Bucharest to which he used to take me, I heard him say – "One eats for the pleasure of drinking." I thought it was up to Oscar Wilde standard and I kept it in my mind for twenty years before I used it in the Trilogy.'

In the opening volume of the Trilogy there is a scene where Guy, rather the worse for drink, asks Harriet, 'Do you think I look like Oscar Wilde?'

'You do a little,' she answers.

Then, as he climbs into bed beside her, he says with inebriated satisfaction, 'Old Pringle's all right. Old Pringle's not a bad chap. Old Pringle's not a bad chap at all.'

Many years later, in Venice with Olivia and the Braybrookes in 1966, Reggie would come back to the Casa Frollo after a heavy night of boozing and make his way up the stairs alone. Neville and June would then hear him telling the cats of the *pensione*, 'Reggie's not a bad chap, not a bad chap at all.'

It is one of the minor characters – Klein, a Jewish financier – who provides a key to the Balkan Trilogy when he says, in 1940, that Romania can be likened to a foolish person, 'who has inherited a great fortune' only to squander it. But Olivia herself sees 'the great fortune' as something different. In her second volume, *The Spoilt City*, she describes Bucharest as a city in the process of selling itself to the Nazis. The whole country is falling apart, while the English colony can only look on appalled. For

Harriet and Guy 'the great fortune' has become life itself, which they must preserve as best they can, whatever the odds against them. Earlier on, Guy has quoted to Harriet, 'There is no wealth but life.' It was not until 1976, when Olivia read *The Letters of J. R. Ackerley*, where this quotation is printed on the title-page, that she learnt that it came from Ruskin. 'We must remember those words when bank managers become tiresome!' she told June. Both women always did – to their advantage.

In *Guests at a Marriage* (Olivia's unfinished draft) Maria Tanase, the famous Romanian gypsy singer, is called 'Dola Polksa' and each evening at Pavel's finishes her final song 'with a last elemental howl of sexual fury that drowned even the applause'. In *The Great Fortune* (the second volume of the Balkan Trilogy) Maria Tanase is called 'Florica' and now ends her performance at Pavel's with 'an elemental screech that was sustained above the tremendous outburst of applause'. There are many similar changes between the first manuscript and the final published text.

Among Maria Tanase's English fans in Bucharest were Geoffrey Household, the author of the best-seller *Rogue Male*, Denis Hills and the Smiths.* In 1940 the Minister of Information, Ionescu, had been Maria Tanase's latest protector. When the Balkan Trilogy came out twenty years later neither the singer nor the politician was alive. But Olivia was less fortunate with her account of the assassination of the Prime Minister, Armand Calinescu, which occurred on 21 September 1939. In her novel she wrote that his entire family had been wiped out. In 1968 Barbu Calinescu, son of the Prime Minister, brought a successful libel action against the author and her publishers on the grounds that the opening two volumes of the Balkan Trilogy had made him appear an impostor. Not only had he, his mother and a number of other relatives in fact all survived, but since 1940 he had been a resident in England. 'Ex-Premier's Son Receives Apology' was a headline in the *Daily Telegraph*.

As the war entered its second year in September 1940, King Carol abdicated in the first week of that month. In one sense Romania was

---

* In the television version of the two Trilogies, presented under the joint title *Fortunes of War*, Kenneth Branagh, who played the part of Reggie, caught him to perfection when he put up both his hands above his head to applaud Maria Tanase as she took her bow. 'That was an inspired re-creation of Reggie,' said T. P. McKenna, the actor, who knew him well.

already an occupied country, with the swastika displayed in many shop windows along the Calea Victoriei. Maria Tanase sang with greater abandon than ever about the city's disappearing freedom. 'But where will the Jews go?' Olivia kept asking Reggie during these last days.

'I don't know. The Council will look after us. They've places for us in Cairo and Athens. But that doesn't answer your questions about the Jews – or the gypsies for that matter.'

Now that the King had gone into exile, peasants were being herded into cattle trucks so that they could be transported to Germany to become part of the Third Reich war machine. As they boarded the trains, they went happily enough, sometimes singing: many of them thought that they were being sent to fight for Great Britain, their old ally.

On 7 October the Germans officially marched into Romania. As they entered the capital, the army of occupation passed through the city's Arc de Triomphe. In the past the Arc had always been roped off against all traffic, except the ex-king's limousine.

Just one step ahead of the Nazis, Reggie and Olivia decamped to Greece.

Chapter 12

Among Friends and Heroes

Olivia fled first. She travelled to Greece a week before Reggie was able to do so. Some women who had opted to wait for their husbands were critical of her precipitancy.

On their separate journeys both of the Smiths had to touch down at Sofia airport in Bulgaria, where they transferred from Romanian planes to Lufthansa ones. Lufthansa was, of course, a German company, but at that stage of the war still prepared to carry passengers, whatever their nationality, over neutral territory. Nevertheless, there were stories in circulation about planes in mid-flight being diverted to Vienna, where Allied personnel and passengers had found themselves interned on landing. In Athens, Olivia worried greatly about Reggie. During her week of waiting for him she had nightmares about 'R. being kidnapped' or 'being beaten up by the SS'.

Reggie brought with him little luggage – a suitcase and a rucksack. He was twenty-seven and still had the look of a student.* Into the rucksack he had put several changes of pants, shirts and socks; into the suitcase he had crammed as many books as possible and some lecture notes. 'What about your suits?' Olivia asked as they passed through the airport lounge.

'I had to leave those behind,' he apologised. 'Just not enough room. You can buy suits anywhere.'

She retorted, 'Books can be bought anywhere.'

'Yes,' he answered her, 'but not signed copies or first editions.' Among his proud possessions were some first editions by D. H. Lawrence. She was so happy to have him with her that she did not bother to pursue the

---

*There were those who remarked that he retained that look even in his sixties. Olivia used to say, 'All his life he's been happy to doss down on anyone's floor.'

argument any further.

Olivia and Reggie had to acclimatise themselves, in more ways than one. When they had left Bucharest, the signs of winter were on the way; but here in Athens, where people were still sitting in the outdoor cafés, it seemed that summer would last for ever. More important, the Smiths' marriage was entering a new phase. In Bucharest she had arrived as a new bride. 'Our marriage was so sudden', she would explain to new acquaintances, 'that we only received a minimum of presents and the odd cheque.' Those whom she then met were friends whom Reggie had made during his previous stay in the capital. Now, in Greece, any new ones would begin by being friends of both of them.

There was another difference between Romania and Greece. In Romania the English colony consisted of those who worked for British institutions, or for British companies with an interest in the oil fields at Ploesti. In addition, there were a few English governesses, who had long reached retirement age but had been kept on as retainers by rich families living in Bucharest. The British colony had therefore been largely a working one, as Olivia explained to her parents. In contrast, in Greece, the British colony contained many leisured immigrants, who had begun arriving there in the 1930s. These saw the country as a place of retirement and some had even brought their dogs with them. After the outbreak of war, Greece had also been absorbing Poles, White Russians and Jews. There was a Russian Club with Russian food – though one did not have to be Russian to eat there, since nobody was ever turned away.

Greece, like Romania, had many beggars – but there was a difference. The Greek beggars were less mutilated and less aggressive. 'At least they take no for an answer and do not swear at you,' Olivia said to Reggie.

Reggie was not happy about this comment. 'A beggar is a beggar anywhere,' he insisted. 'A beggar is a hungry man.'

All Olivia said in reply was 'You're too dogmatic' – and there the matter rested until some quarter of a century later when she was at work on *Friends and Heroes*, the third volume of the Balkan Trilogy, and he happened to look at a page that she had just typed.

He spoke cautiously: 'I don't want to influence you, for you are after all the author, but I must repeat what I have said before – "A beggar is a beggar wherever he is."' Olivia listened politely, but stuck to her view that the Greek beggars were pleasanter than the Romanian ones. That very morning she had been writing about a beggar whom they had met in their last week in Greece, before the German invasion began. '*Dhos mou psomi,*' he had said to her. She had then opened her hand to indicate that she had nothing to give. He had passed on without a word. Had she been in Bucharest, 'Some deformed creature in a similar circumstance would just have spat at me.'

Reggie was able to make friends wherever he went. Olivia did not have that talent. Reggie could come into a room and within ten minutes know everyone. Olivia was able to deal with only two or three at a time. 'I get lost in a crowd' – that was her verdict on herself in November 1940. R. A. (Reg) Close, a member of the British Council, recalls the period in Athens:

> She shrank into a shell out of which my wife and I several times tried to coax her, so as to have her with us at evening parties or on weekend excursions . . . She preferred to stay in her room, writing and writing but not telling us what.

Her project remained her book on Stanley and his rescue of Emin Pasha from equatorial Africa in the 1880s. Close continues,

> She saw little of what was really happening in Greece, and seemed to have met few, if any, of the interesting and really worthwhile characters who crowded the Athenian scene. [She had] an almost paranoiac fear that colleagues were doing Reggie down.

The last comment has a degree of truth. Olivia did suffer from recurrent paranoia and did, at times, exaggerate Reggie's importance in the British Council.

Olivia's nervousness at social gatherings was something that she tried to get over, but never completely conquered. Harriet Pringle would try 'to endure the situation by distancing herself from it' and watching the company as she would watch a play. Olivia, in fact, missed little and after parties liked to indulge in post-mortems. By all means read Frances Donaldson's history of *The British Council* (1984) for a straightforward account of the Council and its 'First Fifty Years', but read the Balkan and Levant Trilogies for an insider's view, admittedly not always impartial or fair, of the petty intrigues and squabbles intermittently waged within the organisation.

Reggie had his phenomenal memory for passages from books read months and even years before. Olivia could match this with her phenomenal painter's eye for detail and place. She could look at a scene for a short time only, yet years later re-create it down to the last detail. On a patch of grass, at the airport at Athens, she had stood in October 1940, waiting for Reggie to arrive. In *Friends and Heroes* she re-creates the scene as it was – and recalls 'the withered tufts of airfield grass'. Ralph Todd, a friend in Athens at that period, remembers her saying after she had met Reggie off the plane, 'For once he was punctual – or rather the Lufthansa plane was.'

'Romania is abroad,' Olivia would say, 'but Greece is home.' She never went back to Romania: but to Greece she returned many, many times. Soon after she had arrived in Athens in the autumn of 1940, she was seated at the then fashionable café, Zonar's, reading a copy of *The Times* in which was reported the sinking of seven German submarines. A waiter was looking over her shoulder: 'I don't think he could read English – but I think he got the drift of what I was reading. Imagine it! He started to clap! You see, one had only to be English to be appreciated.' Certainly this was in sharp contrast to her last months in Bucharest, where nothing but British defeats were broadcast on the Romanian radio.

On the night of 28 October General Metaxas, the Greek Prime Minister, had rebuked the Italian minister when he called at 3 a.m. Could his visit not have waited until a civilised hour? Then Metaxas learnt that Grazzi had brought with him an ultimatum demanding that Greece should agree to an Italian occupation. '*Ochi*,' said Metaxas. '*Ochi, Ochi.*' Thus, overnight, Metaxas became a Greek hero. So, too, while his nation slept, Greece entered the war. Next day, the hall porter at the small hotel at which the Smiths were staying said in broken English, 'We now your allies. We fight next you.'

At the end of November, against all expectations and Mussolini's proud boast that he would overrun Greece in ten days, as Hitler had overrun France, the Greeks crossed into Albania and captured the town of Koritza. Reggie jubilantly quoted Thucydides to Olivia: 'They are daring beyond their power and they risk beyond reason and they never lose hope in suffering.'

She said, 'If Dumps knew history as you do, he would be quoting that.' To both father and daughter the glories of war were something to be celebrated.

But there was a downside as well. Treated as friends by everyone else whom they met, they found that their welcome by officials was cautious. 'You would think we were aliens, not allies,' Olivia said to Reggie one night in their bedroom. For days she had been followed by a plain-clothes detective because on her passport her name appeared as 'Olivia Mary Smith'. Early one morning she was called down to the hotel desk, where two policemen waited to escort her to the police station. There she was interviewed by an official who had on his desk a file labelled 'Maria Schmidt'. Some time before, a 'Maria Schmidt' had, for some unrevealed reason, been ordered to leave Greece. The recent appearance in English guise of an Olivia Mary Smith had made the police suspicious. Olivia wrote,

> I was questioned through an interpreter and in the end the official had to admit that I was to all intents and purposes an innocent Englishwoman. In his disappointment, he opened the file that lay before him. There was nothing inside in it.

Before Olivia had met Reggie, she had had her affair with Hamish Miles, so tragically terminated by his unexpected death. Hamish had instructed her 'in the delights of sex', as she put it in an article on 'First Love' commissioned by the *Sunday Times* in the 1970s but mysteriously never published. Sometimes she would say that she had been born into a generation which was not supposed to know about such matters. 'Reggie taught me differently.'

During the war she remained faithful to Reggie, though over his own behaviour during the same period there hangs a question mark. Ivor Porter in his autobiography *Operation Autonomous* (1989) claims, 'When he returned, married, to Bucharest [he] continued to sleep around as if nothing had happened.' Some friends say this is an exaggeration. At all events, everyone believed that he really loved Olivia – albeit in his own erratic fashion.

To say that Olivia remained faithful to him during the war years does not mean that she was not attracted to other men. She was always concerned with the question of whether she might be losing her sex appeal. In Romania she had learnt as a new bride to be 'something of a camp-follower' as she trailed after Reggie and his friends from bar to bar – and then, nine times out of ten, decided to go home on her own. Yet

Reggie always returned to her – eventually. It was simply that it could take him anything up to three hours to tear himself away from a carouse. 'I was often a lonely wife,' she would complain to her women friends.

This did not go unnoticed among the male fraternity of the British Council, nor by many of the other members the English colony. Those who tried to take advantage of Olivia's loneliness found her generally withdrawn. On occasion she would open up a little and indulge in mildly flirtatious behaviour – which was eventually to grow bolder. Meanwhile there were those who hoped for something more from her and, if disappointed, they would sometimes mutter in rage 'bitch, bitch', as Clarence Lawson does to Harriet in the Balkan Trilogy. Clarence, who has known Guy since he first came out to Eastern Europe in 1938, accuses Harriet of having turned Guy into a bourgeois husband – changing him from an eternal student who will doss down anywhere to a man who wants to spend the night in the warmth of his own bed in his own home.

One of the men whom Harriet attracts in the Balkan Trilogy is Charles Warden. The character is based on Terence Spencer, a lecturer for the British Council in Rome and Athens prior to 1939. The war then interrupted his academic career. He was mentioned in dispatches and rose to being a lieutenant-colonel in the Military Mission. In 1954 he brought out a learned study of literary philhellenism from Shakespeare to Byron. What he offered Olivia was companionship – but a companionship that he would like to have taken a step further. Wearing his knowledge lightly, he knew both classical and demotic Greek. On one occasion he explained to her how the River Ilissus ran much of its way underground through Athens. She was to use this information in *Friends and Heroes*.

Olivia found Terence romantic, protective and a useful escort, but she was relieved when he was posted from Athens. When Charles accuses Harriet of wanting him to be 'some sort of *cavaliere servente*', it is wise to remember the qualification 'some sort of', for this is what Harriet/Olivia was continually looking for. Reggie's treatment of his wife could often be neglectful, yet if he was ever criticised for this, he would fall back on the argument that Olivia was a part of him, as he of her. In this respect he never changed. It is a key to his character and their lasting marriage.

During this period Olivia was jotting down occasional poems. She was to write far more than she published; less than a dozen appeared in her life. Probably the best of these, 'Written in the Third Year of the War', eventually published in *Personal Landscape* in Cairo in 1942, had begun to germinate in her mind in 1940, when she saw the shop windows in Athens decorated for Christmas with palms and bays in honour of the Greek heroes on the Albanian front, and with olive branches in anticipation of victory in early 1941. She had stood in the streets with the people cheering and applauding as the soldiers were driven off to war. Farriers had brought their horses into the capital so that they too might be used by the Army.

On the boat from Dover in 1939 Reggie, like many others, had optimistically thought that the war might be over by Christmas 1939. In Bucharest, many shared this view and were disappointed when it did not happen. In Greece in 1940, there had been the same anticipation of an early end, but by late January everyone realised that victory might not be so near, or indeed so certain. As Olivia put it in her poem:

> We felt then a thing unknown to our generation, the sorrow
> and terror of defeat.

By defeat, she was thinking of the Greek Army, for she was convinced that the Greeks would remain Britain's allies. In March her morale, and that of other expatriates in the English colony, received a boost. Anthony Eden, the British Foreign Secretary, had arrived in Athens and she and Reggie had seen him being escorted on a tour of the Parthenon. Transferring her remembered feelings of 1940 to Harriet Pringle, she later wrote of how seeing Eden was 'as though some part of England itself had come to be with them here in their isolation'. She speaks of being 'transported' – a term which she employs some half-dozen times in the novel, though not always in the same context. Harriet is 'transported by the glory of war' when a young Greek soldier catches her by her hands and says in English, 'We are friends.' When Harriet sees a mother embracing her small son and pressing his head against her bosom, she is 'transported by the sight of these two human creatures wrapped in love'. When Charles Warden is 'transported by rage' because he thinks that she has exploited him as a *cavaliere servente*, Harriet feels that, in witnessing that rage, she has suddenly come to know him as well as if she had lived with him for half a century.

Dumps had told his children many times the story of how, at Thermopylae, the Spartans had stood to the last man guarding their pass against the invading Persian forces. Now, in Greece in April 1941, Olivia was aware that she was watching the Greeks make a similar last stand against the Germans. She had been in Athens when Metaxas had declared war on Mussolini and she had watched women throwing flowers of valediction to their soldiers as they left in lorries for the front. The very air she breathed was alive with the spirit of heroism. Now defeat was imminent – but the earlier heroism was not forgotten. The women threw flowers as tokens of consolation to their retreating men as they made their way back to Athens, a wounded and outnumbered army.

By mid-April, the Greek people knew that all was up. In anticipation of evacuation, the Smiths had packed, having been forewarned that each of them might take only a small suitcase. Most of their books they gave to Greek friends to keep for the duration. Among their precious possessions was a painting that the famous Greek artist Ghika, later to marry Barbara Rothschild, had given to Olivia. It was of one of the Greek islands – 'mostly blue and white, very sharp and clean as though a wind blew through it'. She was afraid to take it with her lest their ship be torpedoed. So Ghika promised to keep it until the war was over.

The next time Olivia saw the painting was after the war at an exhibition of Modern Greek Art in Grosvenor Square. It was priced at £150 – a sum of money that she did not then possess. She remembered how Ghika had told her when he had first given it to her, 'You *must* have it.' He now repeated these words at the exhibition: 'It is yours. You *must* have it.'

But thinking that he must still be far from rich, she said, 'If you can get so much money for it – then you *must* sell it.'

However, Ghika went on insisting that the picture was hers. He was now doing well, he said, he was no longer desperate to make money. Didn't she remember that his last words to her in Athens had been 'Yours for ever', as he had taken custody of the picture? He recalled how desperately she had wanted it when she first saw it in Athens. Now in London he repeated the words 'Yours for ever'.

Olivia was profoundly moved by his generosity. But when she returned to the exhibition for a second time: 'It had a terrible red dot on it and I knew that meant it had been bought.' Friends told her she had been a fool not to have had Ghika put her name and address on the back of the picture.

A few months later when she saw the picture reproduced in the 1946 issue of *Horizon*, she felt suddenly very angry: 'The picture was mine but someone else had bought it and I would probably never see it again.' Nor did she – though she always kept an eye open in case by some miracle she might once more come on it and be able to buy it back. In her last two decades she bought a number of modern pictures, often in the company of Francis King, who shared with her an interest in collecting contemporary art. She was shrewd at finding a bargain.

During these last days a terrible hush fell over Athens. On 18 April Korizis, the new Prime Minister who had taken over from Metaxas in January, committed suicide. Pro-German elements began to appear everywhere, as they had in Bucharest after King Carol's abdication. The Greek radio station sent a final independent message to its listeners. The owners of shops gazed out vacantly from their doors. Some of these shops were already boarded up. There was no food to be bought.

The *Erebus*, which had been commandeered for the British, lay at anchor in the harbour. Among its passengers were R. A. Close and his wife, and the novelist Robert Liddell. Reggie said to them, 'We are journeying people.' None of them knew if he was quoting – or if the line had come to him out of the blue. He began quoting Cavafy: 'It is the Barbarians who are coming today' – then stopped: 'It's too long a poem.' On the deck he soon settled down to making notes for a lecture on the Sonnets of Shakespeare, which he intended to give some day in the now unforeseeable future.

'He is like a student in a library,' Olivia said proudly to those around her – a statement on which she was to elaborate in the final pages of the Balkan Trilogy: 'He spent the day absorbed, like a student in a library.' Then she added that Reggie had begun to sing to himself so low that probably only she knew what the words were. They were:

> If your engine cuts out over Hellfire Pass
> You can stick your twin Browning guns right up your arse.

Olivia decided that this showed heroism of a sort.

Before that, as they had walked up the gangway to the *Erebus*, Reggie had hummed 'Tipperary'. It recalled for Olivia one of their first nights in Athens. In a taverna smelling strongly of aniseed, one of the musicians had played the tune on a concertina as a welcome to them as honoured English guests.

After a voyage of three days, Olivia and Reggie reached Egypt safely. They heard that the swastika was now flying above the Acropolis.

Chapter 13

Land of the Pharaohs

When Reggie and Olivia arrived in Egypt they had been without food for three days. In Athens they had been warned to bring provisions to the ship, but the shops had been bare. Olivia carried with her a bag of oranges as well as a small suitcase, and they had been surviving for the past week on a diet of wine and oranges – plus 'a feeling of exaltation brought about by the Greek spring'.

At Alexandria, where the *Erebus* docked on 21 April, they saw troops on the quay unpacking shipments of arms – shells and spare parts for anti-tank guns. Some of the passengers shouted to the men, 'Have you got anything to eat?' Others took up the chant of 'Eat! Eat! Eat! We want to eat!' The men went to a store at the back of the quay and returned with several large branches of bananas. Slowly they divided them and then threw the fruit up in ones, twos and threes. Olivia caught a bunch of three and took it to Reggie. The notes that he had made on the voyage, about Shakespeare and the Sonnets, he folded and put in his back trouser pocket.

The nightmare was over. They had not been torpedoed or dive-bombed on the voyage. 'Now we are safe,' Reggie announced to those gathered around him as he clutched his banana. 'We are anchored to Africa.'

'Come off it, Reggie,' his wife said. 'Don't be so damned dramatic. Eat your banana instead.'

After they had landed, the military checked their passports and shepherded them to a canteen, where they were offered bacon and eggs. 'The tea was so sweet a fly could trot on it,' was Reggie's verdict. Swarms of flies, unnaturally large, greyish and greasy-looking, kept circling them. Olivia assumed that these must be descendants of the flies that had been one of the plagues of Egypt. She and Reggie passed the time swatting them with rolled-up newspaper. The corpses littered the floor, until ants carried them away.

Early in the evening they were put on the Cairo train. On one side of
the line ran the Nile delta, while on the other the sand stretched to
infinity. How often as a child she had imagined this desert scene now
before her. In her last terms at Portsmouth Grammar School she had tried
to capture it and similar Egyptian scenes in a series of pen-and-ink
drawings.

From the carriage window, as the train sped through fields rich with
beans, flax, barley, tobacco, cotton and pomegranate trees, she watched
the peasants walking home. She pointed out the irrigation channels to
Reggie – who put on his spectacles so as to see them better. Then they
glimpsed their first camel. Reggie began to recite a Tommy Atkins poem
by Kipling in which camels appear. The Hindustani word for camel is
'cont', pronounced to rhyme with 'grunt':

> O the cont, O the cont, O the commissariat cont
> With 'is silly neck a-bobbin' like a basket full of snakes;
> We packs 'im like an idol, an' you ought to 'ear 'im grunt
> And when we get 'im loaded up 'is blessed girth-rope breaks.

Olivia tried to silence Reggie: 'People will think you're being obscene.'

Reggie would have none of it and went on reciting the remaining verses.
'Kipling's a damned fine poet,' he said when he got to the end.

As the sun set, so the train glided into the midway stop of Tanta, with
its mud houses and rickety balconies. Fat men awakened from their siesta
and came out in striped pyjamas to stare at them. Was it for this dun
colour of unbaked clay that the Smiths had exchanged the marble
splendours of Greece? Would Cairo have better things to offer? Already
Olivia was disappointed. As the train pulled out of Tanta, she saw the
beggar children run beside it for a few yards, thumping on the windows.
They shouted, '*Muskine! Muskine!*' 'It must have something to do with
money,' was Reggie's comment.

Twilight was brief – then darkness came upon them suddenly like a clap
of thunder. When they drew into the station at Cairo the platforms felt
even hotter than had the carriages just left. 'We could smell the heat of the
spicy, flaccid Cairo night,' Olivia was to note in an article that she
contributed to the *Sunday Times Colour Supplement* a quarter of a century
later in 1967.

An army sergeant had been delegated to meet the train. Those who had the right currency hired taxis to take them to Shepheard's or the Semiramis and waved the rest goodbye. But Reggie and Olivia had no more than a few drachmas and fell in dutifully behind the sergeant. He led them down narrow alleyways to a requisitioned hotel. The street lamps had been painted blue as a precaution against air raids, but from the shops and houses the lights shone out. No one seemed concerned to pull the curtains or close the shutters. In the darkness of the streets figures in white robes floated past. There were no blackout rules enforced, as there had been in Athens. Olivia was told by one air force pilot that the Nile was always visible. 'The Huns would just have to follow it,' he said.

Everywhere there was the stink of rotting vegetation and piss – a smell that Olivia was always to associate with the Middle East. The requisitioned hotel was a former brothel, which had changed its status during a recent upsurge of morality. It consisted of two dormitories – one for men and one for women. Each had a solitary light bulb hanging above the naked floorboards.

The next morning Reggie rose early to get an advance on his Council salary through the British Embassy. When the ex-brothel owner presented Olivia with a bill, Reggie took it and settled it. It was as high as if they had been staying at Shepheard's – and prompted Reggie to make his first feeble pun on Egyptian soil: 'You can say we have been well and truly gypped.'

Before the morning was over, they had settled into a *pension* in the east of Cairo. The city was alive with rumours and false alarms. Within their first week the owner of the *pension* was telling the Smiths, 'You British finished. The Germans already here.' These alarms, or 'flaps' as they were usually called, were a part of living in Egypt then. The local population was always on edge.

Olivia herself was jittery too. She had been jittery since the time of the air raids on Athens. No sooner had she unpacked at the *pension* than she talked about getting away from the bomb that might lie in store for them. Reggie tried to allay her fears: 'Those who live in bombed cities *do* survive. The only danger is if the bomb has your name on it. Our deaths are preordained – but we just don't know the time or means.' Olivia thought it rather rich for an entrenched materialist to talk about things being 'ordained'.

At that time Cairo was the clearing house for kings, princes and heads of state from Eastern Europe, along with their statutory attendants and hangers-on. Rivalries and fights flared in hotels and restaurants. Sir Miles

Lampson, the British Ambassador, referred to the city as having become 'the dumping-ground for refugees'. Meanwhile, the western desert was a theatre of war, where Allied and Axis forces pursued each other backwards and forwards across some 600 miles of terrain. It was a tactician's paradise. Tobruk was captured by the Germans in June 1942, only to be recaptured five months later by the British. Thus the fortunes of war swung to and fro.

When the Smiths arrived in Egypt General Montgomery had not yet appeared on the scene. General Auchinleck, one of Olivia's heroes, was still Commander-in-Chief of the Middle East force and she often watched him from the opposite pavement walking along the Suleiman Pasha. Indeed, she saw him there on his last morning in mid-August before he departed from Egypt for good. In 1977 she recalled,

> He was a very tall man with a grave, handsome face and a broad brow: the ideal of those leaders, those demi-gods, whom she had seen ordering the lives of common men, yet he, too, owed obedience and had been sent away. Though she had not met him and would probably never see him again, she felt a profound sadness as she watched him disappear into the indifferent crowd.

Occasionally Olivia fell into conversation with squaddies in the streets. She never allowed her chats to become too protracted, always revealing that she was a married woman with a husband working in Egypt. But she kept them going long enough to gain whatever information she wanted. Two unwritten laws of desert warfare that she learnt this way were that the enemy never attacked those burying their dead or vice versa, and that neither Spitfires nor Messerschmitts strafed soldiers at play, when they were kicking a ball about. Both sides held Rommel in high esteem. Cairo and the war in the desert were to form the backdrop to Olivia's three fine sequels to the Balkan Trilogy. Known as the Levant Trilogy they were the novels *The Danger Tree* (1977), *The Battle Lost and Won* (1978) and *The Sum of Things* (1980).

Wartime Cairo was a happy hunting ground for girls looking for husbands, boyfriends or 'meal tickets'. Olivia had never before heard the last term. The demand far exceeded the supply. 'Distressingly ugly girls could become as tiresome as prima donnas,' Olivia noted. It was a period, too, when young officers did not admit to their titles. Lords preferred to be known by their Christian names – so that in the Levant Trilogy the Irish peer Lord Lisdoonvarna turns up merely as 'Peter'. Dobbie Dobson, who is partly based on Adam Watson, informs Harriet, 'Titles are *de trop* for the duration.' Levantine hostesses were quick to catch on.

Social equality increasingly asserted itself with the war, as newly commissioned officers just out from England brought with them a sense of being 'all in it together'. When the war was over, the old sense of hierarchy quickly returned. Passing through Cairo on her way to Suez, Harriet is asked by an English woman friend, 'You know Lord Lisdoonvarna, don't you?' The familiar days of calling him 'Peter' are over. Levantine hostesses were again quick to catch on.

Shortly before the outbreak of war Stevie had written to Olivia, 'Like the Old Testament prophet Samuel, we authors must be attentive to what we hear.' Olivia interpreted this to mean that she must be an eavesdropper, which was not hard in her case. 'Never speak too much, for everything comes to those who listen' was one of her mother's sayings. So it came about that, one day when she was sitting beneath a table umbrella at Groppi's, she found herself riveted as she listened to a group of middle-aged homosexuals discussing boys. They complained that the local boys made no pretence at love or affection: they only wanted to be paid – and then to rush off. 'It's something to do with them being Orientals,' said the oldest man present.

Within a month of their arrival in Cairo the Smiths had left their *pension* and moved into Adam Watson's flat at 13 Sharia Ibrahim Pasha Neguib, overlooking the British Embassy. Watson was a second secretary there. From their bedroom window they could see mango trees and myrtles, and banana palms with purple blossoms. An early morning weekly visitor to the garden was a snake-charmer. He came to collect snakes and, to everyone's amazement, always left with a sackful of them. What a delight it was to be woken by a reed pipe, repeating the same delicate phrase over and over again. Later, another kind of music was to become familiar to the Smiths when a guest in the flat bought a record of Mozart's Clarinet Quartet, which he played every afternoon on his gramophone. In 1969 it was Olivia's fourth choice on her *Desert Island Discs*.

From the lawn beneath, which stretched down to the Nile, could be heard the continual hiss of water sprinklers. This preserved the greenness – 'O green I want you green,' sang Olivia slightly out of tune as she walked about the flat. But the wet grass spelt danger, for some foreign Embassy children who played here had contracted bilharzia from contaminated water. Bilharzia, according to Olivia, had so enervated the Egyptian peasantry over the centuries that it had left them with little desire for revolt. One European mother approached Olivia: 'My son seems to have no strength.'

'Then don't let him play on the lawn,' Olivia advised.

Illness was Olivia's constant fear in Egypt. In her more imaginative moods she felt that it was a country in which one breathed in sickness. On one occasion she had danced at the Turf Club with an officer who had been feverish. The next morning he had gone down with smallpox and everyone who had been at the party was re-vaccinated. For more than a fortnight she dreaded that she might be similarly struck down. Reggie tried hard to calm her, but he found it difficult work. All his life he himself had known only robust health. If she reminded him about his appendix, he would dismiss it: 'It was just an unlucky blip.' Once, foolishly, he went on to generalise, 'A woman's lot is to be ill.'

But Olivia was not prepared to let him get away with this. 'Your father was frequently ill and your mother had to take over. Don't forget that.'

Reggie never cared for being defeated in an argument and on this occasion tentatively suggested that it might be best if she went back to England. 'The climate would be so much kinder to you,' he urged.

She was indignant: 'Wherever we go, we go together. If we return home, we both go. I won't have the war separating us. End of story.'

In comparison with many of the civilians the Smiths were fortunate. They shared a pleasant flat and enjoyed meals prepared by an efficient servant. Each night Olivia would put out her white leather shoes to be cleaned. To her parents she confided, 'Snow-white shoes are *de rigueur* for ladies who move in Embassy circles.'

Olivia could be spiteful in her behaviour. On board the ship on which she and Reggie had sailed from Athens there had also been the Welsh scholar Harold Edwards, author of a pioneering book about the poet John Skelton. He was travelling with his well-to-do Greek wife, Eppie, and the two couples had shared the same cabin. Neither woman cared for the other and Olivia became enraged by the way that Eppie insisted on keeping her hatbox, with its smart Paris hats, in the cabin. Some half-dozen times she put it in the gangway outside, saying to Reggie on the last occasion, 'I'll give her something to think about.' She did not elaborate.

When Eppie and Harold reached their bedroom at Shepheard's and Eppie opened her hatbox, it was to find a rusted chamber pot pressed on top of a hat of which she was particularly fond.

In September 1941 Olivia had been overseas for two years without a break. As a writer she had collected a fund of material – enough for at least half a dozen books. But from the start, since she had left England with only a smattering of French and even less German, her lack of languages had been a disadvantage. Yet she was a gifted, shrewd and often obsessive observer. Early in the Balkan Trilogy there is a telling description of how Harriet Pringle passes much of her time: '[She] had spent most of the day watching from the window.' This was an occupation in which Olivia indulged. 'Watching is part of a writer's work,' she would say.

Romanians, Greeks and Egyptians have reacted variously to Olivia Manning's novels about their countries. Countess Drobska, who knew her in Bucharest and was a fellow guest with her and Reggie at Adam Watson's Cairo flat, spoke with affection of her and added that Olivia had helped her greatly on several occasions. She remembered Olivia explaining to her that, whereas Reggie came from the working class, she came from the lower middle class. Countess Drobska believed that the Smiths' was a true love match, if not exactly a conventional one: 'Olivia was often left to fend for herself. Still, no woman calls a man "Bear" unless she really looks up to him and Olivia called Reggie "Bear".' Of Olivia's attitude to foreigners the Countess was more critical: 'Olivia got them incredibly wrong. Where she succeeded best was in presenting small circles of British people living abroad, such as those of the British Council or the Legation. She has prejudices – but then English people always have them. A novelist by nature is a prejudiced person.'

When she had gone to Romania in 1939, Olivia was a provincial girl with little knowledge of 'abroad'. 'I was open to any experience, but I had first to get my sea legs,' she told June Braybrooke. 'I was the daughter of a sailor who had served much of his life on the lower deck.' Her father had, however, impressed on her that, if she became a writer, doors would open to her. That was what Olivia was to discover as her fame as a novelist grew. In 1960, when Francis King invited her to lunch with Antonia Fraser at a Chelsea restaurant, she said to June Braybrooke, also a guest, before they set out, 'Pour me a stiff gin. I'm nervous. How proud my old father would be to know I was lunching with an earl's daughter.'

Commander Manning had brought up his daughter to believe that the

British Empire reigned supreme. When she went abroad in 1939, she fully believed this. As the war progressed, she accepted another of her father's beliefs – that the British always fought best with their backs to the wall. Dunkirk, in June 1940, had been one example of this. She felt certain that Greece would rise again; the Nazi occupation would be a passing phase.

But in Egypt she had to come to terms with the fact that the British occupation of the country had never been popular among its people and was growing less so with the war. Her father had drummed into her that it was the British who had introduced the Egyptians to justice and prosperity. Like Harriet Pringle, Olivia still indulged in imperial dreams. Although she was fully aware of anti-British feelings as she walked through the streets and bazaars, she was never in any doubt that in the end the British would triumph over the Axis.

Reggie shared these convictions. He discussed with Olivia how British troops never made fun of Rommel or told sexual jokes about him, while Hitler was subject to both – as were most of his top henchmen. 'Our cartoonists are helping to win this war,' Reggie would say. It was a simplistic view of history – but it had its truth. When he had put on shows for the troops in Athens, he had readily grasped what figures of fun Europe's two dictators could be made out to be. Tommy Handley, on home radio, had shown that already.

In October 1941 Reggie and Olivia moved temporarily to Alexandria, a three-hour car journey from Cairo. Here, they lived in a flat rented by the novelist Robert Liddell, whom they had first met in Greece and travelled with on the *Erebus*. The two men had been offered teaching posts at the new Farouk el Awal University. Olivia and Reggie were fond of Robert – but he could be tricky and malicious, as they were to discover. But what is a friendship if it cannot endure these things? Olivia, Reggie and Robert remained friends all their lives. Despite the malice between Robert and Olivia, there was a basic loyalty. As dedicated novelists, they shared a common aim and Reggie, as a voracious reader of novels, respected their sometimes selfish or vainglorious sense of vocation.

By comparison with Cairo, Alexandria was cool – but the war was closer. The city was being continually bombed in preparation for a winter offensive. Then, another sort of bomb landed at their door: it was a letter from Olivia's parents bringing 'the saddest news possible'. Her brother's plane had disappeared into the sea off the Dorset coast. Olivia, who had been devoted to the dashing Oliver, was devastated. Not even the wreckage of his plane was ever found. In *The Remarkable Expedition*, the book on which Olivia was then working there is this dedication:

> To the memory of my brother lieutenant Oliver David George Manning, A.R.I.B.A., R.N.V.R., killed on active service October 7th, 1941. He has no grave but the sea.

She composed a poem, which was found among her papers after her death. It is entitled 'Dying in Kind':

> Engine's error or the pilot's failure
> Cleavered a decade of increasing hope.
> Remaining, ready to have died in forfeit,
> The father fallen into long silence,
> The distracted mother; both too old now ever to recover.
>
> In the sharp, autumn waters, darkening
> As the plunge deepened, death's confusion
> Caught temperament, eyes, furies doubling
> Mine. To meet extinction thus by proxy
> Is to be proof-holder of one's own mortality.
>
> Remembering him – secretive, in emotion
> Violent, ambitious in long studentship,
> Or brilliant for companion's sake,
> Feigning, in recklessness, indifference –
> I am led again to questions asked of the young dead.
>
> In childhood's desolation, adding
> By our impatience to the anchor's weight,
> In listing needed miracles, he'd accuse me
> Of charming fortune. Who has gained her now?
> Dying in kind – he once, I with him endlessly in mind?

At the time when she wrote the poem – between late 1941 and the beginning of 1942 – she was heavily influenced by Auden. Walter Allen and Reggie had constantly talked to her about him and she knew his work well. Some of the implications in 'Dying by Kind' were to be worked out further – in *The Play Room* in 1969 and in the Levant Trilogy. From neighbours in Laburnum Grove she had heard that her father and mother could hardly bear to talk of their tragedy. '134 Laburnum Grove became a silent house,' wrote the couple living opposite. Her father was eighty-four when his only son died.

The Smiths did not stay for long in Alexandria because the bombing of the city made Olivia nervous and edgy. Robert Liddell was relieved when she returned to Cairo, for it meant that, when the sirens sounded, she would not be there to insist that they must all troop to the basement. Sometimes, when she heard the sound of a car horn and mistook it for a siren, she would seize Robert's arm in terror. 'I have bruises to prove it,' he complained to his friends. At that time the Cecil Hotel in Alexandria used to advertise in *The Egyptian Mail* that, in addition to the usual amenities, they could provide 'comfortable air raid shelters'.

In 1946 Olivia Manning published a short story called 'A Spot of Leave', which began:

> At five o'clock, when the afternoon was deepening into violet-scented, spring twilight, Phillip and Aphrodite met for tea at Larides'. This was the hour when the Alexandrine Greeks drank coffee. Sometimes men dropping into the café from offices, and women pausing in their shopping, would stand at the counter and eat with a silver, two-pronged fork, a couple of cakes. The counter displayed immense chocolate-boxes tied with ribbon.

Larides' was in fact Pastroudi's — described by Olivia in 1967 as 'Alexandria's wartime equivalent of Groppi's in Cairo'. She noted how officers would dine and dance there as well as consume sticky cakes. Among them had been the writer Keith Douglas, who was a tank commander.*

Some years after the war, on a return visit to Egypt, Olivia asked an ancient waiter at Pastroudi's whether the officers had behaved themselves.

---

* Keith Douglas was a poet whose work she grew increasingly to admire. One of his last poems is called 'Behaviour of Fish in an Egyptian Tea Garden'. The Tea Garden is Groppi's in Cairo. He was killed not in the desert but during the Normandy landings in June 1944.

He rebuked her, 'I am ashamed you should ask such a question, Madame. Only the privates went round the streets drunk and singing.' When she passed this on to Reggie, he said, 'You see, nothing has changed, or rather there has been no change for the better in the things that matter. But something that does matter is that the belly-dancers are no longer allowed to show their midriffs. That's due to Egypt having become a republic.' The source of this information was Tahio Carioca, now a retired belly-dancer, who had been the most famous of all belly-dancers in 1942 – the year in which she was presented with a shooting stick inscribed by a group of army officers.

The short story that Olivia set in Larides' depicted a scene that she had frequently witnessed – namely, a passing affair between an officer and an Alexandrine married woman. Aphrodite wants to sleep with Phillip and sees no reason why she should not do so, since she has an open-ended marriage with her English husband, a banker. 'We agreed we'd be modern,' she tells Phillip. When Phillip nonetheless decides against such behaviour, the story closes with her confessing to her husband, 'He did not want me. Now I know I am getting old.'

Age haunted Olivia. Both her father and her first lover, Hamish Miles, had been womanisers who were married. She had thus learnt a good deal about unfaithful marriages. Throughout her life she never had any intention of letting her own marriage disintegrate. But there were many times when she felt lonely and deserted by Reggie. He was so gregarious – it was as if the whole world were his wife. In Greece she had had an *amitié amoureuse* with Terence Spencer, alias Charles Warden in *Friends and Heroes*. Constantly, Olivia needed to reassure herself that her powers of sexual attraction were not declining, for this was one of her great fears. It explains why she liked causing young men twinges of jealousy, as indeed Harriet causes Clarence Lawson in the Balkan Trilogy. She was not, however, interested in cold, calculated seduction. She identifies with Phillip's reaction to Aphrodite's direct suggestion that they should sleep together: 'Hell, let's drop the subject.'

Olivia observed the relationships that she had seen briefly flourish and then abruptly die at Pastroudi's, and noted how they were subject to the swings of fortune. A 'flap' in the city, an advance by the Afrika Korps, and the most agreeable flirtation was brought to a jarring halt. Army leave would be cancelled and everyone would be on the alert.

Olivia also brings a domestic note to bear on the scene in Pastroudi's.

At one point she records, in the person of Harriet, how the Wrens and nurses proved more exacting than the regulars by insisting that the old tea be emptied out of the pots and fresh tea put in for each customer. Olivia had been ashamed when she discovered that Reggie sometimes made tea without putting a kettle on to boil, but merely by drawing hot water straight from the tap.

On her return to Cairo from Alexandria, Olivia managed to get a job as a press attaché to the American Embassy, where one of her tasks was to keep up to date a map of troop movements in the western desert. Looking at the map one day, an American officer had said to her, 'Fortunes of war are like a see-saw, ma'm.' She was to remember this when she began her Levant Trilogy in 1976.

Reggie travelled to Cairo most weekends but for the time being continued to work in Alexandria. For the radio station there he produced Sean O'Casey's *Juno and the Paycock* and also ran a fortnightly variety programme. At the beginning of 1942 he began editing *Citadel* for the British Council. It was a little review that appeared monthly and cost two piastres – or, as its editor would say, 'the price of a beer'.

Towards the end of 1942 Olivia Manning completed a 5000-word article on a group of writers – mainly poets – whom she had met in Greece and the Middle East. A friend managed to 'squeeze it' into the diplomatic bag. It was addressed to Cyril Connolly at *Horizon*. He published it in November 1944 under the title 'Poets in Exile'. Olivia had concentrated largely on the work of Laurence Durrell and Bernard Spencer, two of the editors of *Personal Landscape* (the third editor was Robin Fedden). She also had several things to say about Robert Liddell. She recalled how in 1941 he had rented a house under the Acropolis escarpment and there engaged on a translation of Politis's *Eroica*: but when news came that the Germans had broken through at Thermopylae, he had fled to Piraeus and there boarded the *Erebus* with the Smiths.

Her comments in *Horizon* on Keith Douglas constituted the first critical notice that he was to receive in England. She wrote, 'He is the only poet who has written poems comparable with the works of the better poets of the last war and likely to be read as war poems when the war is over.' High praise and prophetic words. His wartime poetry made a greater mark on her than that of any other poet whom she had met at this time.

In the course of her *Horizon* article Olivia also mentioned the poets G.

S. Fraser and Hamish Henderson. Fraser was to write of meeting her in Cairo, 'She was slim and tubular, with a face at once oval and birdlike whose pattern she completed with a turban, so that an artist of the school of Wyndham Lewis might have drawn her as a swathed, beaked egg balanced on a cylinder.'

Hamish Henderson in a journal kept at the time describes her thus: 'She was a languid, alert woman.' Of Reggie he adds, 'I took a liking for Smith – he is one of those beefy intellectuals, who go barging their ways through criticism; he said his wife scented the "phoney" from afar.' Henderson had met them both when on leave in Cairo.

Olivia, Reggie and their circle would amuse each other by producing satirical limericks and short poems. Hers were usually sharper than his. Often she wrote such verse to get her own back on those she suspected, with her incipient paranoia, had not sufficiently appreciated Reggie's talents. One which she circulated was about C. F. A. Dundas, who had been appointed the first Representative of the British Council in the Middle East. His 'villainy' in her view was that he had been slow to find her husband a job. It circulated under the title 'Dundas in the Desert':

> I'm so like the desert
> And the desert's so like me
> We're lean and bare, and full of hot air
> And we haven't got the OBE.

Dundas was known for despising 'the long-haired brigade' in the Council, whom he instinctively wrote off as 'pansies'. Reggie, though not long-haired, did have 'a generous crop of curls': but to Dundas he was suspect mainly because of his Marxism – which caused Dundas to harbour doubts about his suitability to be in charge of foreign students.

Olivia carried her dislike of Dundas further. In her fictional portrait of the Director of the British Council in Greece and Egypt, she presents an effete and ineffective man called Colin Gracey. Outwardly Gracey in her novels, and Dundas in real life, could not have been more dissimilar. In Cairo, for instance, Gracey spends long hours on a houseboat on the Nile, owned by a rich Turk. The name of the Turk is Mustapha Quant, but among the inner circle he is nicknamed 'Mustapha Cunt'. The parties on the houseboat are for males only. This was not Dundas's scene at all, but Olivia clearly derived pleasure in pretending that it was. Sometimes, when challenged to defend some such travesty, she would say, 'You cannot know the absolute truth about anyone. The most macho or crusty may have an effeminate side.' In her Levant Trilogy Olivia made up several short poems about 'Gracey of Gezira', which she attributed to Guy Pringle.

Her mocking portrait of Lord Pinkrose, who comes to a violent end, is partly based on the Irish poet Lord Dunsany, who died in 1957 in a Dublin nursing home. In Mark Amory's 1972 biography of Dunsany there is no mention of the Balkan or Levant Trilogies. But Amory does report, as Reggie did to Olivia, that Dunsany thought T. S. Eliot's plays 'frightful nonsense'.

Before January 1942 ended, Olivia was already dreading the summer. In Cairo there was no spring or autumn, only the soft warmth of winter to be contrasted with the fierce heat of summer. Soon the hot, gritty wind would blow through the streets, foreigners would melt in their clothes and squaddies newly arrived from Britain would become 'kippered'. Whereas in pre-war years the American Embassy moved its staff out to Alexandria, where there were refreshing sea breezes, in wartime they remained firmly implanted in the capital. The American Embassy was the only one that insisted on its staff forgoing a siesta. After the lunch break staff had to be back by 2 p.m. sharp. 'Everyone, except the Americans and I, go to bed in the afternoon,' Olivia informed Stevie ungrammatically in an air letter.

The evenings were the rewards of the hot summer days. The local populace strolled out on to their balconies, or put chairs in front of their houses in the street. This was the ideal time to hire a horse-gharry. Gezira Island appeared to float like a basket of flowers on the Nile. If one looked between it and the other island, Roda, the Pyramids could be seen in the distance. How impressed Olivia had been when she had first glimpsed them! But to Reggie they had meant nothing. He reacted to them as he had to the Parthenon – a popular site to be avoided and later dismissed from the mind as quickly as possible. Was this an affectation? Affectation or not, it was part of an attitude to 'beauty spots'. The Pyramids in his view were neither useful nor beautiful.

The Berka was the red light district, out of bounds to soldiers. Olivia was anxious to visit it, and so the Smiths and some friends formed a party one evening to do so. One of the sights was said to be a fat, middle-aged woman who coupled with a donkey.

The girls sat behind open windows upstairs; when they leant forward to speak to those in the narrow streets below, it could be seen that only the tops of their bodies were covered. 'How many men do the girls have in a day?' Olivia enquired of a major.

'I have heard the figure thirty mentioned,' he replied. 'Some of the houses are run like conveyer belts. It depends which you choose.'

Olivia's party had made its way to an establishment that promised sex displays. In the basement, a student entered. He was naked and had his trousers over his arm. Immediately he mounted a woman who lay supine with her kimono open and her legs apart. Their union was over in seconds. 'Should I go and speak to the chap?' Reggie said, as the student hurriedly dressed. The woman in the kimono handed a 1000-piastre note to the young man as he buttoned up his shirt.

When Reggie came face to face with him, the young man, clearly ashamed, excused himself by saying, 'We Egyptians like to do these things in private. But we need money.' Reluctantly he took the note that Reggie held out. Olivia was to write about this incident in the second volume of the Levant Trilogy, *The Battle Lost and Won*.

In the summer of 1942 the Berka was closed down. But many of the girls continued to carry on their activities, often in the backs of the horse-drawn gharries. Artemis Cooper in her book about *Cairo in the War: 1939–1945* (1989) states that the closing of the Berka halved the incidence of VD contracted in the city. Until then the monthly figure had been some 900 cases.

1942 – with 'Rommel at the gates' – was the year of the greatest 'flap' of all, which occurred on 1 July and was known in Cairo as Ash Wednesday. That evening as Olivia, Reggie and Adam Watson walked beside the Nile, sheets of charred paper came floating down it. The Embassy and GHQ were making a bonfire of their files. Ice-cream vendors later that week were spotted selling cones wrapped in papers labelled 'Top Secret'.

Reggie had been offered a post in the Broadcasting Service in Jerusalem in the autumn – and had accepted it. His problem was how to persuade Olivia to go ahead of him at once, before the possible arrival of the Germans. Then suddenly he thought of exactly the right thing to say. 'You will be my advance party,' he told her. 'You will prepare the way.'

Though a little hesitant at first, she was soon won over. She said to Adam, 'What Reggie suggests seems to make sense.'

On their last day together – a Thursday – they heard that there was a run on the banks, but this was something which no one could confirm. Among the British colony there were few signs of agitation. It was in the nature of 'flaps' that they seldom lasted more than a few days.

The next morning Reggie drove with Olivia to the station. There they found the train packed with women and children – nearly all refugees. The Egyptian porters slung their luggage about with reckless abandon. With difficulty Reggie found his wife a place. 'You go – Germans come,' shouted the porters; they were having a high old time and the future seemed a great joke. *Ma'alesh* – or 'What does it matter?' – was a philosophy in which they had been brought up. For centuries Egypt had been ruled by foreigners.

Olivia turned to those in her compartment, as Reggie passed her some oranges and bananas for the journey. 'The porters know nothing,' she said authoritatively. 'Germans come? I never heard of such a thing. Tell that to the Marines.' Her final sentence was lost on her companions. Only Reggie was there to appreciate it – and remember.

Chapter 14

Hanging on Hopefully in Jerusalem

One of the first things that Olivia did on arrival in Jerusalem was to contact the *Palestine Post*. Soon she was on their staff as a reviewer. John Connell, its then editor, refers to her in his memoir *The House by Herod's Gate* as 'a formidable lady'. He was the first but not the last person to say so in print.

Already she was someone who attracted disparaging remarks. For example, Lawrence Durrell wrote to Tambimuttu, the editor of *Poetry (London)*, 'I see that the hook-nosed condor of the Middle East Olivia Manning has been writing about us in *Horizon*. She's determined to be *dans le mouvement*.' Olivia did not warm to Durrell. Once, when Reggie had suddenly been taken alarmingly ill with food poisoning, Durrell had immediately gone out, leaving her to cope on her own. She also felt that he treated his wife Nancy abominably. Indeed, when this marriage broke up, Olivia was responsible for finding Nancy work on the *Palestine Post*. She also introduced Nancy to E. C. (Edward) Hodgkin, soon to become Director of the Near East Broadcasting Station in Haifa. Nancy and Hodgkin were to marry in 1947.

Olivia's stay of three years in Jerusalem proved to be primarily a time of preparation for future literary work. Her book about Stanley and Emin Pasha called *The Remarkable Expedition* was more than half completed by 1945. Derek Mahon described these years as 'a kind of pencil-sharpening for the future'.

Stephen Haggard wrote to a friend in London, 'I've met a girl who is a writer. She says that Mrs Belloc Lowndes, who is a relative of hers, used always to say, "Never a day without a line."' Olivia's claim that she was a relation of Mrs Belloc Lowndes was, of course, no more than an empty boast. From her schooldays she had had a weakness for claiming literary relationships. At one time she had wondered if she might not be related to Frederic Manning, whose novel about the First World War, *Her Privates We*, had been widely praised when it came out in 1930. She was disappointed to discover that, born in Australia in 1882, he was no relation whatsoever.

Stephen Haggard worked for the department of Political Warfare and had recently been posted to the Middle East. Before the war he had been acclaimed as a rising young star in the theatre, where he had played Konstantin in *The Seagull*. Reggie, who had joined Olivia in Jerusalem now, recruited him to play the leading roles in his productions of *Henry V* and *Hamlet* on local radio.

In the spring of 1943 Olivia made a visit to Petra and wrote a prose-poem about it. The poem shows how carefully Olivia had read the *Guide to Petra* by Lankester Harding, bought a month 'before setting out on this adventure'. He writes of the entrance to the great ravine of Petra where 'no sound is heard except the rattling of pebbles under horses'. This becomes in the poem:

> Our Bedu, screaming higher than hoof-clatter,
> menace the silence.

Apart from 'hoof-clatter' there are many other hyphenated adjectives and nouns: 'tedium-frictioned memory', 'heat-hazed' and 'long-sought arrival'. Once more early Auden casts its shadow – not too happily in lines such as 'Inoculating distances eke thin illusions of escape; denounce a compensate fidelity'.

She also ventured as far as Damascus and Cyprus. She read Tolstoy's *War and Peace* for the first time – she was then thirty-five – and told Robert Liddell what an unforgettable experience it had proved, especially since it had followed within months of the great Alamein victory in late 1942: 'I read it in November non-stop, pausing hardly to eat.'

The Alamein campaign was a series of battles, beginning in late August, and culminating with those of late October and early November. During the final stages Olivia and Reggie and a group of friends in Jerusalem had sat up one night in a dimly lit room reading and quoting poems to each other. One of their company had been the Greek poet George Seferis, who in 1936 had translated T. S. Eliot's poem *The Waste Land*. Olivia later wrote,

> Many of the poets out here are refugees; all are exiles. Seferis
> [feels] that he should have remained in Greece with his
> friends. The sense of a missed experience, that no alternative
> experience can dispel, haunts most of us. Seferis should have
> suffered in Athens; we should have gone through the London
> blitz.

Reggie was acutely conscious of his absence from England. He
frequently felt ill at ease at being in the reserved occupation of British
Council officer, even if his poor eyesight would almost certainly have
exempted him from being conscripted. There was, in his view, something
shameful in holding such a post, when other men were risking their lives
defending London from air attack, or serving in the front line in the
desert. Olivia, on the other hand, had no qualms about Reggie not being
a combatant – especially after she received the news of her brother's death
on active service. Later, she was always to be defensive about Reggie's
unheroic war.

Shortly after her arrival in Jerusalem, Olivia decided that one of her Arab
colleagues, Iqal, at the Public Information Office, was already preparing
for a probable switch of masters. To his face, she accused him of having
suddenly started to learn German. He hotly denied this. His family, he
said, had always been pro-British. He had been educated at nearby
Victoria College, where he had learnt Latin, Greek and cricket. When the
war was over, his father would be sending him to learn commerce in
England.

'But *now* you are learning German,' Olivia persisted.

'That is a lie. Who said such a lie?'

'Nobody. I saw it with my own eyes. I saw you in the office copying
German phrases from a textbook.'

He waved a white handkerchief between them. 'Please be peace,' he
said. 'If the Germans come we must look after ourselves. Between Arab
and English there is love. But you betrayed us – you promised us freedom.'
Then he declared, 'We do not betray you – we just look after ourselves.'

Olivia reported the exchange to Reggie. His advice was wise: 'Write it
down. Keep it for a novel.' Changed a little, the incident was eventually to
be incorporated into her first post-war novel *Artist Among the Missing.*

After the final Alamein battle, with the Germans in full retreat, Olivia began to plan how she would deal with it in fiction. Reggie told her not to be too hasty before putting pen to paper: 'Let the events set in your mind. Remember you are an artist, not a journalist.' So, whenever the opportunity presented itself, she began to have conversations with people involved in the conflict, from actual combatants to 'the armchair chaps behind the scenes at Cairo HQ.' Many years later she was to emphasise that this had been 'a preparation of the mind': 'I noted in my mind what I was told. Fortunately I have a good memory.'

Many years later, too, the title for Olivia's novel about the war in the desert had come to Reggie when he was rereading *Macbeth* in preparation for a lecture. Almost as soon as he had opened the text, he was forcibly struck by the Act I lines:

> When the hurly-burly's done,
> When the battle's lost and won.

He rushed into the kitchen of their flat, where Olivia was preparing high tea for their Burmese cat, and announced, 'I have your title.' He then recited the lines.

'Absolutely dead on,' she replied. The next morning she wrote across the manuscript in capitals: THE BATTLE LOST AND WON.

In her 'Middle East Letter' in *Modern Reading*, Olivia suggested that the western desert, with its no man's land where men dug in the sand, took up positions in the sand and were completely surrounded by the sand, could have been a subject for Kafka. Here was an enclosed world, where a man might stoop to pick up a tin of bully-beef and be blown to smithereens on the instant. In the Scriptures there is a reference to the desert blooming like a rose: under the flashes of gunfire soldiers saw it momentarily turn pink or orange.

Olivia thought the poet Keith Douglas's reports of his life as a junior tank officer the most accurate and satisfying of all such testimonies. In his crusader Mark III tank he had kept a small shelf of books, including *Alice in Wonderland* and David Gascoyne's *Short Survey of Surrealism*, published at the age of only sixteen. The two books, declared Douglas, were easily relatable. In his own memoir, *Alamein to Zem Zem*, published posthumously in 1946, Douglas was to write of lorries 'like ships, plunging their bows into drifts of dust and rearing up suddenly over crests like waves'. Olivia liked his sea imagery and was at times to employ it herself.

Olivia read history with a poet's eye. She also saw the present with a poet's eye. Egypt was a land of mirages, and sometimes she would speak of seeing the islands of Gezira and Roda on the Nile as 'mirages of uninhabitable places' although she knew well enough that people lived and worked on both of them. All her life she had vivid dreams. That in dreams one could see round corners she took as a possible indication of the wonders that awaited one in another world. She was always open to wonders, and for a time she believed in space ships – but finally decided that they were no more than the imagination at work.

Olivia learnt that Montgomery had gone to bed early with a novel on 23 October, the day planned for the final part of the Alamein battle to begin, so as to be as rested as possible when zero hour struck at 23.40 hours. She was reminded of Drake finishing his game of bowls before preparing to meet the Armada in 1588. She thought that both men in their imminent confrontation with history had displayed an ice-cold calm.

Olivia's father shared her admiration of Montgomery. Many of the phrases that Montgomery now used had always been common in the Manning home: 'hitting the enemy for a six', 'accepting what the doctor ordered', 'taking your punishment like a man'. These were not simply clichés, they had been rules by which Olivia and her brother had been brought up.

When the battle of Alamein was being fought Olivia was thirty-three. She referred to the new generation of soldiers as 'schoolboys'. Many of these schoolboys were innocents. In the two years that Olivia had been in Egypt she had met many such subalterns. Her character, Simon Boulderstone, is married, but has never been in a red light district. When, during the battle of Alamein, he looks at his watch and finds it to be 4 a.m., it is 'the latest he had ever been up in his life'.

It took Olivia some while to get used to the 'newness' of Jerusalem. She had not expected to find Cubist architecture, frosted lamps and overhead wires. She had been conditioned by the oleographs – many in sepia – which had been displayed on the classroom walls of Portsmouth Grammar School. She had also been conditioned by the illustrations in the family bible at home, with its brass clasp.

Travelling about Palestine, and further afield, was easy for the British. There were army drivers, male and female, who were willing to give one a lift more or less anywhere. Technically there were orders against this, but they were easily got around with a little ingenuity or persuasion. E. C.

Hodgkin claimed that 'some people had scrounged lifts as far as India'. When Reggie arrived from Egypt, Olivia greeted him with the words 'You can travel for virtually nothing. Everything's at His Majesty's expense.' Harriet's wide travels, which are described in the last volume of the Trilogy, are quite within the range of possibility. Moreover, Olivia was adventurous by nature.

In 1944 Olivia found that she was pregnant by Reggie and could not have been happier. All her worries and stresses of the last months fell away. They both hoped for a son. Reggie became attentive to his wife's every need and spread the good news among those whom he met. Robert Liddell, in a letter to her, supposes that the child is going to be a girl and adds, 'I'm glad Miss Smith isn't troubling you. What is she going to be called?' He tells her that literary talent improves from one generation to the next, as in the case of Fanny Trollope and Anthony Trollope, or Leslie Stephen and Virginia Woolf. He predicts a bright future: 'Miss Smith will grow up to be a famous novelist like her mother.'

Olivia began to take it easy and took up painting again, executing some watercolours of irises in the Jordan hills; she also did some knitting in anticipation of the baby's arrival. She found herself watching other mothers with their children, and began to see mother and child as blending into one. During these months she became sentimental about her own mother and used her razor-sharp tongue only seldom. In the heat she began to feel her increasing size, with her once small breasts straining against the constriction of her silk shirts. Sometimes Reggie accompanied her to the doctor, but so strong did the tie grow between doctor and expectant mother that after the third visit he decided it best if they saw each other on their own. She started to eat ravenously and the weeks fell into a rhythm – long, plodding walks in the morning and in the afternoon daydreams about the tiny creature swimming within her.

Then, early in the seventh month, lying in the bath one morning, she noticed a curious crease across her stomach. The distended flesh had shrunk and she suddenly knew for certain that the child had died within her.

As she stepped out of the bath, she placed her hands on her stomach and sensed a lack of life. She called Reggie in. 'Little monkey's paw,' he said taking her hand in his, 'I'm sure everything is going to be all right. I'll ring the doctor all the same. I don't want you to be worried.'

He telephoned the doctor, who assured him that all would be well: 'Mrs

Smith has a vital imagination. Ladies do at these times. But if you wish to bring her to me, please do so.' Reggie phoned for a taxi and half an hour later watched his wife go into the examination room. When she came out, he realised that her worst fears had been confirmed. As they left, she refrained at first from taking Reggie's hand – then grasped it tightly.

At the time it was common practice in the Middle East for mothers whose children died prematurely in the womb to go the full term. The fear was that if the child were removed earlier, the mother might haemorrhage. 'I am like a walking cemetery,' Olivia would say, as she waited despondently for the two months to pass. 'I had knitted a sock and a half for my child,' she confided to June Braybrooke many years later. Only once in a book did she write directly about this experience and that was in 1974 in *The Rain Forest*. There the child is referred to as a girl, but Olivia told June that it had been a boy – 'a perfectly formed boy'.

Olivia never fully recovered from the experience of losing her baby yet going through labour. She would rarely even speak about it.

Reggie would have made an excellent father. He liked children and often turned up at friends' homes with a haversack filled with different bars of chocolate for their offspring. Sometimes he was known by them as 'Father Christmas'. He was also good at encouraging talent in the young.

Olivia was unable to have further children. She now transferred her maternal feelings towards animals in general and cats in particular. Her last cat Miou, a Burmese, she would constantly cuddle and call 'My boy'. She believed that many animals, especially domestic ones, had a place in the afterlife. On one occasion she wrote to Dodie Smith to consult her about a possible animal faith healer for her twelve-year-old Siamese who was dangerously ill. Dodie Smith confirmed by letter that a faith healer had cured a Dalmatian of hers of a mysterious liver complaint, so that he had lived for another five years. Reggie Smith commented in a letter of reply, 'We Smiths must consult each other more often.'

To help her get over the loss of her child, Reggie took Olivia for a month's holiday to Cyprus in October 1944. She kept a three-page record of their stay. In the opening sentences she claimed that the holiday would be an escape from the hatred, greed, aggression and rudeness that she had come to associate with both the Jews and the Arabs. This document is highly subjective and overshadowed by her recent tragedy. There is a good deal of paranoia. 'I am angry with the world,' she repeats.

In fact, as Reggie was later to report to his bosses, she was having a nervous breakdown: 'She has terrible feelings of foreboding. She thinks I am going to be blown up in my office.'

Her mood on boarding the Cyprus boat remained one of looking for trouble. On the gangway she showed her fury when an Arab porter nearly dropped her suitcase in the water. Once on board, they could not find any deckchairs and so had to spend the night separately in communal cabins labelled 'male' and 'female', in which the portholes had been blacked out. The intense heat did not help: each lay awake, drenched in sweat. 'A horrible night at sea,' was her conclusion.

When they docked at Famagusta, she remained suspicious of everything. Did the apparent kindness of the islanders conceal a baser motive? When the train driver walked down the platform of each stop to enquire how the passengers were getting on, was there an ulterior purpose behind his show of hospitality? In Nicosia, after she had bought some English tooth powder and a disinfectant for the washbasin in their room, she began to feel slightly less persecuted. But she remained discontented with almost everything. Reggie's good humour must have been tested to the utmost. This was a period when, according to the poet Louis Lawler, she addressed Reggie constantly as 'Smith'.

On a visit to an olive press, they encountered Mr W., an oil man from Iraq, who, as he waded with their party 'through the dark brown olives on the floor of the press, managed to pick up twenty-eight fleas, although no one else did'.

Later Reggie was to question her: 'How do you know there were twenty-eight?'

'Poetic licence,' she answered.

This is the only light relief in the piece she wrote about the holiday. When they spent the evening at a nightclub, the place was said to have 'the bareness and ugliness of a Presbyterian church'. The girls sitting at the bar were dismissed as 'an unremarkable lot', who offered 'glamour of a sort' to an audience of rich wine merchants. After a while the girls changed into evening dress and each in turn performed a simple little dance to a sentimental tune. These dances had been in their nightly repertoire for more years than it would be kind to remember. 'Depressing' was the word Olivia used about the entertainment. She used the same word about the rain.

When they arrived at Limassol, it was to find themselves at a two-star hotel, which offered 'the comforts of the slaughter-house'. The food was reasonable, but the crude local oil used in the cooking and salads upset her stomach. Even at the best hotels she found the sanitary arrangements 'appalling'. Reggie was due to lecture at Larnaca one night, but the occasion had to be cancelled because the Cypriots wished to spend their time celebrating the beginning of the liberation of Greece. Olivia's stinging comment was, 'The Cypriots are all obviously convinced that Greece has been liberated by the Greeks, aided possibly by a handful of British guerrillas.'

None of Harriet Pringle's qualities of nobility were to be found here. There was no attempt to make the best of things and the tone was one of constant complaint. Close to the end, the black mood lifted for a moment, when Olivia wrote of how beautiful shells were when still wet from the sea. Olivia loved shells and collected them on holidays. She delighted in the beauty of their names.

Although Olivia was better for the rest and holiday, she was still far from well on the return to Jerusalem. For most of the time that Louis Lawler, also in Jerusalem at that time, knew the Smiths, he thought her 'a difficult and strange woman'. In comparison, Reggie was 'wonderfully patient'. One incident still remained particularly vivid in Lawler's mind in 1996. The setting was the King David Hotel:

> Olivia sits on Arthur Koestler's lap as he and Reggie play chess, in the otherwise deserted lounge. O rather ostentatiously strokes Koestler's hair. He appears a bit contemptuous about R's chess and to take little notice of O – rather as if her attentions are merely his due; he was given at that time to seeing himself as God's gift to women . . . I thought – still think for that matter – that I would not have put up with O's behaviour had she been mine. R was calm, kindly, concentrating on the chess, not noticing or not seeming to . . .

There is no doubt that Olivia, though usually shy, could also be bold and provocative. Lawler noticed a great contrast between her in the Middle East and in early post-war London, which he defines thus: 'Discontented in Jerusalem, smiling and kindly in London.' When he repeated this to her in her flat in Shepherd Market, she said she thought she was happy now because she was writing. This was certainly true. During the war she had been able to write only when she could find a free hour or so. Now, with peace in the world, she could concentrate all her energies on being a writer.

Olivia's years in the Middle East had left her subject to liver attacks and a victim of amoebic dysentery. In the years ahead she was often to put her spells in hospitals in Egypt and Jerusalem to literary use, so that, for example, her stay in the American Hospital in Cairo was later incorporated into *The Battle Lost and Won*. In it, Dr Shaffik tells Harriet,

> 'You are getting better. Are you glad you did not die and go to heaven?'
>
> 'I thought there was no heaven for women in your religion.'
>
> 'Wrong, Madame, wrong. The ladies have a nice heaven of their own. They are without men but there is a consolation: they are beautiful for ever.'
>
> 'If there are no men, would it matter whether they are beautiful or not?'

By 1944 Reggie accepted that he had a sick wife on his hands. In 1945, with the war ended, he decided that she must be got back to England ahead of him. But those above him were totally unsympathetic when he asked for leave, so that he might accompany her to Cairo and from there to a ship at Suez. On his own decision, therefore, he took a few days off, went with Olivia to Cairo and then on to Suez, and saw that she was installed in a cabin on the boat. On his return to Jerusalem no one questioned Reggie about his absence; but he took the precaution of making it widely known that he thought the man who had refused to sign his pass of leave was 'a pompous fool'.

It was during this short stay in Cairo that Olivia was to hear a story that she was to include in the opening chapter of the Levant Trilogy. In the novel the incident takes place in 1941 – but in fact it occurred in Cairo in 1943, when she and Reggie were living in Jerusalem. Sir Walter Smart and his wife had an eight-year-old son called Mickie. Sir Walter was the Oriental Secretary and Minister Plenipotentiary in Cairo, while his wife

Amy was the daughter of Dr Fares Nimr Pasha, founder of the newspaper *el Mukkatam*. She became a painter and writer, and contributed a piece about Cavafy to *Personal Landscape* in 1945. The Smarts patronised the arts and highly approved of Lawrence Durrell's writings. They also entertained Reggie and Olivia, but Olivia felt that neither she nor Reggie was given her or his due. 'We are not part of their inner sanctum,' she wrote. 'They did not think us grand enough.' Olivia had felt something of the same thing about C. F. A. Dundas.

In the Levant Trilogy the Smarts appear, thinly veiled, as Sir Desmond and Lady Hooper Tree. In January 1943, the Smarts' young son was playing in the desert when he picked up a hand grenade, which exploded and killed him. In *The Danger Tree* there follows an imaginary scene, in which the dead boy's father attempts to feed him by spooning gruel into a hole which has been blasted in his left cheek by the bomb. Three times the gruel pours back over the cheek. At last the father gives up.

Later in the book, the poet Castlebar (partly based on Bernard Spencer) remarks, on hearing of the event, 'Egypt's a weird place. Feeding the dead's an ancient custom, but it still goes on.' On radio Victoria Glendinning spoke of how memorable the scene was. Indeed, when the novel came out in September 1976, many other reviewers also singled it out for mention.

Sir Walter had died in 1965 and his wife in 1973. Nonetheless, on 20 September 1978 the solicitors Blackett, Gill & Swan despatched a letter to Weidenfeld & Nicolson, who had published *The Danger Tree*. They were writing, they said, on behalf of the immediate Smart family and other surviving relatives, to protest about the inclusion of this scene and to say that in the following volumes of the trilogy there must be no reference to it or to Sir Desmond and Lady Hooper Tree. Reggie said to Olivia, 'Remember an action for defamation dies with the person defamed. The solicitors are on thin ice.' Olivia felt confident. She wrote to the solicitors, saying,

> I have already made a written statement to Messrs Weidenfeld's legal department. In it I declared that the character of Angela Hooper is not based on the late Lady Smart. The real woman and the imaginary character bear no resemblance to each other. Lady Smart was Syrian or Egyptian of subdued temperament . . . The very fact that

Angela Hooper, as you say, is 'immoral or ridiculous', while
the conduct of Lady Smart was 'beyond question', is a proof
that Angela Hooper does not relate to Lady Smart in any way.

In the two volumes that followed Olivia ignored the solicitors' request that
there should be no further reference to the incident. There are passing
references in both.

Joan Leigh Fermor, who began by telling Olivia that she and her
husband, the writer Patrick Leigh Fermor, had always admired her novels,
took her to task for this. E. C. Hodgkin also did not care for the reporting
of this tragedy. David Abercrombie, with whom Olivia and Reggie shared
Adam Watson's flat, wrote to the Braybrookes on 3 December 1990 to say
that he was deeply distressed: 'Putting this scene in the book seemed in the
worst possible taste.' Penelope Lively, who was brought up as a child in
Egypt, described the passage as 'one of the more insensitive translations of
experience into fiction'. Robert Liddell, a friend of the Smarts, also
strongly disapproved.

Now, more than half a century since the child's death, there is no one
left to be hurt.

Chapter 15

Home Sweet Home

Olivia returned to Liverpool on the *Aquitania*, feeling 'tolerably well'. She was in high spirits at the prospect of once again seeing her own country and hoped that she was leaving for ever this 'land where one ate sickness'. 'I pray that I have had my last attack of amoebic dysentery,' she wrote to Stevie. In this she was mistaken. There were to be recurring attacks for the rest of her life.

For the first twenty-four hours of the voyage Olivia found herself in a cabin fitted out to accommodate eight others. None had turned up. Then, on the second day, she was transferred to a smaller cabin, where there was one other woman with her child. 'The child woke every morning at 6 and saw that everyone else did,' she wrote to Reggie. It was a long and affectionate letter, which she posted on her arrival in Liverpool. 'My dearest Love' it began – and in the middle broke off to say, 'Darling, I long for you to come home. I worry so much about your safety and think about you all the time.' In Jerusalem, especially in their last months together, she had heard that Reggie was on 'a hit list'. They had heard the same thing during their last months in Bucharest. She ended her letter by saying that, whatever ship he returned on, she would be at Waterloo to meet him with a taxi waiting. She had heard that taxis were in short supply in London and expensive: 'You get a black look apparently if you give only a sixpenny tip. Oh! dear!'

The voyage passed swiftly. Two details stood out for her – Gibraltar with its lights blazing, and the small island of Lampedusa, looking 'like the back of a whale'. As the ship approached England she began to appreciate the temperate warmth of the sun. In Egypt she had thought of the sun as an enemy.

Olivia was still very much in love with Reggie. She told friends on landing how fortunate she had been to have such a husband by her side. She had learnt quickly to take his political views with a pinch of salt. She was – though she might have denied this in 1945 – a Tory at heart. Admittedly on several occasions her name was linked to Communist activities, but that was because Reggie always added her name, along with his own, to letters to the press. For this reason many people assumed her to be connected with the International Committee of Intellectuals and with the Women's International Democratic Federation – both well-known Communist front organisations in the late 1940s.

How greatly Portsmouth had changed since before the war! Her home town had been heavily bombed and there were ruins everywhere. A phrase, 'the seed beneath the stone', swam into her mind. She passed some bombed architectural offices where her brother had worked. Parts of the city had been so much destroyed that 'roads netted it like paths in a desert'. That was a simile that she was later to use in her novel *A Different Face*.

With her brother dead, she felt that she had returned to 'a city without a heart'. Her parents never got over his death. His body was never found; his grave was the sea, as his sister repeated to everyone who had known him. Sometimes she would look at her father and think how much he had declined: 'It was heartbreaking to see cashiers at shops cheat him out of his change.' But when Olivia saw him cheated, she thought it best not to notice lest a comment of hers might humiliate him. Her mother refused to admit how frail Dumps was. The food cuts had affected them both, as they had affected everyone else – except those who had found black market ways to dodge them. 'Such people are not patriots,' the Commander would say scathingly. Her mother suffered inwardly because she could no longer provide friends with the feasts of pre-war days – 'I remembered with nostalgia those parties Mother had organised for my brother and myself when we were children.'

Once more in her Laburnum Grove home, Olivia knuckled down to help. Each day she eagerly awaited the post for news of Reggie's return. One thing was certain – she and Reggie would live in London. There was no place to match it. Moreover, for her London was the capital of the publishing world. In America several of her books were published – but sales were usually disappointing.

Her immediate concern in Portsmouth was what Reggie would do when he returned to England. He had much of the actor in him, just as he also had much of the teacher. Yet she could not really see him in either role. In Bucharest, once he was word perfect in *Othello*, he began to show signs of boredom: his interest shifted from playing the main part to his production of the play. 'Thank God this is a short run,' he had said to Adam Watson, who was playing Cassio. 'I would not care to be doing this night after night.'

The first priority, thought Olivia, would be for Reggie to have a good month's rest. With this in mind she arranged to borrow a flat from some friends who lived in Knightsbridge.

Reggie returned that summer – but did not rest, as she had hoped. He kept her on the go from the moment that he landed. The month sped by as he visited friends here, there and everywhere. From time to time he went down to spend an odd night with his mother in Stratford. If Olivia complained about his restlessness, people would say to her, 'Reggie is Reggie' – and that was as far as they would go in any criticism of their much loved friend. She was both pleased and relieved when, through the help of Louis MacNeice, who had been a witness at their wedding, Reggie at last found a job in the radio Features Department of the BBC.

MacNeice and Reggie had been friends since they had first met at Birmingham University. Reggie took MacNeice home to meet his father, where all three – Reggie advising Louis – would play chess until two in the morning. 'Reggie is the least class-conscious man that I have ever met,' Louis said shortly after they were introduced and added, 'He has a fine understanding of poetry and his admiration for old D. H. Lawrence knows no bounds. He plans to write something about him.' Reggie had made several D. H. discoveries, he claimed – among them that in Mexico the writer had once bartered some poems for a pot of home-made marmalade. Reggie believed this told one something about the equality of wealth.

'What does it tell one?' Olivia asked him peremptorily.

'Oh! Something,' he muttered and then shut up.

In 1939, on Reggie's leave from the British Council, he had stayed with Louis in his flat overlooking Primrose Hill. He had refused to sleep on a bed and instead put up on a sofa in the sitting room, scattering his clothes and belongings everywhere. This only lasted for a week or two because once he had met Olivia – and it was love at first sight – he moved straight into her flat in Bloomsbury.

During this particular leave, MacNeice remembered Reggie for his irresistible cheerfulness. He was as happy in the British Museum Reading Room as he was at the Holborn Empire, where Max Miller was one of his favourite acts. In the British Museum, Reggie made notes for his Lawrence project, while MacNeice made notes for a book about W. B. Yeats. At the entrance, Reggie's rucksack and Louis's briefcase were searched lest they might conceal IRA bombs.

Hedli Anderson, Louis's second wife, liked Reggie and once summed him up as someone to call upon if you were in a spot or wanted heavy luggage moved around; but she was suspicious of Olivia, who she thought might be envious of her red hair – which Hedli liked to describe as 'Titian'. Louis himself had mixed feelings about Olivia and in his autobiography, which he abandoned in 1941, refers to her as Reggie's 'girl'. He knew that there had been many previous 'girls' and suspected that there might be many more. Numerically he was right. What he did not allow for was Reggie's enduring admiration for what he regarded as Olivia's genius. MacNeice could be, and was, quite spiteful about that 'genius'.

Louis and Reggie were seasoned drinkers, who liked girls; but their friendship was at its best when there were no women about.

Laurence Gilliam, who at the time was the Assistant Director of Features at BBC radio, got on well with Reggie. It was a golden period for the Features Department and its standing, until the Drama Department took over in the late 1950s, was never higher. MacNeice was a regular writer and producer, and Reggie a producer. Olivia was an occasional contributor. She kept on sending in ideas for programmes, though during 1945 to 1946 she gave most of her time to completing the book on Stanley and Emin Pasha that she had begun before the war and that she had continued to work on during it. She, too, used the British Museum Reading Room, where she checked facts, dates and research already done.

Over the next few years she and Reggie rented flats in Westminster, Shepherd Market and Baker Street, before finally renting a house in St John's Wood in 1951. Laurence Gilliam thought Olivia had 'potential genius as a scriptwriter' – but not as a broadcaster. Like P. H. Newby, he thought her voice 'too thin'.

One great advantage that Olivia had was that she could write to order, providing scripts for *Mrs Dale's Diary* or adaptations of novels by Arnold Bennett, George Eliot, Ada Leverson and William Gerhardie. She also submitted a synopsis for a programme about Sir Thomas More but, to her disappointment, nothing came of that. History had a great interest for her. She lived long enough to see her books about the Second World War regarded by a new generation as something from the past. 'I suppose I must regard myself as partly a historical novelist,' she said the day after she handed in her last book, *The Sum of Things*, in 1979.

Olivia wrote only one biography, and that was the one about Stanley and his rescue of Emin Pasha. She found completing *The Remarkable Expedition*, as it was called in England, an exhausting experience, for it had dragged on over eight years. At last in 1946 she gave the manuscript to the literary agency Gilbert Wright Ltd. The firm was then run by her friend Kathleen Farrell, who straight away sold the book to Heinemann. On 18 November the two parties signed a contract, with the author being offered an advance of £50 against future royalties. Less than a week later, Kathleen Farrell sold the American rights to Doubleday & Co. – who were to bring out the book under the title *The Reluctant Rescue*.

Olivia drew the endpapers for her book, which provided a map of Africa and showed in red Stanley's unexpected route across Africa from the mouth of the Congo on the west coast to Dar es Salaam on the east coast. Olivia herself had never been to this part of Africa. Her creation of the Ituri Forest, the legendary heart of darkness left blank in early maps, is a masterly feat of imagination.

Commander Manning had all his life been an admirer of Stanley and there was a copy of Stanley's two-volume edition of *In Darkest Africa* (1890) in the Manning home. Dumps, who regarded him as an all-time hero, often spoke about him to his son and daughter. But Olivia's initial interest in Stanley's rescue of Emin Pasha had been prompted by a short monograph called *Emin, Governor of Equatoria* by A. J. A. Symons, which she had read shortly after coming to London.

The main protagonists in her book are Stanley and Emin, though it soon becomes apparent that the author's sympathies lie with Emin, the White Pasha of Equatoria, who was born in Prussia and whose real name was Eduard Schnitzer. He was a doctor by profession and never happier than when observing the life of plants and animals. One night he recalls how he watched chimpanzees on their way to rob some local orchards and saw them lighting the pathway with flares. Such details delighted Olivia. Emin was also a surgeon – a profession much after her heart: 'If he made any large sum by performing an operation he at once distributed it among those poorer than himself.' His maxim was 'Be to your patients in the first place a friend, then a doctor'. Through his efforts many zoos in Europe acquired rare animals, and he was constantly sending papers about natural history to museums and learned societies.

Olivia had mixed feelings about zoos – and in the end decided that it would be best if they were to be phased out, especially in cities. In Cairo's zoo she had seen a polar bear and had stopped, appalled, at finding an arctic animal in such a climate. In her short story 'The Man who Stole a Tiger' she describes the Jerusalem zoo as 'miserable'.

Olivia was to discover, as she worked on the book, that Stanley had a reputation for ruthlessness among his contemporaries. When she read passages aloud to her father, who was losing his sight, she omitted some of the accounts of his more savage behaviour. Even so, Edward Beaver in a *New Statesman* review of the book accused the author of not concentrating enough 'on the dark shades' in Stanley. She omitted, for instance, any mention of Burgari, who was given 150 lashes for stealing half a goat, then escaped from Stanley's camp and, when recaptured, was executed on Stanley's orders.

On the whole the book received an encouraging press and won generous reviews from Roger Fulford in the *Listener*, H. A. Manford in *John O'London's* and Hugh Kingsmill in *Punch*. The last of these declared that it deserved to become 'a classic in the literature of exploration'. The book remains comparatively unknown, has never been reprinted, and is never listed in the bibliographies of books about Stanley and Emin. This sometimes happens when a writer who is regarded primarily as a novelist writes a one-off biography.

Chapter 16

Back in the Literary Swim

Olivia Manning's first post-war book of fiction, published in 1946, was a collection of short stories entitled *Growing Up*. The dedication reads:

To my Husband
R. D. SMITH

Surprisingly, perhaps, Reggie did not appear in any of the thirteen stories. The book sold well and was recommended by the Book Society. Some reviewers favourably recalled her first novel, the 1937 *The Wind Changes*. Elizabeth Bowen, then chief fiction reviewer in the *Tatler*, thought that the publishers had been wise to provide a note of how during the war Olivia had worked in various organisations such as the British Military Mission in Greece in 1941 and later as a press attaché to the American Embassy in Cairo, for it showed why, though a born writer, she had such a small body of work behind her. Nonetheless those very facts had provided her 'with an almost masculine outfit in the way of experience'. In *Growing Up*, Elizabeth Bowen felt that she was only just beginning to draw on this material – which 'might last her a life-time'. These were prophetic words.

C. P. Snow praised the book to Olivia. But although, in the years ahead, he could be relied on always to be laudatory, she never greatly cared for him either as a man or as a novelist – describing his work on one occasion as 'clodhopperish'. In 1972, when Snow's novel *The Malcontents* received a blistering notice in the *New York Times*, she took pleasure in sending out twelve photostats of it to selected friends. The review began, 'It would be difficult to imagine anyone with less natural aptitude for writing fiction than C. P. Snow . . .' Nonetheless Olivia remained a close friend of Snow's wife, Pamela Hansford Johnson.

Pamela would share confidences with Olivia, which Olivia, who thrived on gossip, could seldom refrain from passing on to others. One such item (or so Olivia would have people believe) was that before Snow reached his orgasm, he had to be encouraged: 'You are the greatest! You are the mightiest! You are Tolstoy!' Olivia would also often relate how, when she and Reggie arrived at a party given by the Snows, they were greeted by Pamela at the door with the words, 'The butler has walked out! You'll have to pour your own drinks.' Since the Snows never employed a butler, many people thought that this tale, like many others, must have originated in malice and imagination, rather than in fact.

One day, Olivia showed Reggie a cutting from the *Irish Times*. It recorded that her book had been banned in Ireland. He read it carefully. 'Don't worry, darling,' he consoled her as he put it back in the bulging envelope. 'You could not be in better company. Patrick Kavanagh is banned on the same list. Also Alan Moorehead and Simone de Beauvoir. I think this calls for a drink – four drinks perhaps. One drink for each of the banned!'

The stories in *Growing Up* are grouped under four headings: 'Children', 'Growing Up', 'At Home' and 'Abroad'. The title story, running to sixty-three pages, is based largely on Olivia's love affair with Hamish Miles. She was never to reprint it – though in the 1970s she reworked part of it into another story, entitled 'Let me tell you before I forget'. This was never printed, being considered unsuitable by the *Sunday Times*, which had commissioned it. When she subsequently offered it to *The Times*, they too turned it down. In 1988 Frances Spalding was to draw on it in her life of Stevie Smith.

In the 1948 version Hamish Miles is called Lewis Mitchell and there are a few elementary changes to his circumstances: his publishing office is situated in Great Russell Street, not Bedford Square; Peter Jones, for which Olivia worked in the Thirties, is referred to as 'a big shop'; and the heroine, based on Olivia, is an orphan whose parents have been killed in a car crash, leaving her to be brought up by an aunt in Carlisle. Harriet Pringle in the trilogies, a child of divorced parents, is also brought up by an aunt.

Early in the story, Lewis says to Anna in her bedsitting room, 'You're growing up,' and leans forward and kisses her on the mouth. A moment later he remarks, 'I refuse to believe you are surprised and innocent.' He is only half correct, since their affair, which is just about to be consummated, does not surprise her. She has already expected that this will be the way their relationship will go. But she is certainly innocent. At the start of the affair she is unaware both that he is married and that he has a mistress. A loss of innocence is therefore a stage in growing up for her. Later, when Lewis brings their affair to an end because of his mistress's divorce and subsequent freedom to see him whenever she wishes, Anna has to accept the situation. On the phone Lewis congratulates her on her newly acquired maturity: 'Ah! Now you are growing up.' As a man who has broken many hearts, he adds, true to type, 'I'm sure you will be happy one day. Good-bye, my dear.'

The last story in the volume was 'The Man who Stole a Tiger'. On one level an adventure story, it is about a soldier, Tandy, who steals a tiger from a zoo in Jerusalem and eventually gives himself up. The narrator is a prison chaplain, who visits Tandy, an ex-Borstal boy, in his cell. Tandy, who has spent most of the war in a sanatorium at the top of Mount Scopius after having survived the sinking of a troopship in the Mediterranean, has a sentimental heart. Seeing the tiger confined in a cage, he is determined to rescue it. He tells the chaplain how he stole a lorry, chose a Saturday for his escapade because he remembered that orthodox Jews were not allowed to work on the Sabbath and escaped successfully with the animal. He drove through the British frontier controls in Palestine and north Egypt, and made for Khartoum, where he camped on the outskirts of the city. Next he aimed for the grasslands of Uganda and ultimately reached the Congo, where he could see the dark forest that was his goal. A mile into that forest he released the beast. At this point in his narrative, Tandy is interrupted by the prison chaplain: 'Tandy, there are no tigers in Africa. The tiger is a native of India . . .' So, through his lack of education, Tandy has unwittingly condemned the animal to a life of solitude or even death.

From 1951 Olivia rented for many years a house in St John's Wood. To help with the running costs, she needed lodgers. Among the most talented were two young men – the novelist and dramatist Julian Mitchell, and Tony Richardson, the film and theatre producer, who was later to marry Vanessa Redgrave. Olivia was not an easy landlady. 'She might knock on the door when you were having a bath,' Richardson recalled. 'That could have been accidental, or had she an ulterior motive . . .?' When Richardson read 'The Man who Stole a Tiger', he saw it in terms of a short TV feature and in his mind cast George Cole as Tandy and Alfred Burke as the prison chaplain. But, remembering the knocks on the bathroom door, he proceeded cautiously. An internal memo, dated 5 November 1954 and now held at the BBC Archives Centre at Caversham Park in Reading, explains his predicament in guarded language:

> Could you please clear copyright on 'The Man who Stole a Tiger', a short story by Olivia Manning, published by Heinemann . . . Mr Richardson thinks that Miss Manning may be difficult about the dramatisation: if so, he does not wish to negotiate, but will abandon this story to another.

All went well, however, and Richardson adapted and produced the programme. 'The Man who Stole a Tiger' is the only short story of Olivia's ever to be televised.

Chapter 17

'Our Beloved Physician'

When she died, Olivia's papers filled a large metal trunk. They included manuscripts, typescripts, beginnings of articles and reviews, letters to friends, receipted bills, dividend vouchers, bank statements and press cuttings. Another box of her papers, this time a cardboard one, included passports, cheque stubs, a small commonplace book which she had kept in her twenties, photographs of herself, a box of dried-up paints, two pen-and-ink drawings and a tiny shoe that had belonged to her as a baby. On the sole of the shoe she had written 'Olivia's first shoe'. At the top of the metal trunk she had placed three photostats of a typed letter. Neither dated nor signed, it began 'My dearest love . . .' Evidence suggests that the letter was typed in Athens, in the spring of 1949, when she was on holiday in Greece with her friend Kathleen Farrell. It runs as follows:

My dearest love,

I miss you more than I can say. At first you seemed still to be with me and the journey passed like a dream. The only reality was my life with you. Then, in the middle of the night, I woke up alone, and felt the train rushing forward into darkness and the distance growing between us. I remembered the lonliness [*sic*] and the long periods of desolation before I met you. I wanted you unbearably.

Darling, I love you. I love you. I love you. I have been wandering about this city – which is delightful, full of flowers and sunshine – and I have thought of nothing but you.

I can only think that in April . . . became my lover. You asked me once if I would give up everything for you and I replied 'Everything' and I meant everything. You may think

I have not, after all, so much to give up. You have much more – and yet all my life I have only wanted to be an artist. All the affirs [sic] of which you made me tell you, were secondary to that one ambition – they were all a background to the thing I felt I must do. Now, for the first time in my life, I am in love in such a way that it comes before anything. I cannot tell you why.

You have often asked me why I love you and I have tried to think of reasons I could tell you. I have already told you most of them – because for me you are a man, and have been from my first awareness of you; but, alas, because part of your nature is feminine, and part of mine masculine, and these parts fit so perfectly, it seems at times we must be one person. And because physically and mentally and spiritually we belong, and are in sympathy, and understand each other.

I have never felt any need to deceive you. I tell you the truth about everything because there is no need to do anything else.

I thought of other reasons for loving you, but they don't seem to matter now. Surely I do not need to give you reasons when we have come together so closely, we are almost part of one another. When we lie wrapped around each other, my arms about your shoulders, feeling the movements of your muscles, and your flesh – the most delicious flesh in the world – your breast to my bosom, your mouth to my mouth – then it is as though we have loved each other from the beginning of time.

You accuse me of having been unaware of you the first time you took my hand. It is true. I had tried to cut myself off from people and emotional relationships. I did not want to be aware of anyone. I tried to shut myself away and say 'It doesn't matter' and 'I don't care', and expect nothing, and tell myself I wanted nothing.

Only something I could not resist, could break in one that [sic]. When I did become aware of you, I felt our relationship inevitable. There must be intercourse. And complete intercourse. Indeed, I feel now if we withheld ourselves from each other in any way, it would be more of a sin against ourselves and each other than anything we could do together.

What else can I say? If I read this through I shall probably not send it: so it must go unread. That is all. My beloved is mine and I am his. Saying that, I have said everything.

This letter to Jerry Slattery was, it would seem, written but never posted. Olivia had fallen in love with Jerry, and he in turn is reported to have said of her, 'I shall love this woman until I die.' The letter may have been written merely to get her feelings down on paper. There are several mistypings in the photostat which are not corrected. In placing it on the top of her papers it would appear that she intended that anyone opening the metal trunk would immediately see it – perhaps a future biographer, or biographers. Perhaps, too, she feared that there might be attempts after her death to hush up this side of her life. Already that possibility has deterred one potential biographer. But 'A Life', as Olivia used to say, 'means a whole Life or nothing.' She thought biographers should not restrict themselves in any way but tell the truth, however unpalatable to some.

Note in the letter the reference to the recipient's desire to be told all about Olivia's 'affirs'. In 1935, there had been her first with Hamish Miles, which ended two years later with his death. Her second affair – though a question mark hangs over this – may have been with the detective-story writer John Mair, the son of G. M. Mair, who worked on the *Manchester Guardian*, and the renowned Irish actress Maire O'Neill, for whom Synge wrote the part of Pegeen in *The Playboy of the Western World.* Reggie told friends that, when he first met Olivia, 'she was living with a young chap called Mair'. Some friends found this hard to credit. All that is certain is that when Olivia told John Mair that she was going to marry Reggie, his reaction was 'You cannot marry a man called Smith. Fancy being Mrs Smith for the rest of your life!'

After the Second World War, Olivia confessed to having had affairs with William Gerhardie and Henry Green. These appear to have been brief and some people close to Gerhardie have questioned whether in fact the second ever occurred. Olivia told both Kay Dick and Francis King that Gerhardie and Green had been her lovers.* Both Gerhardie and Green were well-known womanisers living in London, and both were novelists

---

* King mentions the affairs in his autobiography *Yesterday Came Suddenly* (1993).

whom Olivia greatly respected. There was talk at one point of Henry Green preparing an introduction to a reprint of her volume of short stories *Growing Up*. In letters to William Gerhardie, whose work she did much to promote after 1945, she would sometimes sign herself 'Your Literary Wife'. Olivia had some sympathy for the view that, if one has slept with a writer, one might better understand his work. 'This, though, is not a necessity,' she would then add in a tantalising way.

With Francis King, whom she appointed to be one of her three literary executors, she had a long and rewarding friendship, which began in 1957. The fact that he never made any secret of his homosexuality may have meant that she could speak more freely with him than with a male heterosexual confidant. In 1971 she wrote to June, 'The danger with heterosexuals, as we know, is that if you are too self-revelatory about yourself they may think that you are making a pass.'

Like her father, Olivia was highly sexed. Her Trilogies provide accounts of orgies, sexual exhibitions in brothels and tales of men who suffer from premature ejaculation and in consequence have to be restrained with cold water. In *Friends and Heroes* there is a scene where Yakimov on a balcony sings mournfully to himself as he pees over those standing below: 'He displayed the organ the secondary function of which is the relief of the bladder.' In *The Battle Lost and Won* there is a scene where a drunken squaddie sits by the roadside and displays his rampant cock, across which he has balanced his spectacles, for all to see. Such details are so carefully integrated into the text that they have gone hardly noticed by most readers. Only one reviewer in her lifetime – John Miller in the *Evening News* – ever warned his readers that the author went pretty close to the bone. But in 1985, after her death, Bernard E. Dold brought out a dual monograph *Olivia Manning and Tom Sharpe*, in which he censored her for coarseness of detail and for language which was 'almost Australian [*sic*] at times'.

At parties, when Reggie used regularly to go up to women and ask them if they were interested in any extramarital fun, this was usually considered acceptable behaviour since he was a man. Olivia felt that she would sometimes like to do the same but, since she was a woman, it was out of the question – at least for a woman of her generation. Nonetheless at home and elsewhere she did make attempts, as in her pursuit of Tony Richardson, only to be rebuffed. Until Francis King told her, she appeared not to have grasped that Richardson was bisexual. This information at once assuaged her sense of rejection. Sometimes she was bolder. After one party in 1962 she invited an admirer of her books home, plied him with vodka and said, 'I want to be fucked.'

There were many occasions in her life when she felt frustrated – particularly when she witnessed others enjoying what she herself could not enjoy. She was a fascinated observer of the sexual exchange and mart in wartime Cairo – and wrote about it in detail. On her return to London, when she and Reggie rented a flat in Shepherd Market, she was an equally fascinated observer of the activities of the prostitutes in the area. She was not the first writer to have been so fascinated. Others before her had included Michael Swan and Anthony Powell, both residents in what was then a raffish quarter. Diana Tighe and her journalist husband have spoken of the excitement of living there in the late 1940s and not knowing, as one left one's flat, which famous politician one might bump into, following a girl up the stairs.

Jeremiah Slattery, who had been born in 1917, had begun his career in the office of his father, a Kerry solicitor. After a short spell, he decided that the law was not for him and took a medical degree in 1940 at Trinity College, Dublin. Two years later he joined the RAF and became Medical Officer to New Zealand Squadron 489, serving in Burma, Ceylon and India. Later, he specialised in gynaecology and was elected a member of the Royal College of Obstetricians and Gynaecology. In 1949 he put up his doctor's plate in Chalk Farm and built a practice which included many people from the theatre, such as Peter O'Toole, T. P. McKenna and Robert Shaw; from journalism, such as James Cameron and Mary Kenny; and from the literary and political worlds, such as Edna O'Brien and Michael Foot. Michael Foot he regarded 'more as a literary patient than a political one'. Olivia was on his books as a patient.

Olivia told Jerry everything about herself. He deeply cared about her and in a 1960 diary that he gave her he wrote, 'To Olivia with love from Jerry' – and underneath it added, 'Great Success in 1960', which was the year when the first volume of the Balkan Trilogy was to come out. He wrote in the diary her name and address, and by the printed entry 'Driving Licence No.' put the word 'Soon!'. He was a gregarious man and had only to arrive in a room for Olivia to feel better. Jerry, his wife Johnny, Reggie and Olivia became a well-known quartet at parties and theatres, and always got on well. The relationship between them appeared a thoroughly

civilised one. Johnny kept open house for Reggie and Olivia, and the four
of them spent nearly every Christmas together. Jerry was a devoted father
and husband. His problem – not an uncommon one – was that he loved
two women simultaneously.

One Sunday Jerry invited another Hampstead doctor, Michael
Laurence, and his Persian wife Parvin, living close by, to midday drinks.
The couple found they were still there at teatime. 'He opened a new world
to us,' Parvin said afterwards. 'It was like attending a wonderful salon.'
Later, in 1976, Michael Laurence, who was a surgeon, carried out a hip
replacement operation on Olivia. He and his wife became two of Olivia's
staunchest and most valued friends.

Olivia dedicated the first volume of her Balkan Trilogy, *The Great
Fortune*, to Johnny and Jerry, and in 1969 dedicated her novel *The Play
Room* to their children Jane and Jonathan. Reggie and Jerry rapidly took
to each other and became drinking companions. In their cups they would
agree that one could love more than one woman. In pubs it was usually
Jerry who called the shots: 'That's enough, Smith. We ought to be going.
Let me finish your pint off' and, taking Reggie's glass, he would down it
at one go. If Reggie protested, Jerry would retort, 'I'm pulling rank. I am
your doctor after all.'

The news of Jerry's death in November 1977 was broken to Olivia by
Michael Laurence. He remembers that she remained extraordinarily
composed, saying, 'It will be a great loss to us all.' When Francis King rang
to console her, she surprised and disconcerted him with her calm reply: 'I
don't know where I'll ever find another doctor so good.' To June
Braybrooke she wrote,

> Our dearest friend, Jerry Slattery, died on Saturday evening
> . . . I realised from your letter that you did not know . . . I
> could scarcely bear to speak or even write of it. He is lost to us
> and now I don't know how we will go on living without him
> . . .

The tactful 'we' speaks volumes and she carried herself with dignity
through the sad days that followed. She confided to June, 'One has to go
on living, alas . . . I . . . wish I did not have to wake up again.'

On the day after the death she rang *The Times* to ask if they would like her to write an appreciation of Jerry, but an authoritative voice informed her 'We seldom run pieces on general practitioners by their patients'. 'That', she said caustically, 'put me in my place.' Next she tried the *Guardian*, only to discover that they had commissioned James Cameron to prepare a piece. In the end she contacted her local Hampstead paper.

Cameron recalled how Jerry would sit on his bed in hospital and say, 'Come, me boy. We'll have a small one on the survival of your living soul and we'll get the Sister in.' Mary Kenny, in her piece in the *Sunday Telegraph*, remembered how Jerry had once told her that babies did not need the perpetual washing recommended by Dr Spock, but needed much more the warmth that only a mother could offer by cuddling her child. She remarked on how once she, Jerry and Olivia had passed the house in Hampstead in which the Tory MP Norman St John-Stevas lived. A papal flag was flying. 'I'd have more sympathy with that man's opposition to abortion if his house was full of orphans,' Jerry had commented as they passed.

The Slatterys as a family were well known for their hospitality. Their home in Eton Villas was a place where friends made other friends. Olivia ended her obituary piece in the *Hampstead and Highgate Express* with these words: 'Their home was never more crowded than on the Sunday when the news went round that our beloved physician was lost to us. Where shall we find another like him?'

Chapter 18

Mad Dog and Englishman

Olivia's first post-war novel, *Artist Among the Missing*, was published in the early spring of 1949. She set great store by it and said to Reggie on the eve of publication, 'I remain anxious but hopeful.' It received a wider press than her volume of short stories, but the reviews were more critical. It is not the easiest of novels of which to provide a synopsis. She herself prepared a draft, which was used by Heinemann in their catalogue and in the 'blurb'. This is how, in her last few sentences, she summed up her book:

> Miss Manning's subject is a painter who before the war found expression in his art. Now, in wartime, the realities of existence had deprived him of this, and have walled him into a kind of living grave. The walls that press upon him are the anxiety for his wife's fidelity, for his art, for his health. He is as much a casualty as the wounded soldier in the desert; for the artist at the Base can also be amongst the missing.

Five years later, in 1954, the *Times Literary Supplement* was to give William Gerhardie a whole page in which to review her fourth novel, *A Different Face*. The review was unsigned, as was to remain the paper's tradition until 1974, when John Gross took over as editor. Gerhardie set about his task by discussing the whole of Olivia's fiction – then five books in all. When he came to *Artist Among the Missing*, he summarised, 'A novel about a young man afflicted with the fears of hydrophobia in the Near East during the war.' He then continued that here was a most powerful indictment, in terms of horror, of the Second World War: 'It is war seen in a compass so narrowed down that the lens scorches and all but ignites the paper.'

Olivia was pleased with what her old friend, who was now fifty-five, had to say. But she was also puzzled by a sentence in which he wrote that 'Olivia Manning inevitably labours under the exacting handicap of being, however dimly conscious of it, also a mystic'. When Reggie came home that evening, 'Am I a mystic?' she greeted him as he opened the front door.

Laughing his way out of the question, he said, 'Well at least you're not a mystic like Miss Tick.' Olivia and Reggie thought it fun to give their friends nicknames and theirs for Kay Dick was 'Miss Tick'.

Olivia, however, was not best pleased when she discovered that she had her nicknames too. At a party, at which Peter O'Toole was present, she had learnt with dismay that she was known by some friends as 'Ollie Beak' – a nickname first given to her by Francis King. 'People are not always kind,' she said reprovingly. But then nor was she. By the 1970s she was calling Charles and Pamela Snow 'The Snows of Yesteryear'. Sometimes she would add, 'Pamela looks so puffy and has become so vague.'

William Gerhardie believed that writers of genius were usually mystics, since he saw himself as both. It was a view that left no place for those like Ivy Compton-Burnett, whom Olivia admired above all living women writers – 'I feel I am in the presence of genius whenever I enter her flat in Braemar Mansions.'

One of the reviews of *Artist Among the Missing* that most pleased Olivia was by Elizabeth Bowen in the *Tatler*, where she referred to 'a masculine impersonality in the work'. This is a vital key to an understanding of Olivia's whole oeuvre. Julian Symons made the same point in the *Manchester Evening News*, declaring that had the novel been published anonymously 'one would not tell easily if the author was a man or woman'. Always Olivia preferred to think of herself not as a woman novelist but as a novelist who happened to be a woman. Her male characters far outnumber her female ones, and when women do appear they are frequently self-portraits. She believed in Women's Rights and held the suffragettes and their leaders in high admiration. But she was less sure about the Women's Movement of the 1960s. She felt that it had been manipulated by big business. In 1970, in a Hampstead bookshop, she had found Jean Rhys's novels stacked under 'Fiction', whereas Doris Lessing's were stacked under 'Women's Studies'. 'I am grateful to see I am a part of "Fiction",' she said tartly to the manager.

In 1949 Olivia Manning won the Tom Gallon Award, administered by the Society of Authors, for her short story 'The Children'. The judges were A. L. Barker, T. O. Beachcroft and L. A G. Strong. Olivia was pleased with the news – but curious. 'Who is Tom Gallon?' she asked. She was told by Victor Bonham-Carter, the then Secretary of the Society, that he was a prolific writer, who had lived at the turn of the century. She went to look him up in an old *Who's Who*, where she found some thirty novels and plays listed. Not a single title rang a bell. She learnt from the same entry that illness had prevented him from continuing to be the secretary of a provincial mayor and that therefore from 1895 onwards he 'had had to bunt for stray guineas in Grub Street'. She complained to Reggie, 'Tom Gallon seems to have been a nobody. I'd much rather have won the Katherine Mansfield Prize.'

Short stories of hers were entered for the Katherine Mansfield. She never discovered the true reason for her failure to win it, since Rayner Heppenstall's *Journals* did not appear until six years after her death. Part of his entry for 4 August 1971 reads:

The three PEN judges for the Katherine Mansfield prize are Nicolette Devas, Kathleen Nott and myself . . . This afternoon, with David [Carver, General Secretary of PEN] joining us later, Katie and I went to Nicolette's house in Chelsea. We all lacked enthusiasm for any of the stories we nevertheless thought might do. David and Nicolette, like myself, thought that, this being so, the final choice might not improperly be affected by what we thought rather of the authors than of the stories specifically offered, and that we might even allow ourselves to be influenced by such consideration as whether we could expect the chosen author to be agreeable company [on the trip to Menton, where the prize, financed by the municipality, was awarded]. Katie, very properly of course, took the view that we must judge the stories themselves on their special merits . . . Olivia Manning was thought by David and less emphatically by my fellow judges to be particularly unlikely to be agreeable company, while even my reluctant fondness for her was tainted by the feeling of certainty that if she won she would insist on bringing Reggie, whom none of us wanted . . . Stonewalling, I batted for the Orcadian George Mackay Brown. A variety of mark-awarding voting systems was tried, and by flagrant cheating, I carried the day, which ended with Katie and myself not on speaking terms.

From 1964 until 1978 she herself was to be a Tom Gallon judge, first with Arthur Calder-Marshall and Selwyn Jepson, and later with Arthur Calder-Marshall and Francis King.

Chapter 19

Anglo-Irish

Before Olivia had received the proofs of *Artist Among the Missing* she had begun work on another undertaking. This was to be a travel book, concerned with Ireland and her Anglo-Irish background. It was the only travel book that she wrote, although Ivy Compton-Burnett was to say later to Barbara Pym, 'A great many novels nowadays are just travel books . . . Olivia has just published one about Bulgaria.' Ivy was in fact referring to Olivia's *The Great Fortune*, the first volume of the Balkan Trilogy. Abroad was abroad for Ivy, and there was not much difference for her between Bulgaria and Romania. Subsequently, in 1962, Olivia dedicated to Ivy the second volume of her Balkan Trilogy, also set in Romania. No doubt she did so with her tongue slightly in her cheek. A kind friend, in the way of kind friends, had relayed to her Ivy's comment about the first volume.

Olivia's Irish travel book, commissioned by Evans Brothers for their series 'Windows on the World', borrowed its title, *The Dreaming Shore*, from Yeats. Olivia was to find it a tiresome and expensive book to complete. On 18 May 1948 she wrote to Stevie Smith from Hanratty's Hotel in Limerick,

> I'm spending an awful lot. I've already gone through £50. I shall spend much more than my advance altogether, as I spent nearly £100 last year on the Donegal part, and then I have to write the bloody book before I get the other half of the advance. No more commissions, never again. I simply hate writing to order and as to travelling to order – God save me from it!

The book became 'a millstone', as she told June and Neville Braybrooke.

Its plan, though, had been simple enough. Its aim was to record a series of bus journeys from Cork up the west coast to Donegal. In the beginning she thought that the research could be completed during one stay, but it involved two more. During some of the time Jerry joined her. Reggie never came over during this period – though he had a great love of Ireland.

Jerry left his mark on the book – although he is never mentioned in it. A footnote about St John's church, in Sligo, reads, 'Churchyard soil changes into adipocere. Yews will not grow in it unless planted in pits filled with imported soil.' Jerry was responsible for the information about adipocere, a grey-white fatty substance generated by corpses in damp ground. Reggie is mentioned in the main text and also provided the information for two footnotes. One of these concerned a playbill for a production of *Hamlet* in Limerick in 1793, which stated that on the advice of the local priest, Father O'Callaghan, the roles of the King and Queen would be omitted 'because their lines are too immoral for the stage'. The other related how the word 'limerick' had derived from an early nineteenth-century nonsense verse which had begun, 'Will you come up to Limerick?'

There are some superb descriptive passages in the book. In a review in *Tribune* Alan Ross demonstrated this by quoting one about County Donegal:

> . . . It was one of those exquisitely still, mild days that are so becoming to Ireland. The hills were dark blue but with a grape-bloom on them that gave them a tinge of violet. The colour varied from hill to hill and on the nearest it was as richly deep as the blue of a sloe. A cloud, very white in contrast, had drifted down and lay like a fleece around the peak. At the edge of the Lough a small, colourless wave curled and uncurled on the flawless sand.

One of the first things to notice about *The Dreaming Shore* is that Olivia's endpapers show a map of Ireland drawn without frontiers. Her mother used to repeat 'a people is indestructible', and when Olivia was a child she and her mother and brother used to move from north to south and back again in complete freedom: 'There may have been police and border guards – but we were never aware of them.' By the 1920s things had altered. In *The Wind Changes*, which is set early during this period, there is a scene in which an old woman has her cottage burned to the ground for not having warned the Black and Tans about a Sinn Fein ambush. Yet, as the author remarks, had the old woman warned them, the Sinn Feiners would not merely have burned down her cottage but also probably shot her. There are a number of references to the 'Troubles' in *The Dreaming Shore*. But the Troubles would pass, Olivia believed, and one day Ireland would be once again united. She knew by heart Roger Casement's speech from the dock after he had been sentenced to death in 1916, and quotes it in the chapter 'Tralee and the Dingle'.

> If English authority be omnipotent – a power as Mr Gladstone phrased it, that reaches to the very ends of the earth – Irish hope exceeds the dimensions of that power, excels its authority, and renews with each generation the claims of the last. The cause that begets this indomitable persistency, the faculty of persevering through the centuries of misery the remembrance of lost liberty; this, surely, is the noblest cause men ever strove for, ever lived for, or ever died for. If this be the cause I stand here indicted for and convicted of sustaining, then I stand in goodly company and right noble succession.

Reggie also was fond of reciting this speech, for he too believed in an eventually united Ireland. For him, as for Olivia, Casement remained a hero. In her student days, Casement had been the cause of many arguments among her contemporaries. There was no doubt about his Irish patriotism and that the British wanted to hang him as a traitor. But some of the more narrow-minded maintained that a patriot could not be a pervert. Others countered with the argument that a pervert would not carry an *Imitation of Christ* everywhere as Casement had done. But there were whisperings about black deeds. Access was not given to Casement's black diaries until 1959.

Only many years later, when Reggie was lecturing at the University of Coleraine in the 1970s, was Olivia to hear from him that after Casement's judicial hanging a prison doctor had been sent to examine his anus and found evidence of sexual malpractice. The doctor had acted on orders from the British government. 'How sad and ridiculous grown men can be in their persecution of the invert,' Olivia wrote to Reggie. Jerry agreed with her: 'I remember hearing a lot of Irishmen saying that if a pervert preached freedom, the freedom he spoke of would be perverted.'

Reggie blamed the 'Troubles' of the 1970s on a few hundred hotheads, or psychopaths, who had access to bombs. He maintained that the protection money they collected from publicans and shopkeepers ensured that their arsenals were continually stocked. Once, during a bomb alert in a hotel on the outskirts of Belfast in 1975, he found himself sweeping up an old lady and running down a passageway towards the open street with her tucked under his arm. 'It was as if she were a rugger ball and he was out to score a try,' said Walter Allen. Reggie's views on the IRA of the 1970s may have been simplistic, as Olivia often said, but they carried a good deal of truth. She felt proud of his rough chivalry towards the old lady.

Olivia had 'the usual Anglo-Irish sense of belonging nowhere'. This was a statement that she inserted in her biographical notes for the paperback edition of the Balkan and Levant Trilogies. She had said something similar in an early short story, though in a different form, when she had referred to Belfast people being 'mongrels'. In *The Dreaming Shore* she is more explicit, recalling in the final chapter how there was a time when Ulster was the most Irish part of Ireland and the chief centre of revolt. A change came when James I, employing the supposed conspiracy of the earls as a pretext, ordered a seizure of 'the six counties'. He then forced the native Irish to flee west and introduced bands of Scottish settlers to provide a bulwark against the South. Nonetheless many of the displaced Irish made their way home as soon as possible, married those whom they found there and, with a strong mixture of Scottish blood, produced in the six counties a unique people that was energetic, conservative and loyal.

Olivia argued that the Irish in the South were anti-British rather than pro-German during the Second World War. She also argued that the English and Americans had a better understanding of Hitler's territorial ambitions than did the Irish. These views she aired in *The Dreaming Shore* and none of the reviewers in Dublin quarrelled with them.

Olivia had been brought up by her mother and her Irish relations to regard Cromwell as 'a black Puritan'. In her travel book she writes of how, when Cork surrendered to him in 1649, he ordered the church bells to be taken from their belfries and melted down. The protests of the local people were to no avail, because he told them that 'since gunpowder was invented by a priest, the best use for church bells was to have them turned into cannon'. Nor were any of the women and children spared from his army of butchers. Olivia writes at one point, 'He can scarcely be judged with the sane.'

Olivia liked to consider herself as Anglo-Irish – partly for snobbish reasons. When, in a conversation with her, Elizabeth Bowen observed that 'it made you feel grander', Olivia agreed. But the concept of Anglo-Irishness was one that she believed would pass away before the twenty-first century ended. There would be just English and Irish. In 1949, as she progressed with her book, she decided that Gaelic was dying as a language.

In Dingle Olivia lost a large silver brooch of Indian design that Reggie had given her. She told everyone whom she met about her loss and even persuaded one of the local priests to mention it before his Sunday sermon. She advertised, too, in the *Kerryman*, offering a reward. When all these efforts met with no success, she suffered from great guilt, for this had been her first present from Reggie. She was luckier when a white flannel bush jacket, once owned by her now dead brother, went missing. She had sent it so many times to the cleaners that it had now shrunk to her size. It soon transpired that a waitress in a café at which she stayed in Letterkenny had 'borrowed' it. When, a week later, the proprietress returned it, Olivia caught a glimpse of the girl, hurrying out of sight. She wanted to say to her, 'It doesn't matter. When you get to London you'll have the time of your life.' But the words froze in her mouth. Some weeks earlier, Olivia had kissed the Blarney stone. Her reaction was, 'Never much of a talker, I find I'm not improved.' Often she wanted to say kind things, but shyness overcame her.

Many pages in *The Dreaming Shore* read like entries in a journal – which is what they are. When she came back each evening, she would go to her bedroom and write up the experiences of the day. There are several sections about ghosts, hauntings and people who possess a sixth sense. On Achill Island, as she walked back to her hotel, she felt that she was not alone and had the impulse to take to her heels – although there was no one to be seen. The proprietor later told her that she had just passed over the most haunted area of the island.

The Dreaming Shore did not receive so wide a press as Olivia's three previous books. Apart from Alan Ross in *Tribune*, only one well-known writer had been asked to review the book: Louis MacNeice. The rumour was that Olivia had herself, typically but unprofessionally, proposed him as her reviewer. He proved, however, to be in rather a snappish mood: yes, the author was definitely a good writer, but it had been a mistake for someone so highbrow to embark on a guidebook. Her reconnaissance of Ireland's imponderable west coast was 'too calculated'. In her book she had tried to 'serve both God and Mammon'. This was a pity, because she possessed 'a mind with fingertips' and could obviously feel in a tree something more than what Mallarmé called 'the intrinsic deadwood'. He thought that she had only given of her second best which, however, was 'still something to welcome'. Some of MacNeice's censures were justified. The book is bitty and there is an excessive concentration on famous beauty spots. But it also contains some excellent writing. Time and again Olivia's feelings for animals come through. She sees rubbing stones put up for them in Kerry and Cork. She is appalled when she notices a donkey with a deformed hoof between the shafts of a cart, but her sympathy is put in perspective when a countrywoman tells her, 'He's got to earn his living.'

Olivia dedicated the book to her mother (now a widow), who was delighted. Once again, she made sure that everyone in Laburnum Grove heard about her daughter's success. 'My Olivia is a terrific reader. When she asked for a reading lamp in a hotel in Clare, the manager asked her, "What manner of lamp would that be now?" Did you ever hear the beatings of it?'

Chapter 20

Five in a Row

For five years running, from 1947, Olivia Manning published a book a year. They were *The Remarkable Expedition*, *Growing Up*, *Artist Among the Missing*, her Irish travel book *The Dreaming Shore* and, in the autumn of 1951, *School for Love*.

Olivia was beginning to be known. 'You have made your break-through,' Reggie exultantly congratulated her. To his friends he would boast, 'My Olivia is now what might be called an established author.' But at about the same time he confessed privately to Bill Bailey that he had made a mess of his marriage. 'Olivia has another,' he said, referring to Jerry. Yet Reggie's pride in her literary achievements never dimmed and he continued to be her best editor. 'Everything has to survive his scrutiny,' Olivia told Stevie Smith in 1950.

School For Love is about a boy growing up in Palestine during the last months of the Second World War. When it opens Felix Latimer, aged sixteen, has lost both his parents: his father has been killed and his mother has died of typhoid. The friends who have temporarily put him up in Baghdad send him to stay with Miss Bohun, a distant relative. There he becomes one of her lodgers in her house at Herod's Gate in Jerusalem. Later they are joined by a new guest, a young widow whose husband has been shot down in flames as a rear gunner in the RAF. Felix falls for Mrs Ellis – admiring her painted nails, the rattle of her bangles and her long elegant legs. He goes with her to cafés and for the first time hears the names of Kafka, Palinurus and Sartre. In the Café Innsbruck middle-aged exiles from Central Europe play chess; some read newspapers attached to stands; and there are a few always staring in a melancholy way at nothing at all. Mrs Ellis is pregnant and, increasingly interested in the child growing within her, she becomes slightly bored, even irritated, by Felix's perpetual questions about everything. In his affections he then replaces her with Miss Bohun's female cat, Faro, with whom he has long conversations.

Miss Bohun disapproves of cats lying on beds or sofas. 'Oh, no, young woman,' she addresses Faro, 'you are here to catch rats. Out into the garden you go, the woodshed's full of them.' It is Miss Bohun's regret that, though Faro will kill rats, she will not eat them, which means she has to buy her camel meat in the market: 'Oh dear! The expense!' For the past twenty and more years she has been the pastor of the local 'Ever-Ready Group of Wise Virgins'. In her house a room has been prepared for the Second Coming, for which she charges the group rent. The outbreak of war in 1939 has meant that Armageddon may be at hand.

Reviewers were to describe Miss Bohun as mean, miserly, a humbug, sanctimonious and a scrounger. She was all these things – and more. In her frugal housekeeping she palms off fried slices of aubergine in batter as fried fish. She tells her guests how Indian sages eat nothing but vegetables. When Felix asks if he may have a reading lamp to help him study for his matriculation exams and says that he will even pay for the plug to be fitted, she tells him that he must not have the ceiling light on at the same time. Those who live in Herod's Gate grow accustomed to hearing the ping of their one-bar electric fires being switched off by Miss Bohun as they leave the house.

Mrs Ellis and Miss Bohun are so different that it is inevitable that they never quite hit it off. Mrs Ellis begins by thinking the older woman an entertaining joke, but soon tires of her mean, eccentric ways and her sudden bursts of aggressive cheerfulness. When Mrs Ellis finds that Miss Bohun has been prying into the paternity of her unborn child, she thinks this 'damned insolence' and even has doubts about her sanity. 'Mad' is a word that regularly comes into her mind. In a final encounter she calls Miss Bohun 'a hypocrite, a liar, a cheat, a dirty-minded old maid'. The two women are standing on the staircase during this altercation, and the sound of a hard slap being administered is heard. Mrs Ellis loses her balance. She reels from side to side of the staircase and tumbles down it, to lie slumped against the fumed-oak dresser at the bottom. Felix shouts, 'You've killed her,' as Miss Bohun runs down the stairs. It is not revealed who administered the slap to whom. When Miss Bohun sends Felix to fetch a doctor, the doctor asks him point-blank if he saw what happened. 'No,' he replies, 'I was downstairs.'

Dr Klaus advises him, 'Ah, then it is well to speak with caution.'

Felix and Miss Bohun never see Mrs Ellis again: the baby is dead by the time she reaches the hospital. The war in Europe has ended on 5 May and Felix has been told at short notice to be prepared to leave, because although the priorities are first women with babies and then troops, a vacancy may suddenly occur on a ship homeward bound. This happens. Felix then takes Faro with him. A collar, basket and a scratch-tray prove the most expensive things that Felix has ever bought in Jerusalem.

Miss Bohun is a magnificently realised character. In *World Review* Stevie Smith wrote of her as 'a maniacal Adventist'; Richard Church in *John O'London's* compared her with Betsy Trotwood in *David Copperfield*; and Frederick Laws, the literary editor of the *News Chronicle*, came up with the paradox 'likeable in an unattractive way'. Over the years, several film options have been bought on the novel, but none has ever been renewed. Miss Bohun remains a star role waiting to be filled – a dry stick ready to be kindled into life.

Shortly after *School for Love* was published,* there was talk that Robert Graves's sister, Clarissa, whom Olivia had met in Jerusalem and on whom she had in part modelled Miss Bohun, might bring a libel action. In anticipation of this, Olivia had made some rather obvious changes: Miss Bohun is 'tiny', whereas Clarissa was tall; Miss Bohun is 'tuneless', whereas Clarissa sang in a loud, tuneful contralto. Olivia also devised an 'early history' for Miss Bohun, totally unlike Clarissa's. Two resemblances between the fictional and the real-life character are that Clarissa, like Miss Bohun, gave English lessons and that she would not buy on the black market. But Miss Bohun refuses to deal on the black market because she thinks the prices prohibitive, whereas Clarissa was wary of it because her brother Richard (Dick) Graves was a British official in Palestine. Miss Bohun's 'Ever-Readies' are based on the Christian Scientists, in whose Jerusalem circle Clarissa moved and was a force. Miss Bohun says with

---

* In the general chorus of approval, Pamela Hansford Johnson declared in *John O'London's Weekly* that *School for Love* appeared to her 'among the ten best novels written by women in the past twenty-five years'. A columnist in the *Bookseller*, called 'Ultra Bold', seized on the statement. 'I hazard the guess,' he mocked, 'that this is among the most meaningless pronouncements by women reviewers in the past fourteen years and a half.' Reggie had a difficult weekend, for Olivia kept saying to him: 'I'm singled out – even when I get a "rave". Find out who this "Ultra Bold" is. I would like to kick him.'

great emphasis, 'We don't believe in illness.' However, the presentation of the group in the novel is so farcical that one doubts whether Mrs Baker Eddy would have acknowledged them.

Clarissa's nephew Richard Percival Graves, author of a three-volume life of his uncle the poet Robert Graves, writes,

> Clarissa was a great moralist. The contrast between brooding one moment, and 'then loudly and carefully' throwing off her worries, is quite characteristic of Clarissa – one of the touches which makes one certain that the character is based on her. As is the occasional irritability; as are the occasionally martyred remarks. As are some of the individual speeches.

Richard Percival Graves says that his aunt had piercing spiritual insights. Occasionally she might be petty, but she was never dishonest. She would never have engaged in the financial chicanery over rents in which Miss Bohun indulges.

In *School for Love* there are already many indications that Olivia was developing into the historical novelist that she was so triumphantly to become in the decade ahead.

Chapter 21

Branching Out

By late 1951, with *School for Love* having proved a minor critical success, Olivia began to look around for other sources of income. She was hopeful that a film company might make an offer for one of her three novels – but no such offers were to come until 1969 and then only one. 'Reggie tells me I must be patient. I must persist with the BBC. "Begin a bombardment," he advises.' In fact, by 1950 she had already turned to the Features Department of the BBC as a secondary source of income.

The bombardment, as Reggie called it, had begun in a minor way when they had settled into their first London flat at 50a Shepherd Market. From 106 Baker Street – the Smiths' second post-war flat in London – she was to continue it, with more success. There, unexpectedly, she received a commission to contribute to the series *A Year to Remember*. The year she decided to remember was from the Greek Easter in 1940 until the following Easter. The Smiths had come from Romania to Athens in April 1940 on a holiday, and on their return to Bucharest had at once noticed that the country was falling more and more under the sway of the Nazis – 'both imported from across the border and home-grown as well'.

During the commissioning of this feature Olivia was to have a battle with the BBC Contracts Department over the fee offered. In the summer of 1949 she wrote to a Mrs Gray in the Copyright Department,

> I am rather surprised that you suggest a fee of only seventy-two guineas for my projected sixty-minute script of A YEAR TO REMEMBER. I have known several writers of no greater reputation than myself and very little broadcasting experience who have received ninety guineas for scripts of the same length.

I have, as you probably know, done a good many serial adaptations for radio and other scripts. A YEAR TO REMEMBER would be purely creative work and I had hoped to receive something nearer 100 guineas for the script.

I should be grateful if you would go into this and increase the fee as I suggest.

Reggie had virtually dictated the letter. 'Stick out for a bigger fee' was always his principle. 'Big corporations can afford to pay.' In the end Olivia received a fee of eighty guineas.

Olivia had many such fights with the BBC Contracts Department. In January 1952 she had come to the rescue when Pamela Hansford Johnson had been struck down with flu. Olivia had taken her place in a discussion programme. After it had gone out, she received a contract offering her five guineas for her contribution. She returned the contract unsigned – and ended her letter with the statement: 'Miss Handsford [*sic*] Johnson received (without delay, I may say) the sum of 7 guineas and I shall be pleased to accept the same.' A new BBC contract was issued for this sum by return of post.

A number of such letters of complaint survive at the BBC Archives Centre.

Early on Stevie had said to her, 'Every publisher is your best friend until you become his author.' Reggie put his wife's pugnacity down to her Ulster blood. She was known for being 'difficult'. In the world of the arts, from early on, she had thought that literary justice was always in short supply. Nor did her views change with age. Michael Holroyd and his wife Margaret Drabble have this memory of her: 'Crowded rooms, parties, cats, Reggie, fury at the Booker prize'. Olivia Manning was never shortlisted for the Booker.

Reggie was fond of the phrase 'Rally the troops'. He would use it to Olivia whenever he felt that she had let a publisher, editor or producer keep her waiting too long for a decision. A case in point was her radio adaptation of Mrs Gaskell's *Wives and Daughters*. 'Darling, I've said to you three times "Rally the troops". Well, rally them fast.' Olivia knew exactly what he meant. Then, by chance, one afternoon a few days later, browsing among her books, she found this comment by George Sand: '*Wives and Daughters* is a book that might be put into the hands of an innocent girl, while at the same time it would rivet the attention of the most blasé man in the world.' So she copied this passage out, posted it off to the producer in question and wrote, 'I don't think that the BBC could ask for more.' Her *Wives and Daughters* was broadcast in autumn 1953.

Although Reggie had his regular job at the BBC, the hours of which he made increasingly elastic, the couple were often strapped for cash. In 1952 Olivia wrote to Charles Lefaux, a scriptwriter at the Drama Department, 'I have two overdrafts. But, of course I always look forward to acceptance of my *Middlemarch*!!!' This was a broad hint about her radio adaptation of the George Eliot novel, already submitted. To a neighbour in Queen's Grove she confided, 'We have nice lodgers, but we could not do without their rents. Let's hope the Inland Revenue never discover.' She had done a stint of novel reviewing at the *Spectator* in the late Forties, and had also written the occasional review for *Public Opinion* and *Punch*. She had kept her contacts going with the *Palestine Post*, from time to time sending them 'A Letter from London'. In a 1952 'Letter' she covered Norman Douglas's collection of aphrodisiac recipes entitled *Venus in the Kitchen*, Terence Rattigan's play *The Deep Blue Sea* and a film version of Stephen Crane's *The Red Badge of Courage*.*

In the opening paragraphs of her 1952 *Palestine Post* 'Letter', Olivia turned to Betty Miller's pioneering study of Robert Browning, in which the biographer had viewed the poet as 'a mother-dominated child, who sought in his marriage a continuation of that dominance'. Olivia thought that Reggie was to some extent dominated by his mother: 'Daughters have to make a break – but it is often painful, as I know. It's even more difficult for sons.' She agreed with June Braybrooke's observation that 'though there is a commandment "Honour thy Father and Mother", there is none for parents to honour their children. Psychiatrists should have spotted this – but then few read their bibles! Psychiatry today is by and large a secular calling.'

Olivia's fourth novel, *A Different Face*, had a Book Society Recommendation – her third since 1949. There was much praise in the

---

* Long after Reggie and she had left the cinema at which *The Red Badge of Courage* was showing, the realism of the battle scenes had stayed with them. 'That's how war should be presented,' he said to her. 'Go and get the novel out of the Public Library.' She did so – and to good effect. In 1978, when reviewing *The Battle Lost and Won* in the *Observer*, Hermione Lee wrote, 'Olivia Manning surpasses herself in her account of Alamein. It is a superbly precise and convincing reproduction, and as moving about a young soldier's first experience of battle as *The Red Badge of Courage*.'

review columns for the author's skills as a writer, but the book was widely thought to be a depressing one. Sadly, among the reviewers were Nancy Spain and Viola Garvin, both then influential. Both were disappointed. Nancy Spain headed her review 'OH! DEAR ME' and spent 150 words elaborating on this, while Viola Garvin summed up the book as 'a dreary tale about a dreary man'.

A Different Face is set in Coldmouth, during the early 1950s. The headline of a review of it in the Portsmouth *Evening News* ran READ PORTSMOUTH FOR COLDMOUTH. Hugo Fletcher, its central character, describes the city of his birth as 'murderous'. He speaks of his attempts to climb out of 'the littleness of Coldmouth'. When he takes a job at the beginning of 1939 in Egypt, he hopes never to return to the place.

When the novel first came out some people thought that Hugo was based on Reggie. Stevie Smith had already anticipated that it would be, because she thought that Reggie would always figure as the male protagonist in any fiction written by her friend. Admittedly Hugo is a schoolmaster, like Reggie in earlier years, and both share a liking for draught ale. But there the resemblance ceases. Hugo is a character closer to Olivia, especially in his loathing of provincial life and everything connected with it. Both Olivia and her fictional hero are children of naval men who gave up their lives to serve King and country, only to be shabbily treated in their retirements over pensions and other promised benefits. Hugo's father, already dead at the start of the novel, is depicted as an embittered man who gambled away a legacy of £15,000 left to his wife. He has none of the benevolence of Commander Manning, who in the 1930s had lent £500 (a large sum in those days) to a friend down on his luck, who then failed ever to repay it. Yet the Commander had no regrets over the loss.

In 1963 Olivia told Kay Dick, 'We were very, very poor in the way that only a naval officer's family can be.' In a 1977 *Spectator* review of an autobiography by Daphne du Maurier, she remarked how in her teens she would repeatedly have to wear the same old washed-out dress. The mothers of her better-off friends would sense in her 'the avid uncertainty of the poor'.

Olivia was to express her hatred of her home town once again, briefly, in the opening volume of the Balkan Trilogy. Reggie frequently urged her to abandon these old, rankling animosities. 'Get on to other things, love,' he would say. 'Try and forget the past.' He understood her very well. He also knew that the past was something from which she could never escape.

A Different Face has been reprinted only once, in 1975, and has never appeared in paperback. Olivia, when in the mood to look on the black side of life, referred to it as 'my least successful book'. Complaining was a part of her nature. Anthony Powell in his *Journals 1987–8* declares her to be 'the world's worst grumbler'. He wrote this, of course, after her death. Had he said it to her face, she would have been furious. 'Only I am allowed to criticise myself,' would have been her response.

As the reviews of *A Different Face* came in, Reggie did his best to be encouraging. 'They think you're a fine writer, but that you've chosen a difficult subject.' In trying to console her about the piece by Nancy Spain in the *Daily Mail* he said, 'Perhaps she thinks you've had too much success. Don't let them defeat you as they silenced poor old Henry Green for *Doting*.' Green, although he lived for another twenty-one years, was never to write another novel. But Olivia had no intention of letting Reggie cheer her up. 'What do you mean I've had too much success?' she demanded indignantly. 'I haven't had the success of Brigid Brophy. Everyone's talking about her *Hackenfeller's Ape*.'

Olivia could always call to mind potential rivals – especially young female rivals. Brigid Brophy had been born in 1929. Later she and Olivia were to become good friends and Olivia was an active supporter of both Brophy and WAG, the Writers Action Group for Public Lending Right of which Brophy and Maureen Duffy were the originators.

In 1952 Olivia had written to Louisa Callendar, a director of Heinemann, 'Have my sales been so terrible that Heinemann have lost all faith in me? I feel I have been a disappointment . . . I really don't know what to do to make myself sell. I don't know at all. I often feel like giving up writing altogether.' This letter, or versions of it, she was to write to every director at Heinemann with whom she came in touch. Nonetheless they were to keep her on their list until 1974.

John St John, in his history of *William Heinemann: A Century of Publishing 1890–1990*, reports that Olivia was to toy regularly with the idea of leaving the firm from 1952 onwards. Apparently even the early sales of the Balkan Trilogy were comparatively disappointing, despite determined efforts by the 'reps' to put over the Trilogy.

In 1968, when a successful libel action was brought over the first two volumes of the Balkan Trilogy, Dwye Evans, the managing director, insisted that she should pay her share – and though she did this, she did so with ill grace and bad temper. 'Dwye is as mean as hell,' she went around telling everyone. However, by the end of 1968 things were patched up and she handed Dwye the manuscript of her new novel *The Play Room* before the year ended. John St John's final verdict on her is that though 'never an easy author to handle . . . being difficult often goes with being a great writer'.

In John St John's book there is a section headed 'Shute, Powell, Frankau, Manning'. Olivia regarded Nevil Shute and Pamela Frankau as novelists whose popularity was based on their ability to buttonhole their readers. Bitterly she would point out that a street was named after Shute in Portsmouth but that none was named after her – despite the years that she had spent there. Anthony Powell, though he sold well, she saw in a more favourable light. He had published one book with Cassell and four with Duckworth before Malcolm Muggeridge (for whom Olivia never cared much – 'more interested in your garters than you') had introduced him to Heinemann. Olivia had bought all twelve volumes of his sequence *A Dance to the Music of Time*, as each volume came out, and had then persuaded him to sign them for her. But after the final volume, *Secret Harmonies*, appeared in 1975 she decided that she would not reread them. 'They are not Proust or Musil,' she said to June Braybrooke.

Olivia met Anthony Powell when he was the literary editor of *Punch*. As contemporaries there were only three years between them – but this Olivia kept as a closely guarded secret: 'I have a feeling that Tony thinks I was born just before the end of the Great War.' When he was signing one of his novels for her she instructed him, 'Don't forget your full name on the title page, so that people will know it is not just any old Tony – posterity, I mean.' Halfway through writing the Balkan Trilogy she had consulted him: 'Do you think I will ever reach the exalted status of being reviewed separately, like Iris M[urdoch] or Muriel S[park]? Or am I just not good enough?' This was a question that she put to many fellow writers at some stage or other.

Powell gave a tactful reply, saying that the best authors were not always recognised during their lives, while fair to middling were frequently overpraised. 'Be patient,' he counselled.

'Worse luck! I may have to,' was her reply. When, during one of her grumbles, Francis King told her that in the house of literature there were many mansions, she replied indignantly, 'Then why do I have to be placed in such a shabby attic?'

The relationship between Olivia and Powell was not always one of her coming to him for counsel and comfort. Sometimes it was the other way round. In 1956, for example, he wrote to her, recalling how disappointed he had been in 1952 with the critics' reception of the second volume in his projected sequence – *A Buyer's Market*. She had replied sympathetically, 'I do not feel you have any reason to worry about the book. The trouble was that the critics failed to appreciate what you were doing.' She added that she saw

> the complaints of the critics as those that might arise if a large painting were cut into squares and exhibited one square after another. There may be some justification for complaints about this way of giving your book to the public – but what else can you do? In time they will have it all.

Meanwhile her counsel was to press on. It is significant that she sees *The Music of Time* in terms of painting rather than music. 'I am not the best appreciator of music,' she would say, 'though I do accompany Reggie to concerts from time to time.' She was, however, a lover of art. Anthony Powell kept all her letters.

In 1966 a row broke out between the two. Twenty years later Powell wrote to Neville Braybrooke to explain the reason. Apparently, during a television interview earlier in the month Malcolm Muggeridge had asked Anthony Powell, 'What about women?'

Powell had replied, 'Do you mean women writers?'

Muggeridge had nodded and said, 'Yes – if you like.'

Powell had then replied, 'I don't think any of them mean a great deal to me.'

Olivia, who had not seen the programme but had had this exchange relayed to her by a friend, had taken it as a veiled reference to herself. Here was another example of her paranoia. As Powell explained to Braybrooke, 'In the studio I was thinking of Jane Austen and George Eliot – two novelists whom I admired but who I did not think could be compared with Dostoevsky and Proust. It was as if one might say "Dickens and Thackeray don't mean much to me, say, in comparison to Dostoevsky and Proust".'

For several days Olivia brooded. Finally Reggie said, 'Write to Tony. Get it off your chest, love.' The truth was that he was getting fed up with her 'continual groaning about this matter' – as he confided in Neville. Finally, she despatched a letter to Powell, together with a copy of his latest book *The Soldier's Art*.

> In spite of your horrid TV comments, I enclose your new novel for inscription or, at worst, signature. Having all your previous books I felt I must have this one.
>
> I do wish that you had told me long ago that you had such a low opinion of my work.
>
> Looking through your letters to find your address, I could not help feeling how misleading were your past comments. It all makes for pain and shock. Nevertheless
>
> Love,
>   Olivia

Powell provided a friendly inscription, as repeatedly in the past, and Olivia then forgave him – though there was nothing to forgive. What she had been told that he had said on the television programme was 'deliberate malice on somebody's part and a lie', he declared. The two became friends once more and in 1973 for the umpteenth time she was to consult him about leaving Heinemann. He advised her to stay with them. He was, he said, perhaps prejudiced or had been fortunate with them – or both. He himself had once been a publisher and so understood their side as well as the author's. It all boiled down to whether 'you got on with your particular publisher or not'. So she stayed on until 1974, when her next novel *The Rain Forest* came out, and then she moved.

At the end of her life she told John St John that her move from Heinemann to Weidenfeld might have been a mistake. 'Weidenfeld got me more publicity, but they didn't get me a solo in the Sunday papers for either *The Danger Tree* or *The Battle Lost and Won*.' Privately he thought that she would be hard to please wherever she went. Always, she had been difficult. 'Still,' as he resignedly added, 'that was what publishing was about.'

Chapter 22

Venus Observed

Titles never came easily to Olivia, as she told Henry Green in a letter in 1953. Sometimes they were only decided upon 'in desperation'. When *The Doves of Venus* appeared in 1958, Michael Swan in the *Sunday Times* and Stevie Smith in the *Observer* both suggested that the title had derived from some lines by Ben Jonson:

> See the chariot here at hand of Love
> Wherein my lady rideth
> Each that is drawn is a swan or a dove
> And well the car Love guideth . . .

Friends who questioned her to confirm this found her non-committal. 'Yes,' she would say, '*The Doves of Venus* is a good title, isn't it?'

In the novel Tom Claypole, an elderly roué, declares, 'Girls . . . They are the doves of Venus . . . little soft white doves that carry our thoughts – where?' He is in his eighties and, an agnostic, has no idea where his thoughts go. His remark might well have been made by William Gerhardie – though he was far from being an agnostic – to whom the book is dedicated. At the time, Gerhardie still spelled his name Gerhardi – the final 'e' only being appended on 4 January 1967 when, in a grandiose announcement in *The Times*, he told the world that this was an earlier, ancestral spelling. His great-great-grandfather, a printer in Amsterdam, had spelt the name with an 'e', he declared. 'Dante has an "e". Shakespeare has an "e". Goethe has an "e". Who am I not to have an "e"?'

When Tom Claypole's niece Nancy hears what her uncle has been saying about girls, she responds tartly, 'It is true doves are sacred to Venus, but so are lots of other birds. Sparrows, for instance.' Nancy enjoys cutting her uncle down to size but also thinks him a sexy old thing – a view that coincides with Olivia's of Gerhardie.

Whether Olivia and Gerhardie ever had an affair is a matter of debate. His niece Christina Street and his literary executor Anne Amyes think it improbable. On the other hand Herman Schrijver, the Dutch interior decorator who lived in London and who often entertained Olivia, claimed that she had confided the affair to him and he certainly believed that it had happened. It was Schrijver who gave Olivia the nickname 'Olivia Moaning', which was then adopted by many of her friends. When she learnt of it she was, surprisingly, not annoyed.

Olivia said to June, 'William used to like beating girls, you know. I was never into that sport.' Harriet Cohen, the concert pianist, confirmed Olivia's comment. On one occasion she had written to William, 'I'm sorry I cried last night – there is a black bruise this morning – sensitive in such a place . . . Personally, I like *love*.'

Stevie wrote to June that she could hardly believe her luck when she found *The Doves of Venus* in her review batch of novels from the *Observer*. 'Terry Kilmartin [the literary editor] must have remembered how much I admire her. I am not so sure of Mrs Kilmartin. I think she does not think I am up to much as a reviewer.' To Kathleen Farrell Stevie said on the day she received the copy, 'I have a treat in store.' However, when she had read it she was disappointed. She confided in June, 'There are *longueurs*. She has included everything under the sun, tally ho! Reviewing can be hard work. It takes ages, it's badly paid, you lose your pals.'

The red-haired heroine, Ellie, is taught how to paint antique furniture. Olivia is here recalling her own early years at Peter Jones. Olivia was then twenty-seven, but Ellie is eighteen and is in seventh heaven, as she learns

> how to make a thin mixture of black and umber, to wash it over the white paint and rub it off, then brush the patina till the crass white surfaces seemed bloomed with age [as] she covered wardrobes, inside and out, tables, bed-ends, commodes, writing desks, chairs.

Never before has she endured such long hours and been so exhausted by the end of the day. But she is also exhilarated. Her wildest dreams are being fulfilled, for she is among artists – even if they are commercial artists. She is also living in Chelsea – even if her bedsitter is so small that there is no room to put up her easel.

Hardly has Ellie arrived in the capital than she meets Quentin Bellot, a philanderer, whose aim is to educate *jeunes filles* in more ways than one. On their first evening together he instructs her first in how to choose dishes from a French menu and later how to make love. Ellie then returns to her bedsitter to celebrate the loss of her virginity. She is now a woman of the world. But her lover is a mean man and decides soon to drop her merely because she is a girl without a proper flat. He would, it is clear, never have married his wife if she had not brought with her a private fortune. He himself has private means of some £2000 a year – quite a sum in 1954. Because Ellie has no flat of her own, he always orders her a taxi to take her back to her bedsitter after their lovemaking in his. Yet he never offers to pay the fare – which beggars Ellie for most of the week that follows. When he buys her a belated Christmas present of face powder, he rejects an expensive one with a pleasant scent for a cheaper with no scent at all.

Things take a sudden change when his wife makes a dramatic re-appearance into his life. Petta Bellot is a heavy drinker and obsessed with the idea that she is ageing. Youth and age, innocence and experience, are the novel's central themes.

Olivia was in her mid-forties when she started this novel. Her aim, she told Reggie, was to write a love story of sorts – and it seems that at first she briefly had in mind a sequence of novels similar to Anthony Powell's, which at that time had reached the quarter-way mark.

Olivia set the boundary between middle age and old age surprisingly early, at forty-five. In later years she was to maintain that she thought middle age the most difficult period in a woman's life. She had found hard to endure the deterioration that she had witnessed in her father as he headed towards his nineties. She told June, 'Since he was almost blind I don't think he saw my tears.' Yet as she herself grew older, she became more and more convinced that medical science would one day discover the elixir of life, in the same way that it had found a cure for tuberculosis. 'I don't think being a hundred will be the rarity it is today,' she said in 1959.

Ellie in the novel is at the age when she wants to go everywhere and meet everyone. 'I want the whole world,' she declares. 'I am sure I am immortal.' She is bursting with ambition. Walking back after work, she cuts home by different ways, searching for new areas to explore. Olivia and

Reggie also did this when on holiday. Quickly they would come to master the geography of towns like Fowey or Ryde, or even cities like Venice and Madrid. When Olivia first went to live in London she told her brother, 'I feel like an explorer.'

Although the press for *The Doves of Venus* was, on balance, favourable and it became a Book Society Recommendation, Olivia, demanding as always, was not satisfied. In the *Times Literary Supplement* the unsigned reviewer declared in the opening paragraph, 'By the highest standards . . . her latest novel is a disappointment.' Reggie was again consulted: 'What does he mean – "highest standards"? Who's standards? Some bloody pansy, I guess.' Her friends gathered round and said they could not imagine what the reviewer was up to. Universally they assumed that the culprit was a man.

Stevie Smith's *Observer* review had given with one hand only to take away with the other. 'Is she now on the *TLS* staff?' Olivia maliciously asked Fred Warburg at a party – with the implication that Stevie had also written, or at least had a hand in, the *TLS* review.

He played it safe: 'I've no idea.'

Olivia, like her own mother and Mrs Parsons in *The Doves of Venus*, was not a forgiving woman. For the sake of an occasion – a family wedding, perhaps – she would draw down a blind. But only on a temporary basis. As soon as it was over it was back to square one. 'Oh no, you're not going to push me into that, my lady,' was a comment made by both Mrs Manning and Mrs Parsons if their daughters suggested a reconciliation with someone once pronounced an enemy.

Stevie was correct in her reservations about *The Doves of Venus*. Too much had been crammed into the fragile suitcase: reflections on youth, age and love, astronomy, the next world, being penniless in this, working as a freelance, joining CND, searching for locations for films, discussing Wyndham Lewis, polygamy and polyandry, reflecting on being Anglo-Irish, bedsitter life, learning to eat with a fork alone, experiencing precognition, believing it unjust that women should be served with smaller helpings in restaurants, the injustice of men's superiority, the fear of loneliness, the desire for separateness.

Chapter 23

A Pattern Established

By 1955 Olivia Manning had been back in England ten years and her life had begun to fall into a pattern. Nor, in the remaining twenty-five years, was it to alter much. After having rented London flats at 50a Shepherd Market and at 106 Baker Street, she and Reggie were now renting an elegant Regency house at 36 Queen's Grove in St John's Wood. In each case she signed the leases and was the party responsible. She kept steadfastly to the rule of 'Never a day without a line', always writing her first draft by hand. Often she thought it a good idea before settling to work to 'rev up' by writing letters to friends. 'I must get down to my novel, so will close,' ends one characteristic letter. The novel was *The Rain Forest*.

If, when Olivia was writing a book, she found herself lost for a word, or that the narrative flow had deserted her, she would make drawings in the margin. These doodles, as she referred to them, were invariably of the same woman's face with large eyes and a Greek nose. Every page of fiction she drafted at least three times – sometimes as many as eleven.

After she had completed a first draft, she would resort to the typewriter. She had been trained as a touch typist and often typed her letters – many of which ran to 1000 words or more. Word processors did not appeal to her. 'They have not the same swing as a typewriter,' she would say. She remembered that it was said that T. S. Eliot at a certain stage used a typewriter when composing his poems. 'A typewriter can become part of you in a way that a processor never can,' was a comment that she made in 1979. 'Better a messy manuscript than an imperfect one,' was another of her sayings. She had said this first in 1951 to a radio producer, who had accused her of presenting untidy scripts with corrections inked in.

Sometimes she would use the backs of envelopes to make notes about her characters. Each morning she scanned the post for unfranked stamps.

Sometimes she would play a game with Anthony Burgess, when he was living in Malta in the 1970s, to see who found the most.

Olivia was neither a neat nor a particularly methodical writer; she would use any folder at hand in which to file away the day's work. Often these folders were those that had brought her company reports. 'I never read them because I leave them to Jerry to check,' she would say. Over the years she had amassed a wide share portfolio, following Jerry's advice to spread her investments. She gained considerably from his financial acumen. With regard to typing paper, Reggie kept her well stocked from the BBC. As a child her father had done similarly: he would make regular raids on the Royal Naval Stationery Office on Whale Island in Portsmouth. When friends moved house, she would ask them if she could buy any of their old stamped or printed stationery from them. If they said she could have it for nothing, that was better still. This explains why a number of her letters were written on other people's writing paper, with their addresses crossed out.

Olivia was always looking for bargains and she bought many first editions at church bazaars. In 1956 Reggie claimed that they had 3873 books – but by the end of their lives that figure had quadrupled.*

Olivia was a perfectionist. She would frequently cut a paragraph from one draft and then add it to a later one with sellotape. Her manuscripts often resembled a patchwork. She noted a passage from *The Letters of J. R. Ackerley* about his poem 'Snow': 'It is hardly possible to give too much trouble and thought to the perfecting of any work that one loves. How bitter it is to see the light when one's work is in print and it is too late.'

Olivia did several stints of reviewing fiction for the *Spectator* and the *Sunday Times*. She was grateful to Reggie when he went through these batches of novels as they came in. Occasionally a consignment would include a biography, to be covered separately. From ten or so novels sent to her, she was expected to cover between four to five – but 'in November sometimes as many as six'. Often she was working in tandem with Julian Mitchell, who at the time was also renting a room in her house. He remembers that his own batch of novels would arrive before she had finished hers. 'They were like a double act,' said Trixi Craig, who lived

---

* When Reggie died their library was sold off by his widow to second-hand booksellers.

close by in St John's Wood. Julian remembers that Reggie would sometimes rough out a review for Olivia, if she was sent a biography and it was of someone who interested him. She had complete faith in his literary judgements. When she worked from his 'roughs', she insisted that he should share part of the fee. Reviewing is one of the few literary occupations in which couples can share – and often do so, unbeknown to literary editors.

Reggie and Olivia had very different work patterns. He did not mind working in a room, or a studio, full of people: however much hubbub there was around him, he was blessed with the power to concentrate. In contrast, Olivia liked complete silence and preferred to be in a room by herself. In her home at Portsmouth she found nothing more infuriating than to be interrupted by her mother with some foolish question when she was writing a letter or review. Olivia wrote to June about these interruptions, 'Such people never allow for the fact that one needs intervals of thought. I don't think they understand thought as we understand it.'

Reggie was far more accommodating. In the best of all possible worlds he might have chosen quiet in which to edit scripts or prepare lecture notes. But, things being what they were, he accepted whatever conditions were on offer. In any case, he was not himself a quiet man, so that at home he usually worked with the radio blaring away. From next door Olivia would sometimes shout out, 'Turn it down, Reggie! Not everyone's a rugger fan.'

'Sorry, love,' he would reply and lower the volume.

When, on a *Woman's Hour* programme in the summer of 1974, Reggie claimed that he was a feminist, Olivia thought that he was talking nonsense. She believed, she declared after having listened to the broadcast, in the rights of women – especially in the matter of literary fees – but she had no sympathy with a number of the activists of the Women's Movement: 'They make such an exhibition of themselves. None can be said to be beauties. Most have faces like porridge.' This, though, may have merely been her attitude on a particular summer's day and she might well by the next day have changed it. Both she and Reggie were inconsistent. Their tolerant acceptance of each other's inconsistencies was one of the things that held them together.

Over their forty years of married life Olivia constantly called on Reggie to help her. She never wanted anybody to see her work before he had passed it. Each of them had lovers – but nothing could break their literary bond. Nor did she ever forget that he was the first person who had called her a genius – something that he was to repeat all through their life together. Once in a fit of anger he had said to her, 'You are a bloody awful woman and a bloody awful writer.' Then he changed tack: 'You are a bloody awful woman but a bloody literary genius.'

There was no doubt that Olivia's affair with Jerry had come as a terrible shock to him. Reggie felt that in some way he had let Olivia down. Have I neglected her? was a question which haunted him. He had learnt of the affair only second-hand when a relation of Jerry's wife, Johnny, had told him. Beti Naylor, an old friend of them all, can remember a time at the beginning when she would drive Reggie early to parties. As they left, she and Reggie would see Olivia and Jerry in another car, waiting for their turn to go to the same party. 'It was like musical chairs,' Beti said. But when the two rivals did meet – which was inevitable – they got on so well with each other that it was impossible to bear grudges or resentments. Reggie was in some ways even grateful, since Olivia's single infidelity made it easier for him to pursue his many ones.

With the passing of time, Reggie and Jerry became close friends. Johnny appeared to accept her husband's frequent afternoon visits to Olivia, but did once telephone her to ask her not to give him too much to drink on such occasions, since he might crash the car on his way home.

In Reggie's early years at the BBC after the war, and into the 1950s, drinking at the George, the pub close to Broadcasting House, was the order of the day in the Features Department. In the 1990s Tony Van Den Bergh was to recall, 'We were pissed morning, noon and night. The "George" was known to us as "the Glue Pot", because we could not get out once we got in . . . We were a load of drunken louts, who produced good programmes.'

Often it was hard for Olivia to drag Reggie from the George. Nonetheless he got his programmes out on time and they did well at the hands of the radio critics. 'He may seem all over the place,' she said, 'but somewhere in him there's an iron core. He has his own rules.'

One rule to which he always kept strictly was to tell Olivia several months in advance when his BBC holidays were due, so that she might make plans for them. Yet this did not mean that he would necessarily be there on the first day of the holiday – or perhaps for the first week.

Sometimes, the night before it began, he would ring to say he had met a couple of students from abroad and the only decent thing would be to show them London. If the next morning there was still no sign of him, Olivia would set off on her own. That night, when she might be in Ryde or Fowey, he would ring to say that he would be leaving to join her the following morning. But the following morning could mean a week later. Sometimes he even left it as late as the day of her return. Offering no excuse for his absence, he would breeze in and announce, 'I didn't want you to travel home alone. I've come to help you pack.'

Olivia played along with such a husband. It was all material for the portrait of him in which she was going to immortalise him. On both their sides there was a degree of role-playing involved. Feckless and inconsiderate though he often was, he did, however, behave like a conventional husband in giving her a monthly allowance by banker's order for the running of their home. That was something she had insisted on as soon as they returned to England in 1945.

Travelling abroad was never easy with Reggie. His intentions were good, but carrying them out was another matter. There was the time in Rotterdam when he suddenly disappeared from the station. She writes,

> All our luggage was aboard. Seconds before the train started,
> I had to take the luggage back on to the platform and watch
> the train go . . . I am not a natural Anxiety Case but Reggie
> has made me much worse than I need be.

But in her heart of hearts she knew that, if she had not let him behave as she did, how dull her portrait of him in fiction might have been. Those who said Reggie and Olivia were a mismatched couple simply did not understand their complementary relationship and how each bounced off the other.

One of Reggie's particularly aggravating habits was that of suddenly disappearing to place some small bet. In Paris, during a five-day break in the city, he claimed that he could ring a London bookmaker and put on a bet within thirty seconds. The sums were so tiny that Olivia doubted that, even if he won, they could have covered the calls – in those days far more expensive than now. Yet at the end of each year he drew up a balance sheet, duly presented to her, which always showed a small, but definite, profit. His father before him had been a betting man.

Reggie never had an entry devoted to him in *Who's Who*. Instead, there appeared annually this reference: 'SMITH, Mrs Reginald Donald: see MANNING, Olivia'. Reggie was happy to play second fiddle, often saying, 'My wife's fame washes over me.'

Sometimes Olivia would view it that way too; at other times she would declare proudly, 'Reggie is famous in his own way.' Although there are far more entries about her in reference books, he is mentioned in many memoirs. When he retired from the BBC in 1965, a party was held for him. During it Olivia turned to a friend: 'At this moment Reggie seems the best-known man in London – but in an ephemeral way.' What did she mean by ephemeral? Probably she was referring to what at times she thought an unnecessary expenditure of energy on activities such as producing amateurs in plays or organising poetry and memorial meetings.

Chapter 24

Cat's Company

The opening sentence of Olivia's book *Extraordinary Cats* begins 'The position of cats is highest when civilisation is at a peak'. She had heard Reggie maintain several times that one of the peaks of civilisation was the Shakespearean age – and cats were certainly important creatures then. Erasmus, after a visit to Sir Thomas More's house in Chelsea, had noted how, in England, it was expected that visitors should kiss not only their host and hostess on arrival but the family cat as well.

Olivia was also of the opinion that cats could be teachers to their owners and, at the end of her book, she made a small anthology of poems to this effect. Among those that she chose was a passage from 'Jubilate Agno' in which Christopher Smart praises his cat Jeoffrey. One of her favourite lines in the poem was 'For by stroking of him I have found out electricity'.

Olivia also included a poem by herself entitled 'Black Cat', which she had written in Jerusalem in 1943. It is not a very good poem. The opening lines are:

> Hist, black and
> Guilty-walking cat!

When the literary editor of the *Jerusalem Post* asked her why she had ended a line with the word 'and', she defended herself by saying that all the best modern poets had done so – 'Eliot, Auden, MacNeice, Empson and Gascoyne'. It is noticeable that there are no women on her list. In 1966, when Kathleen Anscomb was interviewing her for *John O'London's*, Olivia recalled a remark that Vernon Scannell had made to the effect that, when a woman poet was really good, she was superb and reached heights impossible for a man to achieve. Olivia thought for a moment, then replied, 'I cannot think of any women poets who justify Vernon Scannell's belief.' Kathleen Anscomb then mentioned Edith Sitwell, who had only recently died and received some extravagant obituaries. Olivia replied that she considered Edith Sitwell a fake as a poet, except for *Façade*. 'She is, though, quite a good prose writer, but not of the top class.'

At home in Portsmouth the Commander had kept a succession of little dogs and Olivia could also remember him sitting with a cat on his lap. He was the first person to talk to her about Siamese cats and their exotic ways and their resonant voices, which were said to carry up to six miles. When he was aboard HMS *Venus* at the turn of the century, two Siamese kittens had been presented to the ship's company as they lay off Singapore. He could still recall, he told her, how they chased each other up the rigging 'leaping like flying foxes from rope to rope' – a phrase that stuck in her mind and that she was to use herself when she came to write her own cat memoir. Her father also remembered how the kittens had been the delight of the crew.

Olivia was sixteen when she saw her first Siamese cat. Only forty years had passed since the first Siamese cat – called Tiam-o-Shien – had been introduced to Britain by the Consul General from Bangkok. In Laburnum Grove most of the neighbours had either tabbies or Blue Persians as pets. Then, in April 1924, a former school friend of Olivia's, who was a couple of years older and was working in London, brought back to Portsmouth a Siamese kitten. Olivia stroked the cat lovingly. 'Do be careful,' her friend warned, 'they can scratch like the devil.' But Olivia was not in the least frightened. She decided on the spot that she would one day have a Siamese cat herself. Eventually, she was to own three. Her school friend's Siamese had a collar and lead, and her brother Oliver had screamed with laughter at the sight.

Later, when Olivia was to have cats of her own, she several times tried to take them out on leads. It never really worked. Once in Regent's Park, when one of her cats planted itself firmly on the path and refused to budge an inch, some cheeky boys, much to Olivia's annoyance, jeered at her and then rushed off. She never again took a cat to Regent's Park.

The three Siamese cats that Olivia owned were called Eebou, Faro and Choula. Her last cat was a Burmese and he outlived her by six weeks. His name was Miou.

As a young man Reggie had been slightly nervous of cats and even more so if they happened to be oriental. So when Olivia, unknown to him, accepted the gift of a Siamese kitten from a friend, she was uncertain about Reggie's reaction. They were living in a two-room flat in Baker Street, with no access to either a garden or a balcony. 'We have a new member of the family,' she greeted Reggie as he came through the front door. But it was not until an hour later, when she heard him saying to the kitten 'I *love* your little black nose', that she knew all was well. When he went to bed that night the kitten climbed on to his chest. 'She reminds me', he said, 'of a blue-eyed owl.' For several days afterwards they called her 'Owl'.

Then one morning Reggie announced firmly, 'We simply can't keep shouting "Owl, Owl, Owl" after her. It's like King Lear's "Howl, howl, howl".'

'Well what about Hibou then?' Olivia suggested. 'After all, Siam was once a French possession.'

'That's quite true,' Reggie agreed, 'but what can we do about those who don't understand about the silent aitch?'

Finally they settled on Eebou, which Olivia assured Reggie was the Siamese spelling for 'hibou'.

Olivia wrote in her cat memoir, 'Just as there is never a baby like the first one, so there is never a Siamese kitten like the first.' Eebou appears in Olivia's 1951 novel *School for Love*, but under the name of Faro, which was in fact the name of Eebou's one and only male kitten. The change of name and sex in the novel sometimes led to confusion when journalists came to interview the author about her cats and books.

She disliked the term domestic animal, and was delighted when she came across a Japanese poet who had described the cat as 'The Tiger that eats from the hand'. She associated this with Christopher Smart's line: 'For the Cherub Cat is a term for the Angel Tiger'.

When Olivia went to stay with friends, she liked to take her cats with her and would arrive with quantities of food for them and a bag of cinders, since the latter, she would explain, were healthier than cat litter and, incidentally, much cheaper. Reggie came to regard cats as hot-water bottles. But Olivia, always anxious about her cats' health and comfort, would bring a hot-water bottle not for him but them. She thought it barbarous that in so many English houses the central heating went off automatically at midnight and did not come on again until seven in the morning. She could be ruthless in other people's homes and demand that it be left on.

Once, when she rented a furnished house in Ryde in August, she became worried when Faro started to explore the fireplace and chimney in the sitting room. After she eventually had extricated him, she went upstairs, took two eiderdowns from the spare bedroom and proceeded to stuff them up the chimney, where they remained. On the return of the owner of the house in late September, he lit a fire and was not at all pleased when a shower of scorched feathers came fluttering down. Olivia refused to replace the eiderdowns. She thought the man 'a cheeky bugger' to ask her to do so. 'Why don't you just have them cleaned?' she wrote back on a postcard.

Olivia's last two cats were Choula, adopted from a family in the Isle of Wight who were emigrating to Canada, and Miou, a Burmese kitten given to her by a friend. For several months they were wary of each other but then became friends. When Olivia now went away, she left them behind in each other's company. After Choula died in 1974, she reverted to her old pattern of travelling around with a cat in a basket. Miou, however, was not an easy traveller, because he had once fallen from Olivia's third-storey flat in St John's Wood and had had to have a pin put in his back leg. Although the operation had been successful, his mistress was fearful that he might fall again. In her anxiety she became overprotective. Her relationship with vets was often so fraught that she sacked them. She told a Hampstead vet, who particularly angered her, 'I do not pay you to tell me that there is nothing wrong with my animal.' His bill then remained unpaid.

Later, when Miou developed a small lump on his forehead, she persuaded her surgeon friend Michael Laurence – at the time she was staying with him and his wife Parvin at Billingham Manor in the Isle of Wight – to cut it out. Afterwards he remarked, 'I've never before had a patient who sat on my lap when I was operating and peed all over me.' Nor was Olivia averse to trying out animal faith healers. Cats were for her a substitute for children. Her ill-fated pregnancy in Jerusalem had meant that she could never have a family of her own. Often she regarded the behaviour of her cats as that of naughty children and indeed, on occasions actually encouraged them to play up.

In 1970 when Olivia came to stay with June Braybrooke in Cowes in the Isle of Wight, she brought Miou with her. The garden at the back of the house was fenced in and had a high wooden gate. No previous cat had ever been able to find a way out. But one afternoon June observed Olivia showing Miou how to jump up on to the roof of the garden shed and so make his way into the road. There was a side to Olivia's character which enjoyed tempting providence.

On another occasion when Miou had gone missing at Cowes, Olivia locked June's three-year-old granddaughter in the dining room, which was unheated, and proceeded to search every cupboard and room. Then she started going from house to house. Two hours later when there was still no sign of him, she came back in a fearful rage, rushed up the stairs and shut herself in her bedroom, slamming the door after her with such violence that she split a panel of wood. In 1986 a student of literature from Ireland, who was writing a thesis on the Balkan Trilogy, asked if she might photograph the damaged door for posterity.

A theme running through *Extraordinary Cats*, as indeed through all Olivia's books, is cruelty to animals. She believed in the rights of beasts, as set out by the MP Richard Martin in 1804, and in her cat memoir she extends these rights to the bird world, writing at the end of one section,

> Another victim of man is the ortolan, a little bird belonging to the finch family, which is caught and packed around with grain in a dark box. As the ortolan eats through the grain in a frantic effort to reach the light, it grows fat, and when fat enough, is drowned in cognac.

Olivia used to feel physically sick when writing such passages. 'But you mustn't give up,' Reggie would urge her. 'Cruelty, which begins on animals, does not stop there.' She was to repeat this on the last page of *Extraordinary Cats* virtually word for word.

Chapter 25

The Brotherhood of Man

In December 1956 Heinemann brought out a book by Olivia Manning intended for the Christmas market. *My Husband Cartwright* consisted of twelve pieces originally contributed to *Punch*. There had been no illustrations then, but now the publishers had decided to commission Len Deighton to produce some. It was the first time that he had been approached to work on a full-length book.

Cartwright was made up of a series of sketches about Reggie, and so was a forerunner of the masterly portrait that Olivia was later to provide in the Balkan and Levant Trilogies. The book did not attract wide coverage and has never been reprinted. Sections of it were broadcast.* By New Year 1957 Olivia was moaning about its meagre reception. When she saw herself reviewed in a January issue of the *New Statesman* she said, 'It seems I'm a bit of a Christmas left-over.'

---

* On Christmas Day she received, as she told Joanna Scott-Moncrieff, the editor of *Woman's Hour*, a letter informing her that, since *Punch* held the copyright of her book *My Husband Cartwright*, 'the seventy-five per cent promised from Heinemann would not be coming her way for the five extracts which the BBC were to broadcast.'

She always asked Reggie to read through the letters that she typed on business or literary matters before posting them. He noticed in this case that instead of typing *Woman's Hour* she had typed 'Woman's House' in her indignant letter to Scott-Moncrieff. But he let that pass, since he was anxious to shepherd her along to a Boxing Day party to which they had both been invited. 'We're late,' he said. 'Put on your skis. It may snow.'

'But you must agree, darling, that I *am* singled out. I *am* a most unfortunate person.'

'No you're not. You're a bloody genius. You'll become a classic.'

'Maybe. But I'll be dead by then.'

'Hurry up. We're already late enough.'

'Darling, don't be absurd,' replied Reggie. 'If you're a left-over, so are Fougasse and Robert Graves . . . Think what company you're in.' The three authors had been reviewed together.

The book begins:

> My husband Cartwright is a lover of his fellow-men. Lovers of their fellow-men can be maddening. Cartwright's love manifests itself not merely by general benevolence but by a dislike of anything that distracts the eye of charity. While lecturing abroad he suddenly conceived a resentment of 'sights' especially 'useless' sights, such as ruins or tombs. You might suppose that were it not for such distractions as Tiberias, the Valley of the Kings or Hadrian's Villa, tourists abroad would occupy themselves solely in alleviating poverty.

In 1940, when Olivia and Reggie were trudging up the Acropolis, he had talked non-stop to her about social conditions in Greece. The fact that he had been in the country less than four months had not mattered at all. When he first saw the Parthenon, he observed critically that past bombardments had improved it. 'In fact, it must have been dark, ill-ventilated and unhealthy,' he claimed.

Olivia's immediate reaction was, 'It's only a temple, you know, not a block of workers' flats.' Much of the *Cartwright* book is based on such conversations remembered from the past. When she was writing the various pieces, Reggie would frequently jog her memory. He ruefully accepted that he had a comic side and did not care if she exploited it.

A similar story is about a visit to the Pyramids. When Cartwright/ Reggie first sees them, he scarcely gives them a glance. What instead fascinates him is a row of triangular buckets on a narrow railway gauge, used by those on a nearby dig. Pointing to the buckets, he says to his wife, 'I like *those*. They remind me of the tips on the road to Dudley.'

As a young man Reggie had taught at a school in Dudley. Each morning on the bus from Birmingham he would admire the blast furnace flaming in the morning sunlight. They reminded him, he said, of the brotherhood of man, with all comrades harmoniously united together – as in the Soviet Union. Olivia tried to correct him. The Midlanders were as self-absorbed as anyone else, she said – and there was no need to bring Russia into the matter. Reggie would then reply, 'That's what comes of looking at stone and marble monuments instead of looking at humanity.'

In other pieces in the collection Olivia writes of Cartwright's attitude to cricket, children and animals. She is also forthcoming about herself: 'I am not a watcher of games and I need a lot of sleep.' There is a fair amount about her husband snoring. Only those who had had Reggie to stay the night could know the full horror of that. At Venice in 1966, when the couple were staying with the Braybrookes at the Casa Frollo on the Giudecca, Olivia insisted that he be given a room on the first or ground floor, so that he did not disturb the other guests, who usually slept on the second and third floors of the *pensione*. In St John's Wood the Siamese cat Choula would sleep on the pillow beside him, but then Choula was deaf. As the night wore on, so did the sound of the rhythmic snoring. Olivia no doubt had Reggie in mind when she wrote of Peabody in the *Cartwright* book:

> Soon Peabody's snores were rising again to full blast. It was as though a procession of elephants, emerging from the jungle into sunlight, trumpeted in turn.

Looking at this passage over her shoulder Reggie said, 'You know "snoring need not be boring",' then added, 'That's not me – but Queen Caroline. Someone sent me a script about her, which I went through last night.' Reggie did not need more than four hours' sleep and the night was the time when he caught up with his reading – often a pile of BBC radio scripts.

My Husband Cartwright was soon to become a collector's item. On Reggie's sixty-fifth birthday, held at Broadcasting House, Mary Wimbush read some extracts from it to bursts of applause.

There was an in-joke in the book – slipped in by Olivia at her own expense. A journalist known as Pinky Coutts, who flatters Cartwright's wife about her novels merely because he wants to keep in with Cartwright, is later reported by a friend of hers as having said,

> 'What! Read one of *her* books! Not likely. That woman's the sort who loses readers. Dry, sour and chilly.'

Those were three adjectives that Olivia knew were often applied to herself.

Chapter 26

Analysis of a Marriage

By the middle of 1956 Olivia decided that the time had come for some stocktaking about her life and her career. She had nine books behind her – seven of them fiction, including *My Husband Cartwright*, which she regarded as 'something buckshee'. Now, for the second time, she had just appeared in *Who's Who*. 'Being in *Who's Who* makes you somebody,' she told Reggie, who then replied with his usual gallantry, 'You've always been a somebody.'

Olivia had become accustomed to being given pocket diaries at Christmas – sometimes by her parents, sometimes by Reggie's mother, sometimes by Jerry. They contain random jottings – sometimes a quotation, sometimes a record of something heard or seen, sometimes a recipe, even though she was an incompetent cook, as Robert Liddell, a first-class one, often teasingly told her. One such jotting consists merely of two Romanian words, written perpendicularly down the page. An explanation of them is to be found in the opening volume of the Balkan Trilogy, where Bella Niculescu, an Englishwoman married to a Romanian army officer, tells Harriet Pringle,

> 'You're in Blocul Cazacul. That was built by Horia Cazacu, whose motto is *Santajul etajul.*'
> 'What does that mean?'
> 'He's a financier but his income is chiefly from blackmail. It more or less means "Each blackmail builds another floor".'

The significance of the Romanian phrase in the 1956 diary is that it demonstrates that Olivia had already begun work on what she first thought would be 'a double-decker novel about my Romanian experience'. Only when she was completing the first volume did she begin to see the project as a trilogy, with a third volume set in Greece. More than two decades were to pass before she would return to a second Trilogy – the Levant Trilogy – to continue the story begun in the first. Her overall title for these six books was *Fortunes of War* – a phrase used in the final volume of the Balkan Trilogy and again twice in the Levant Trilogy.

Reggie was eager that she should begin. 'It's now sixteen years since you were in Bucharest,' he told her. 'Add another three for writing the book. I have a feeling that 1960 would be the ideal year for you in which to publish. Twenty years is a good lapse.' He then added, 'Remember your great fortune has been life and . . .'

She stopped him in mid-sentence: 'You've given me a title – "A Great Fortune". Now I've only to write it.'

'Yes,' he urged her. 'Start now. Don't delay. Consult Dwye.' Dwye Evans was the managing director at Heinemann and it was to him and his wife that, in 1965, Olivia dedicated *Friends and Heroes*, the concluding volume of the Balkan Trilogy.

Between 1956 and 1964 the Balkan Trilogy was to become Olivia Manning's major project. 'Everything else must be grist for it,' she said. 'I am lucky to have a husband who supports me.' Some of her friends felt that in writing about the war she was taking on too massive a task for a woman, but kept their views to themselves. Meanwhile Reggie went about urging everyone to encourage Olivia. He had an ability to inspire not merely his wife but many of the writers and actors who came into professional contact with him.

Walter Allen, one of Reggie's oldest friends from his Birmingham days, refers to Olivia's painter's eye for colour. In her student days Olivia had talked about 'a palette of memory', which Reggie thought a term to remember. Tennyson and D. H. Lawrence were writers whom she had long admired for their use of colour. In the opening volume of the Balkan Trilogy, Harriet picks up a copy of *Kangaroo* and from it reads aloud three of Lawrence's descriptions of the sunset over Manly Beach, which Guy has marked. They are: 'the long green roller of the Pacific', 'the star-white foam' and 'the dusk-green sea glimmered over with smoky rose'.

To friends on the Isle of Wight Olivia would suggest going for walks along its shores and add, 'You never know what we shall find.' She said to June on one such occasion, 'I do not search, I find.' That was Olivia's approach to life. 'Nothing (I feel) is ever quite fortuitous,' she jotted down on the back of a 1933 envelope.

When a child, she had been told by a woman who lived close by in Laburnum Grove that she possessed potential psychic powers. The same neighbour suggested that one day she might become a medium. Olivia read widely on the subject, but never rushed to join the Spiritualists. 'There is an element of falseness about their public seances,' was her verdict. 'There is such a pressure on the medium to make things happen that trickery is resorted to.' In *The Great Fortune* Prince Yakimov recalls attending seances where ectoplasm oozed out between the black curtains of the medium's cabinet. For Olivia, those who had died in battle were never out of reach. Whether it was the entire Athenian expeditionary force at Syracuse in 413 BC or the casualties of the battle of Alamein within living memory made no difference.

In the last volume of the Balkan Trilogy, just before Greece is overrun by the Germans, a group of English friends, including Harriet and Guy Pringle, sit in a café near the bombed seafront. Among them is Alan Frewen, an expatriate of five years who tells those around him, 'When I camped out on the battlefield of Marathon, I was awakened by the sound of swords striking against each other.' The imminence of the Greek defeat perhaps may make him confess to an experience about which in normal times he might have been silent. Nobody, not even Guy 'impressed against reason', now doubts that he is telling the truth.

Reggie accepted that his wife had psychic powers – though he was never too anxious to discuss them. One night, when the Smiths had been staying in a sixth-floor *pensione* in Alexandria during the war, they awoke to see a journalist – in the Levant Trilogy the character Jake Jackman is based on him – standing in their room, even though they knew him to be in Sicily. Was it an apparition, or had he made the journey from Sicily by means of astral projection? The next morning Olivia questioned Reggie, who replied, 'Yes, yes, I do remember . . . there he was standing by the bed.' But he offered no direct explanation. Like Guy, he remained 'an unpersuadable materialist'. Yet both Reggie and his fictional counterpart would admit, when questioned, that anguish and violent emotions might impress themselves on the ether and so be perceived centuries later by others.

The Balkan Trilogy offers an analysis of a marriage of a young couple, set against the background of the Second World War. The couple flee the

Germans from Romania to Greece and then, in April 1941, escape to Alexandria. An early version of the Trilogy closed with the sentence, 'Little blotches of palms, a flat rather shabby, sea-side whiteness – then we entered the great harbour of Alexandria.' But by the time each part of the Trilogy had reached its final draft, the narrative was entirely in the third person. The separate volumes might be described, Olivia once said, as three long chapters of autobiography, presented in the third person.

Olivia was thirty-one when Hitler's troops marched into Poland and Reggie six years younger. In the novel Harriet Pringle is twenty-one and Guy twenty-two. In the opening chapter Harriet says to Guy, 'I love you' and he replies, 'I know.' This should never be lost sight of. His comment later in the first novel that she is part of himself, reinforced by the statement 'I expect from you what I expect of myself', becomes in the third 'But you are myself. I don't need to consider your feelings.' Harriet's patience is frequently tested to breaking point, but the love persists.

In the opening novel Harriet is still in the stage of early passion. At the beginning, she and Guy are sitting hand in hand as they are driven down the Calea Victoriei in a four-wheeler. The vehicle smells of horse, but 'they are more aware of each other than anything else' and so hardly notice. Just a few minutes before climbing into the carriage, she has given his little finger a lovebite that has made him yelp. She has done this in case he gets 'too good to be true'. In each of the volumes sexual passion is assumed and clues are given, but only the sexual encounters of others are actually described – and sometimes laughed at. Olivia was a passionate woman, who found sex enjoyable, but she was always aware of both the bestial and the funny side of it.

The strongest bond between Olivia and Reggie, unlike that between Harriet and Guy, was not a sexual but a literary one. This is because Harriet, unlike her creator, is not a writer – though she has literary and artistic leanings. What she does, above all, have in common with Olivia is that she is a survivor, who grapples with life.

On one occasion Harriet and Guy have a heated argument about religion – as Olivia and Reggie would often do – while out on a walk. She argues for a life after death; he counters that religion is merely a method of holding the poor and underprivileged in subjection. They become increasingly exasperated. Soon, they are walking a little apart, separated by their differences. Yet, within minutes, she has 'slid her hand back into his'. That was how it was always going to be between Reggie and Olivia.

Twice in the Balkan Trilogy Guy Pringle is shown at work as a producer. In *The Great Fortune* he is producing *Troilus and Cressida*, with a cast which includes Romanian students and members from the British Legation and British Council. In *Friends and Heroes* he is staging an RAF revue at Tatoi near Athens, with the nineteenth-century melodrama of *Maria Marten* as the star item. In each case Harriet is supportive – though, in the first case, if she had her way, 'she would seize Guy and canalise his zeal to make a mark on eternity'. The zeal which he has expended on his Shakespeare production will, she decides, merely 'fill the theatre for one afternoon and evening and be forgotten in a week'. Elsewhere she declares that he is 'profligate of life' and will 'simply waste himself'. She knows that she would never be able to give herself to the ephemeral undertakings for which he shows such enthusiasm.

In her youth in Portsmouth, Olivia had told her brother and school friends, and later those in London with whom she worked at the Peter Jones studio, that when she married it would be for adventure. To Louis MacNeice, when he was the best man at her wedding, she confided that she was not interested in an ordinary marriage. To another witness present she said the same thing.

MacNeice then asked, 'Did you say orderly?'

'No, I said ordinary, but I meant orderly as well.' Like Harriet in the Trilogy, Olivia wanted to possess and be possessed by her husband, to envelop and be enveloped in a relationship that would exclude the two of them from 'the enemy world'. Neither Guy nor Reggie wanted this: they saw themselves in roles in which they welcomed the world, for it held no fears for them.

This was something that Olivia and Harriet had to learn to accept – and as Olivia would say in retrospect, 'It took some time.' She wrote of Guy, 'He belonged to everyone.' In an attempt to define a character at once so unsatisfactory and so admirable, Harriet comes up with the image of radium: 'He seemed like radium throwing off vitality to the outside world – not that he thought of it as an outside world.' Another image was of a whirlwind: 'He was born to expand himself like a whirlwind . . .' Yet she had to admit that there were times when his whirlwind activities – in teaching, broadcasting or the theatre – functioned to a definite purpose. A maxim for her became 'Only someone capable of giving much could demand and receive so much'. There were occasions when she was deeply proud of his achievements.

In Harriet's view, day-to-day marriage was divided between periods of pride in Guy and ones of impatience and irritability. She admitted to herself that, although she knew him in many ways, she did not know him in every way. There might even come a time, she speculated, when she might be bored with him – though that had not happened yet. One thing remained certain: she experienced with him supreme moments of happiness such as she had never known before.

Those who met Olivia during the war often took away the impression of a shy provincial girl. Adam Watson, on whom Dobbie Dobson is partly based, recalled in 1996, 'Olivia knew little of the great world before the war. She had hardly been abroad – perhaps a few days in France, perhaps a few days in Germany. That was about all.' So it was not surprising that Olivia clung tight to Reggie in Bucharest. After all, he had spent a previous apprentice year in the city with the British Council and had got to know a number of Romanians. Harriet saw herself and Guy very much as a unit – one not to be split up.

> 'We're together. We're alive – anyway for the moment.'
> 'The great fortune is life. We must preserve it.'
>
> *(The Great Fortune)*

> 'The only place I want to go to is Greece, but I'm not going without you.'
>
> *(The Spoilt City)*

> 'I suppose we're lucky to be here [in Athens]; and we're lucky to be together.' [Harriet] embraced him because he was with her and alive.
>
> *(Friends and Heroes)*

As the war advanced, so the world was changing. Would it ever be less class-ridden? Harriet asked herself. In Romania it had seemed to her that the old order lingered on, even if the Nazis had brought with them across the border a terrible savage new order that they were determined to impose. In Greece, in 1941, she had found signs of hope. Tavernas and cafés were open to officers and their men alike; rank had nothing to do with class in the Greek Army, only with proficiency. High-ranking British officers disapproved of this. Such diehards represented the forces of reaction for Guy, as indeed they did for his young wife. On their walks in the Bucharest countryside they would smile at the groups of peasants that they passed. This is followed by 'But their smiles grew strained as they breathed-in the peasant stench'. Though she knew that Guy too had recoiled from this stench, Harriet said nothing. Had she done so, Guy would have angrily accused her of class prejudice. She had an answer prepared for that accusation: 'The trouble with prejudice is that there's usually a reason for it.'

Olivia herself came from the narrowest, most prejudiced class in England, the lower middle. Nevertheless, she had successfully declassed herself. What Guy still accused Harriet of being was muddled and lost in childish mysticism. If she was intolerant too, he put that down to her feminine nature. He also thought of her as a romantic – but that was perhaps tit for tat, since she thought the same thing of him and his political views.

In the concluding volume of the Trilogy, Harriet's view of marriage changes and develops. The man whom she married less than a week before the war is no longer the man whom she knows now. She discovers in their relationship new loyalties and dependencies.

> For each thread broken, another had been thrown out to
> claim her. If she tried to escape, she might find herself held by
> a complex, an imprisoning web, she did not know was there.

She and Guy have learnt about each other's faults and limitations; there is no purpose in expecting more than a person can give – on either side. The vital point, in a final analysis, is that each shall not fail the other. She has audacity but feeble health – he has the strength of an ox but is limited physically by poor sight. At one point in this volume Harriet asks, 'How did I come to marry someone so different?' It is a rhetorical question and she replies, 'It was his difference I had married.' The question and answer are among the most revealing sentences that Olivia ever wrote about herself and her life.

It has come to be believed that all three volumes of the Balkan Trilogy had unanimous rave reviews. This was not so. A brief unsigned notice in the *Dublin Evening Herald* dismissed *The Great Fortune* as 'a wasted effort'. 'Never mind,' said Reggie protectively. 'That paper's one of the worst Irish rags.' Twice Olivia protested to London papers about their reviews of *The Great Fortune*. Despite the fact that it carried a foreword to the effect that it was the first of a Trilogy, neither Richard Lister (T. C. Worsley) in the *Evening Standard* nor John Coleman in the *Spectator* seemed to have noticed this. Coleman ended his review, 'A sense of direction – the why of a novel – is conspicuously, fatally absent.'

The Spoilt City, by contrast, had no carping reviews. The general tone was of eager anticipation to know what would happen in the final volume. Moreover, when *Friends and Heroes* did appear three years later, there was wide acclaim. But again there were exceptions. In the *New Statesman* the book was put bottom of the column and David Craig ended, 'The rendering of the characters' inner emotions is dry and schematic. The characterisation is mostly from the outside: if a homosexual or an academic, an officer or a "bounder", comes on stage, he is done in a few conventional traits.' Olivia vented her anger on the literary editor, Hilary Spurling, and became furious with Francis King when he told her that a literary editor could not spike a review merely because she or he disagreed with what his or her reviewer had said.

After she had read the *Observer* review of *Friends and Heroes*, Olivia had gone right back to bed, pulled the covers over her head, turned to the wall and groaned, 'I'm a failure. This is the end of Manning the novelist.' The reviewer was Irving Wardle, who had begun by paying compliments: 'There is a large and strongly characterised cast . . . In terms of straight-forward narrative reconstruction, *Friends and Heroes* is well organised and well written.' The poisoned shaft was left until the last paragraph. There, Harriet is said to be 'a dubious witness. Even the characterisation becomes suspect . . . The undisclosed degree of alliance between Harriet and her creator makes one wary of the novel's larger purpose.'

Reggie tried to calm his wife: 'Wardle's a theatre chap. He should not have been let loose among the novels.'

Olivia hit back: 'I don't care what he is. He's another Stevie. He ought to go and be a pal with her at Palmers Green.'

Fortunately Reggie could fall back on the *Sunday Times* review by Frederic Raphael. 'Listen to this, my love, listen to this. This answers Wardle. You direct Harriet, says Freddie, but Harriet has free will. You are "continuo" and Harriet is "solo". Old Freddie's got the hang of things and Wardle hasn't. Forget old Wardle-boys.'

*

In the Balkan Trilogy, apart from its two central characters of Guy and Harriet, there is only one other character who has a separate entry in the *Oxford Companion to English Literature*. This is the white Russian Prince Yakimov, who sports a sable-lined greatcoat given to his father by the Czar. He is a comic creation of the first order – a mixture between a cultivated Pulcinella and a mischievous Pandarus, the latter being a part that he plays to perfection in Guy's production of *Troilus and Cressida*. In the English colony in which he moves in Bucharest, this Prince of Spongers is more tolerated than admired, for he is by no means trustworthy over IOUs or keeping his word.

Inevitably there have been many suggestions for the prototype of a character so entertaining and vivid. When he was living in Brighton in the late Sixties, Francis King came to know the writer Derek Patmore, grandson of the far more illustrious writer Coventry Patmore and the son of Richard Aldington's valiant and delightful mistress Brigid Patmore. When Patmore told King that he had known Olivia and Reggie in Bucharest during the war and began to talk about his and their life there, King at once decided that here was Yaki's prototype. At his next meeting with Olivia, he asked her if this were possible. Aghast, she told him, '*Never* say that to anyone *ever*! Do you think that I want that awful parasite suing me for libel?' Patmore is now long dead.

Throughout the Trilogy the infighting of British Council life is brilliantly, if sometimes vindictively, portrayed. So too is Guy's attitude to it, for he has always believed that generosity of spirit will be repaid with equal generosity. Now he is to learn otherwise. He can only console himself by saying to Harriet, 'In life, thank God, defaulters are always in a minority.'

Had Olivia required a defence for her Trilogies, she need have looked no further than this sentence of Novalis written at the turn of the eighteenth century: 'Novels arise out of the shortcomings of history.' Both her Trilogies contain details unrecorded by the official historians. For example, in the third volume of the first, when Harriet enters an Athens air-raid shelter in early 1941, she learns that talking is not permitted; this is an order by the Greek government, in case panic should break out. So concentrated is the silence that the whole place is alive with only small animal sounds, 'as though the floor ran with mice'. Later, in April of the same year, she and Guy learn from their servant Anastea that seats may be reserved for 30,000 drachma in a new air-raid shelter being built. They think this is a scandalously large sum. But to Anastea's way of thinking, foreigners who can afford to rent a villa with a bathroom and a kitchen can afford anything. A sum of 30,000 drachma has no reality for her.

The loneliness that Harriet experiences walking alone in the Greek hills is nowhere better conveyed than by the phrase 'the moon her only companion'. It summarises the price she has to pay for having such a gregarious husband; it also underlines Guy's 'selfish generosity' – a phrase used by the politician Chris Patten after rereading the Trilogy in 1977. In October 1940, on Harriet's arrival in 'the longed-for city' of Athens, she waits nervously for her husband to join her in the next few days. Nowhere is her sense of isolation brought home with greater force than when she looks at the posters on the walls, for even there 'the alphabet was unknown to her'.

All these touches indicate a master novelist.

On the penultimate page of *Friends and Heroes*, Harriet sees Guy and herself as 'exiles' when they arrive in Greece and as 'refugees' when they leave for Egypt. It is a subtle distinction, for whereas exiles band quickly together in new countries, refugees remain split up. Harriet's consolation is:

> Still, they had life – depleted fortune but a fortune. They were together and would remain together, and that was the only certainty left to them.

By 1966 critics had begun to compare the author of the Balkan Trilogy with Laurence Durrell, Graham Greene, Anthony Powell and Evelyn Waugh – all male writers. When the third volume came out, Anthony Burgess proclaimed in the *Spectator* that she was 'among the most accomplished of our women novelists' – a phrase which Heinemann was quick to seize upon when advertising the Trilogy and her future novels. Until his second marriage Burgess was always a devoted friend to Olivia. When his first wife died, Olivia put it about that on the following morning he had telephoned to propose marriage to her. 'But I'm already married,' she protested, according to her story. 'Well, get a divorce!' was said to be his reply. From one's knowledge of Olivia, this may well have been fantasy. From one's knowledge of Burgess it may well have been true.

Chapter 27

A Fortnight in Venice

The plan was that during the summer of 1966 Olivia and Reggie should spend a fortnight at the Casa Frollo in Venice and that the Braybrookes should join them two days later. In the event it proved to be three days later, because June was struck down by a bad attack of migraine on the morning of their departure and they had to postpone their flight.

At the Giudecca landing stage Reggie and Olivia were there to meet them. Reggie, always helpful, insisted on carrying their cases the hundred yards to the *pensione*. On the way he pointed out a bar. 'They sell the best grappa in the lagoon,' was his comment.

Olivia then drew Neville aside: 'I do hope June will try not to have a migraine while she's here.'

He replied, 'You can't predict these things.' Olivia would often describe June's migraines as 'tiresome' or even 'a bloody nuisance'.

The two couples spent most of that first evening at Florian's in St Mark's Square, where Reggie kept greeting friends as they passed. At each encounter he promised to meet them later in the holiday for 'a jar or two'. He liked topping up his beer with shorts – whiskies or even liqueurs – and used to claim that he had a cast-iron stomach. He also had an enormous appetite and would regularly ask if he could finish what was left on other people's plates. 'A well-lined stomach is the key to happy drinking' was one of his sayings.

June had no migraine attacks during the next fortnight. Rather it was Olivia who was struck down briefly by malaria, a recurring legacy from her Middle East years.

On the second morning of the Braybrookes' stay there was a tap at the door at eight o'clock. It was Reggie in some state of consternation. 'My Olivia has got one of her attacks,' he began. 'We must draw up a roster between us. I've got people to see and I can't let them down.' Then he paused for a moment or two. 'My idea is that I should be responsible for Olivia during the day and that you keep an eye on her during the evenings. I promise to be back by midnight.' On each of the next two nights he came back on the early morning ferry.

After one of these nights out June spotted in a shop the couple with whom Reggie had been drinking. They were Sir Kenneth Adams, a man high in the BBC hierarchy, and his wife. Adams looked deadly white as he dragged after his wife, who had begun to bargain over the price of a leather bag. Then she rounded on him: 'You're not much help today. Never go drinking with that man again. When I left to return to the hotel both of you were still singing those ridiculous calypsos. You look half-dazed.'

Looking after Olivia was never an easy task. She was a demanding patient. When, in the 1970s, she was having a hip replacement at the Wellington Hospital near Lord's, she had had the head chef summoned to her bedside so as to complain to him in person about the quality of the caviar. During the three days that she was confined to bed at the Casa Frollo, she refused to let her companions call a local doctor, on the grounds that her own London doctor, and lover, Jerry Slattery would be with them before the end of the week. Meanwhile two teenage sisters from the dining room were appointed to look after her and take her orders for meals. They were aged about fifteen or sixteen and it was obvious from the start that they regarded the English signora as a difficult lady. She even made a fuss about entering the dining room. The proprietress, who sat by the door, ticked off the names of the guests as they went in. At her feet were two dogs. Because of her irrational terror of rabies, Olivia would delegate either Reggie or Neville to stand in front of the dogs, so that she could quickly slip by. The girls tittered as she tentatively approached. 'I hope they don't think I'm a joke,' she complained to June. On one occasion she faced a total stranger at a nearby table and announced, 'Rabies is no laughing matter.'

On her second day in bed Olivia's appetite began to return; on her first day she had only wanted to sip water and have a bowl of thin soup. Now she craved something more substantial and told June that she was thinking of a boiled egg. When the youngest girl from the dining room came to take her order, Olivia said to June, 'I'll manage this and tell her what I want.' Rather haltingly Olivia began, '*Prego, acqua . . .*' Then she altered this to '*Acqua, prego . . .*' Searching for the Italian word for 'egg', she came up with '*uva*' which sounded nearly right. '*Prego uva,*' she went on – then stopped. '*Uva, uva,*' she began again. Next she started to improvise: '*Uva bollita, bolleta*...' The girl departed and laughter could be heard from the passageway where her older sister lurked.

Quarter of an hour later the younger girl entered with a tray and placed it on Olivia's bed. '*Prego,*' she said. There was a bottle of spa water and a warming cover over a plate.

But when Olivia lifted the cover she saw only a boiled grape. 'What does this mean?' she asked in English. 'I wanted an *uova,*' she said getting the word right this time. '*Uova, uova,*' she repeated angrily.

The girl looked blankly at her and pointed to the tray: '*Uva, uva bollita, Signora.*' Then, as she saw Olivia reach beneath her bed for a slipper, she made a dart for the door.

Olivia's slipper missed and there was again laughter in the corridor. '*Impudenza!*' Olivia muttered to herself. Then she turned to June: 'Reggie shall hear of this. We shall be leaving in the morning.'

There had been similar scenes before. In other hotel rooms, in Greece and France, Olivia had been known to throw slippers at maids who displeased her. She had an impatient and violent side to her character. But those who worked for her in London never saw this. Alex Priggle, whom she remembered in her will and who had worked for her for many years, said to the Braybrookes, 'I know I am serving a famous star.' Olivia delighted in this when she was told.

After the boiled-grape incident, Neville had to go to the kitchen at the Casa Frollo and make peace. The proprietress promised that she would herself boil an egg for the signora – no, she would boil two. She apologised on behalf of the girls, saying they were *poveri bambini* from a convent orphanage on the mainland. This did little to appease Olivia. 'They were bloody rude and they knew it. They need putting over someone's knee. I shall tell Reggie about it as soon as he's back. We'll have to leave this dump.'

When Reggie returned an hour later she let fly. He listened patiently. After she had finished he advised, 'Be reasonable, darling. Venice is packed, because at the Salute the BBC are sponsoring an international concert during the weekend. There's not a free bed anywhere. Sleep on it. Jerry and Johnny will be here in the morning. We can discuss it then. Besides I'm dead tired' – and with that he left the room.

The next day the Slatterys arrived and Olivia was up, dressed and ready to meet them. Merely by his presence Jerry could bring about miraculous powers of recovery in Olivia. He began organising things almost at once. 'There's nothing that a walk won't put right,' he suggested. Within a few minutes the group set off down the *fondamenta* leading towards the Rendentore, where there was some scaffolding up in the church. At once Olivia decided to climb it. 'Don't expect me to follow you,' Jerry shouted after her. 'You know I've no head for heights.'

At that moment, Jerry was a deeply contented man. Here he was with the two women whom he loved most in the world. To the Braybrookes he seemed, not for the first time, like a ringmaster, immensely skilful at keeping his two fillies bucking and prancing until the final curtain.

Venice is a city famed for its cats. But although Olivia loved this in theory, in practice she gave them a wide berth whenever she saw them. She was terrified that one might bite or scratch her and so infect her with rabies.

Olivia was eager to see any relics of Nini, a famous tomcat, who had died in 1894 but of whom a few early photographs and drawings survived. Nini's home had been a café opposite the great doors leading to the Frari Church. Among his visitors had been Pope Leo XIII, Czar Alexander, Prince Paul Metternich and Verdi, who next to his signature in the cat's visitors' book, had put some notes from Act III of *La Traviata*. Maybe he had added these with a certain irony, for at its first performance at La Fenice on 6 March 1853 his opera had been greeted with catcalls.

Nini's visitors' book was kept wrapped up in brown paper and was brought to Olivia. She rested it on her knees, unwrapped it and slowly turned the pages. At length she said, 'Half the world is here and I am going to add my signature.' She asked Reggie if he had a pen. After she had signed, each of those with her followed suit. When it came to Reggie's turn he paused: 'There's a line in the *Merchant of Venice* where Shylock says cats are "necessary" to this city – also "harmless". Does anyone know the line? It's just before the trial scene.' Their lack of response was an excuse for him to recite, which he loved doing. He began,

> Some men there are love not a gaping pig,
> Some that are mad if they behold a cat . . .

When concluded, this recital drew a round of applause from everyone in the café. Reggie, delighted, now added his signature with a flourish. He next hugged the café owner and promised to be back the following year.

On holiday there was something of the student about Reggie's dress. Seldom did he wear suits, preferring instead trousers that only just stayed up and a shapeless pullover, often with a hole in an elbow, which he hung round his neck in case it should become suddenly cold. He was wearing this rig when he suggested that everyone should be downstairs at half past seven to go across to the concert at La Salute. He had downed a good many pints by then and was confident that the authorities would find six seats for them. 'There's always plenty of space in the side chapels,' he assured them.

Jerry questioned this: 'Are you absolutely certain?'

'Emphatically so,' came the reply. 'That's the purpose of side chapels.'

On the way over a light wind was ruffling the water and several gondolas passed by. 'Which poet was it', Reggie asked at one point, 'who said gondolas look like coffins mounted on canoes?'

Olivia turned to June: 'Reggie's a positive walking encyclopaedia. He seems to know everything. When he's as pissed as this, I'm tempted to try another Cartwright story. I'd call it "The Venetian Blind".'

Meanwhile, Reggie was saying, 'At the door of La Salute I shall announce I am a director of the BBC and walk straight in. You must all follow me.'

Brimming with confidence, he marched his little group up the steps towards the entrance of La Salute, where a doorkeeper stood checking tickets. When the man asked Reggie for theirs, Reggie simply replied, 'I am a director.'

The man looked blankly at him. 'Tickets, tickets,' he insisted.

Reggie then repeated, 'I am a director. No tickets needed.'

A policeman, who had been watching the scene, strode over and uttered the one word '*No*'. Then he went on uttering the word '*No, no, no*', while pointing to Reggie's trousers.

'What's wrong?' Reggie enquired innocently. 'I am a director, a director.'

Olivia intervened: 'Darling, your flies are undone.'

'What am I to do, darling?'

'For one thing – do them up. For another – beat as dignified a retreat as you know how.'

He did what she told him. But it was obvious that his self-confidence had taken a bruising, as he began to retreat slowly down the steps, followed by his friends. Then suddenly his spirits lifted. He had spotted a colleague and chum, the writer P. H. Newby, whom he and Olivia had first met in Cairo. Newby, then Controller of the BBC Third Programme, was sporting a dinner jacket and a rose in his buttonhole. This was Reggie's chance to show the doorkeeper and the policeman that he was a man of substance, with friends in high places. Embracing Newby repeatedly, he kept telling him how well and smart he looked.

'We'll talk after the show,' Newby responded with far less enthusiasm. Then he freed himself to continue his ascent to the church.

Olivia observed, 'That policeman never took his eyes off you. He obviously thought that you were trying to pick P. H.'s pocket.'

'Nonsense! I know where we'll go, love. There's a café beside the church at the bottom. We'll listen to the concert from there.'

Inside the café a huge television screen showed people arriving by gondola and then going up the steps to the church. When the concert at last began, it could be heard twice – once directly from the church and then an instant later from the television set. The result was disconcerting. In the interval, Reggie began to reel off, as he often did, names of imaginary stars from the world of the performing arts. The first was Alexandria Pushover, the Russian ballerina . . . It seemed there could be no stopping him. 'He can keep this up for an hour,' Olivia informed everyone. Fortunately, when the concert began again, he fell silent.

During their fortnight in Venice the Smiths were anxious to see Peggy Guggenheim, whom they had met several times in London. The two went along one morning to visit her at her Palazzo Venier dei Leoni on the Grand Canal and she suggested that they should bring their friends to a trattoria the following night – each paying for themselves, she quickly added. She had staying with her William K. Rose, a professor at Vassar, who had edited *The Letters of Wyndham Lewis* three years earlier. She would bring him along too, she said.

The trattoria that she chose was not far from the Danieli and faced the lagoon. As Olivia followed Reggie to the table, she saw that Peggy Guggenheim had brought with her two of her Lhasa terriers. 'Shall I see if you can sit as far away from them as possible?' Reggie asked.

'Don't worry,' Olivia replied. 'I expect they come from America. They'll be okay.' Olivia could often be inconsistent in these matters. Her only firm rule was that she would never visit animal sanctuaries abroad – though she sometimes sent them subscriptions.

Peggy Guggenheim now invited Olivia to sit beside her at the head of the table. Each woman could be formidable; each had a way of alternating between being reticent and being bold. Olivia had once met a famous woman novelist in Ireland who, she had learnt, had been censorious about her relationship with Jerry. Later on, when she encountered this woman coming out of a Dublin hotel bedroom with a man not her husband, her comment as they passed was, 'Enjoying adultery?'

She now told Guggenheim about this incident and Guggenheim was delighted: 'I wish I could have thought of that. There have been many times when I could have used it.'

By the middle of the evening, no doubt emboldened by the wine – the party had already finished nine carafes – Olivia urged the hostess, 'Do tell us what you didn't put in your memoirs.'

Peggy needed no prompting. 'Pour me another drink,' she ordered. She then began: 'When I was young, I had more money than friends. Friends were difficult to come by and so were lovers. I was in my twenties and virginity was growing burdensome. I had a book of frescoes from Pompeii. It showed people making love in all sorts of positions. I wanted a man who would try all that and my first husband proved the man. He was a wild, wild creature. Laurence Vail was his name. He was an American who had spent most of his life in France and rolled his Rs. My two children are by him, and we had some pretty spectacular times – fights too. When he beat me up he used to rub jam in my hair. Can you imagine that? She looked around the table, but no one spoke. Then she went on: 'He tried to seduce me at the Plaza Athenée Hotel, but I told him my mother might return at any moment. He said he'd go back to his own hotel. So I rushed to put on my hat and went with him. That's how I came to lose my virginity in the Rue de Verneuil. It was as easy as that. You can find it all in my memoirs.'

Next she spoke of her father and how he had owned copper mines all over the world and how her wealth had given her an advantage over her lovers. To John (Oxo) Holmes she had said: 'If you don't rise, neither will the dollar.' She had used this line with others, including Laurence. But he had fought back. 'He told me I was lucky to be accepted in Bohemia, since all I had to offer was money.'

'How do you think of yourself?' William Rose asked. 'Art collector? Patron? Impresario?'

'All those – plus an heiress with a fortune. At one point I used to buy a picture a day. Herbert Read was one of my mentors. Do you still write a sentence a day, Olivia?'

'More or less. What about your other husbands?'

'I've had my say – for tonight anyhow. Another evening perhaps. Laurence Vail is Chapter One.'

'Who's Chapter Two?' urged Bill. 'Tell us before we go.'

'Max, Max Ernst. I didn't want to live in sin in America with an enemy alien. It was the time of Pearl Harbor, so we tied the knot. But that's for another evening . . . He loved to wear fantastic things. In a sheepskin jacket he looked like a Slav prince. "Peggy's a wonderful girl," he would repeat. But enough, enough . . .'

When at last the bill was brought, Peggy scrutinised it item by item. 'Some places try to slip in an extra carafe. But not here. I'll work out what you each owe and I'll include the tips.'

She began to write down sums on the back of a menu. Reggie leaned towards June and said *sotto voce*, 'And to think she's one of the richest women in the world!'

Finally there was the matter of getting across to the Giudecca. Peggy, Bill, Rose and her dogs were going to make the long walk back via the Rialto Bridge, because there was a partial vaporetto strike on and she did not approve of the extravagance of gondolas or motor-boat taxis. 'They go too fast,' she said of the latter, 'they charge too much, they muddy the canals.' Then, turning to Olivia, who was next to her, she said, 'You people had better take the Cipriani launch. They come at a moment's notice. They have their own phone and I'll show you where to ring them. It costs nothing – just pick up the receiver.'

'But when they come do we have to pay for the crossing?' Olivia enquired.

'I never have. The men have a wage.'

'We're not staying at the Cipriani,' June ventured.

'Oh, don't give that a thought! And don't mention it to them.'

Two years later, on 29 March 1968, Olivia sent June a letter with this postscript: 'Venice stays in my mind like a dream.'

Chapter 28

A Year of Bits and Pieces

1967 was to see Olivia engaged on four projects: collecting a volume of short stories; completing her cat memoir; beginning a new novel – *The Play Room* – and making notes for a book about 'Court Life in Europe between 1870 and 1920'. The last of these had been suggested to her by George Weidenfeld – prompting Olivia to say to Neville, 'I think he is really after my novels.' And so it proved, for ten years later he succeeded in persuading her to join his list as one of his novelists. The 'Court Life venture', as she referred to it, never got much beyond the research stage and Olivia returned the advance. The two books that appeared in 1967 were *A Romantic Hero and Other Stories*, in the late spring, and *Extraordinary Cats*, in the late autumn. The blurb to the latter notes, 'She lives with her husband in St John's Wood and cultivates not only a mental garden but a real one.' Reggie's comment was, 'What the hell is that supposed to mean?'

The collection of short stories included eight from Olivia Manning's first volume *Growing Up* and six new ones. The title story, 'A Romantic Hero', she had revised many times since it first began life in 1953 as 'The Smile'. Many considered it the best in the collection.

Harold, the central figure, is in his mid-thirties. It has taken him ten years to climb out of his class and exchange a career in a gentlemen's outfitters for that of an elocutionist. He is a man who, by 'some quirk of nature', is impelled, when looking for intimacy, to shuttle between the sexes. When the story opens he is drawn to girls and has even thought of marrying Angela who, though dumpy and lower middle class, is 'not bad in bed'. She is both possessive and critical of her lover.

Angela is on a fortnight's holiday and Harold is coming from London to spend the weekend with her in a labourer's cottage that she has rented

on the South Downs. On the train journey to Worthing, Harold shares
the compartment with a handsome, fair-haired youth, who is cramming
for the Oxford entrance: his subject is mathematics. When the two men
part, having had a cup of tea with Angela at the station buffet, Harold
gives David's hand a surreptitious squeeze. Although this is not
reciprocated, Harold is confident that it has been 'understood'.

This makes him determined, the next morning, to meet David at
Seaham, a six-mile walk from where Angela is staying. Harold is suscept-
ible to colds and knows that he has a horrid one coming on. When he
arrives at David's bungalow the relationship between the two men is edgy
and Harold gets nowhere. All that happens is that his cold grows worse
and he has to spend the night on an uncomfortable camp bed. It is a
destructive and tortuous experience. He realises that, when he returns to
Angela, his behaviour will have made her weekend a bleak one. But
thinking solely of his own immediate comfort, he decides that for him her
feminine warmth and sympathy are now the most desirable things on
earth. Will he soon set out on yet another doomed adventure with a man?
That is the question that haunts the reader when the story ends.

Many of Olivia's closest male friends were homosexuals and the subject
always interested her. Because of Reggie, she had become accustomed to
entertaining actors and had noticed how uncertain many of them seemed
to be about their sexuality. It was a subject to which she was to return in
her second Trilogy, with the character Aidan Sheridan – a gay actor who
is just beginning to make his name in the West End when the Second
World War breaks out. Often in the company of actors in uniform in the
Middle East, or later at her homes in St John's Wood, she could be
observed watching them and saying afterwards to close friends, 'I wonder
which way that one will finally go?' She observed actresses in the same way.
From Reggie she was to learn that his close friend Nicolette Bernard
alternated between her own sex and the opposite one. Reggie had said
about her that it was 'some quirk of nature' – a phrase which Olivia
applied to Harold in 'A Romantic Hero'.

A sense of mortality hangs over several of the stories, none more so than
'The End of the Street', which Olivia began in 1953 under the title 'At the
End of the Street' and took ten years to complete. Its central characters,
the Partridges, are a married couple living in Kensington. So certain is
Marion of her husband's adoring love that she forgets, temporarily, that
she will ever have to die. He himself thinks that he has a flawless

relationship with her, which will survive the grave. But at one point the chill of reality is felt. She says to him, 'Who knows what happens when one dies?'

He assures her, 'Wherever you go, I will find you.'

She laughs at him teasingly: 'Do you think you could recognise me without my body?' Shortly after that the story closes – but her husband cannot forget her chance remark.

Olivia continued to review and to campaign for the rights of animals, turning her attention for a time to the cruelty of otter hunting. She went to Oxhead in May to observe otters. At home she rallied local friends to try to do something about the wild cats that had taken over the site beside Pond Street in Hampstead, where the new local hospital, the Royal Free, was to be built. But her plans were not practical. Jerry told her that wild cats would tear to pieces the hands of her friends if they tried to rescue them.

'They'll be wearing tough gloves,' she protested.

'Then in that case, they'll tear their faces,' he warned her.

Olivia continued to buy and sell antiques, in a small way and in a typically unconventional and devious manner. On her expeditions she would call herself Mrs Smith and wear a dull, drab mackintosh; she would spin a story that she was looking for a wedding present. Having beaten down the price of some object, she would buy it and then at once offer it to some dealer that she knew – such as Mr Warden Phillips in Cowes – or perhaps even hawk it round Bond Street. Sometimes, if she was selling something, a gallery owner would ask, 'Do you know, madam, if this is an original?'

Her inevitable reply was, 'The family always thought it was.'

Often she would send Reggie ahead of her to test the ground. Whatever the price, she had trained him to protest, 'A bit steep, I'm afraid.' In Fowey, in the 1960s, she bought a beautiful model schooner in a glass case. The shop owner had asked Reggie £7. Ten minutes later she went in and got it for £5. At a church auction for charity in Hampstead, she once bought a David Hockney drawing at a knock-down price, having first instructed those round her to take no part in the bidding. A decorative looking-glass hung in her sitting room, the gilt of which had been chipped in the van that brought it from Kilburn. Noticing this at the front door, she insisted on having the price reduced. The next day she herself restored it. She had lost none of her skills at applying gold leaf, learnt in her early days at the Peter Jones studios.

Towards the end of the year Olivia planned to reread Angus Wilson – but in the end left it until 1968. She was not one of his favourites. When he mysteriously withdrew from interviewing her about the Trilogy on television, she suspected that the cause was that her development as a writer had disappointed him. He did, though, dine out on her 'odd' behaviour. He remembered the savage glee with which she had turned up at a party and told him that his publishers Secker & Warburg were on the rocks. 'Bankrupt' and 'ruined' were the words she had used. He later learnt with relief that there was absolutely no truth in this story, as in so many others of hers.

Olivia tended to be ungenerous to other writers, however helpful and kind they had been to her. So it was with the Snows. Privately she would often be derisive about their work, describing it as emanating from 'The Snow Factory' and then adding, 'Eventually it will all melt away.' She used to warn young writers that the Snows were a powerful literary team, like the Sitwells and the Longfords. 'You don't want to cross them,' she would say. 'They've got publicity going on all levels. Of course, publicity can't do you any good once you're dead – talent has to stand on its own then.'

There was, however, one woman writer about whose place in English literature Olivia had not the slightest doubt and about whose work she had nothing but praise. This was Ivy Compton-Burnett. In 1967, when Ivy was awarded a DBE at the age of eighty-three, Olivia sent a postcard to June: 'I was so glad she got recognition at last – but how slow! Dame Vanessa Redgrave is thirty-one. What a comment on the attitude to literature in this country.'

Olivia had first seen Ivy at a party given by Rose Macaulay, in the basement of a Soho restaurant, before the war. 'I was very young, very nervous and unimportant,' she subsequently told Elizabeth Sprigge. Ivy's friend Margaret Jourdain was with her and Olivia's immediate impression was of the close self-sufficiency of the two ladies.

A few months after Margaret Jourdain's death, in April 1945, Kay Dick introduced Olivia to Ivy. Olivia was apprehensive about the meeting, but Kay, who had a great talent with the shy and the young, assured her that all would be well. That first tea party at Ivy's flat in Braemar Mansions, Olivia used to say, was the most memorable of her life. It sealed a friendship in which there was never a hint of envy or malice, as there had been with Olivia's friendship with Stevie Smith.

It was at luncheon with Ivy that Olivia and Reggie first met Francis King in the Fifties. Robert Liddell had written from Greece to both Ivy and the Smiths to say that King, then, like himself, working in Greece for the British Council, was soon to be on leave in London. Ivy then summoned Francis to luncheon. As was usual on such occasions, there was a joint. For people of Ivy's generation and class, joints were carved only by men or by servants. She therefore asked Reggie to undertake this task. Maladroit as he was, he made a fearful mess of it. Ivy surveyed the chunks of meat, sighed, pursed her lips and said, 'Oh, I do wish I'd asked Mr King to carve.'

Francis King had soon become one of Olivia's closest friends and a confidant. With Reggie he maintained a bonhomous friendship; but since he hated the noisy camaraderie of pubs and usually refused Reggie's invitations to meet him in them, the two men were never close.

Olivia enjoyed giving small luncheon parties at her house in St John's Wood and Ivy was soon on her list of guests. Reggie was seldom present because of his job at the BBC. In any case, he preferred the company of actors and producers to writers and publishers. Jerry, however, usually managed to slip away from his nearby surgery in Chalk Farm and join Olivia's guests for an hour or so.

When Ivy came to lunch, it was a red-letter day for Olivia. Only once did such a party prove a disaster – and that was when Elias Canetti, the future Nobel Prize winner, was invited. This could perhaps be compared with a scene of nearly half a century earlier, in 1921, when Rainer Maria Rilke and Katherine Mansfield found themselves staying at the same hotel in the Swiss Alps and, though each was quite aware of the other's identity, were totally unable to exchange more than conventional greetings when they met in the dining room. It was at Canetti's prompting that Olivia arranged the meeting with Miss Compton-Burnett, as he always referred to her – an author for whom, he said, he had the highest regard and for whom he had already prepared a hundred questions. Yet when he found himself sitting next to her, he was virtually tongue-tied. As he floundered about trying to make conversation, he could not fail to notice how her eager and expectant look turned into one of contempt. On 25 February 1989 Canetti, recalling this dismal occasion, wrote to Neville Braybrooke, 'I feel the shame of our meeting to this day.'

J. R. Ackerley, when he was the literary editor of the *Listener*, used to describe E. M. Forster as 'the supreme reviewer'. Once, when he told this to Olivia at a party, she countered, 'Ivy Compton-Burnett remains for me the supreme novelist.' At this same party she was amazed to learn that Jocelyn Brooke, whom she greatly admired as a *petit maître*, had never read any of Ivy's novels. Later, he was to write to Olivia in a letter, 'I C-B is one of my blind spots. I can see she's very good, and the stylised dialogue is great fun for a few pages, but then I get bored . . . Ditto for Henry James.' Olivia herself had experienced difficulty in reading Henry James when she was living at home in Portsmouth. In fact, she did not really become a reader of his work until after the war – and that was largely due to Reggie's encouragement. A story that Reggie enjoyed repeating to actors, and that Olivia was to use in talks and lectures on the Novel, was of how the Master, having been taken to the music hall in Windsor, had afterwards been asked what he thought of the chorus girls. There followed a long pause and at last he said, 'One of the poor wantons was not wholly lacking in a certain cadaverous charm.'

After the war Olivia paid high prices in Charing Cross Road for a number of Henry James first editions, which were ex-library copies and in rather a shabby state. Later she was to get a shock when Dwye Evans, now at Macmillan, told her that the firm still had in stock many Henry James first editions as late as 1947. Ivy once said to Olivia, 'I respect Henry James, but sometimes I do wish he would get a move on.'

In 1962 Olivia dedicated the second volume of her Balkan Trilogy, *The Spoilt City*, to Ivy Compton-Burnett. Ivy certainly enjoyed Olivia's company and valued their friendship. But she was cautious about praising her work. Ivy did not care for 'abroad' and that there was so much 'abroad' in Olivia's novels.

When Ivy died in the summer of 1969, among her bequests were seven antique mirrors, some of which had originally belonged to Margaret Jourdain. Neither of the two ladies cared to use the word looking-glass and Ivy considered that Nancy Mitford's book on U and non-U language contained a good deal of nonsense. 'Mirror', she would say, 'was good enough for Shakespeare.' Ivy left these mirrors to seven of her friends: Lettice Cooper, Kay Dick, Robert Liddell, Kathleen Farrell, Francis King, Julian Mitchell and Olivia herself.

Olivia considered her mirror the least attractive of them all and slyly suggested to Francis King that perhaps his mirror, a Regency one, and hers had accidentally got transposed. However, when the interior decorator Herman Schrijver told her 'Yours may look plain, but it's a Jacobean mirror, and probably the most valuable of the lot, certainly more valuable than Francis's', she at once forgot about the possible transposition.

On 30 August that year *The Times* included in its diary a piece about the mirrors, in which it was suggested that the bequests 'might hold a hidden symbolism'. Kay Dick had remarked to the diary reporter, 'Ivy had a back-handed sense of humour.' Olivia sent several cuttings of this paragraph to friends: on each she put a question mark next to the phrase 'hidden symbolism'.

When she discussed the matter with Reggie, he expressed the opinion that the mirror left to Olivia might be interpreted as an exhortation to plain thinking and high living. Olivia was not appeased: 'Ivy can't have thought me extravagant. I was always extremely careful to provide nourishing and simple fare for her – nothing fancy or French.'

Chapter 29

The Generation Gap

The Play Room was Olivia Manning's ninth and shortest novel (183 pages). She was anxious to break new ground after the Balkan Trilogy and write a book about the present – particularly teenagers in 1967 and 1968. Determined to find out how teenagers behaved, she thought that a Palais de Danse might be a starting point. She had her sights on the Palais de Danse at Hammersmith, and the Slatterys and Braybrookes eventually agreed to accompany her there. Dates were fixed – and then cancelled. Olivia decided to use other sources and began making enquiries among those of her friends who had teenage daughters.

The central character in *The Play Room* is Laura Fletcher, a fifteen-year-old schoolgirl, who dreams of becoming a famous dramatist, with the collaboration of her younger brother Tom. In their back garden in North Camperlea, a rather seedy area of Portsmouth, she performs her own plays for the benefit of her father, a retired naval officer, who, 'solitary as Ludwig II in his private theatre', generally drops off after the first ten minutes.

At Buckland House School, where Laura is a day girl, she longs to be popular. Particularly, she longs to be the Best Friend of Vicky Logan, who is beautiful, rich and kind-hearted in an indolent way. Once, when Laura has been reduced to tears by the class bully, Vicky lends her a handkerchief. Afterwards, with an eye for the theatrical, Laura draws a picture of Vicky with a halo underneath – 'when all people rejected me, Victoria Logan lent me a handkerchief.'

After reading a history of English Literature, Laura claims to be descended from the Fletcher of Beaumont and Fletcher. She is naïve enough to think that this will make her more sought after by the other girls. Laura is painfully self-conscious about her lack of good looks: she is

Olivia's glamorous brother, Oliver, to whom she was devoted. He died in 1941, when his plane was lost in the sea.

Reggie broadcasting from Jerusalem during the war.

Jerusalem, 1943: Olivia at the YMCA with Reggie (right), the poet John Waller and the architect Paul Hyslop.

The writer Robert Liddell (third from left) and Harold and Epi Edwards, whom Olivia first knew in Greece. Second from the right is Francis King, later to become her close friend.

After the war: Olivia in 1948 at a party given by her publishers, Heinemann.

Olivia wearing a treasured brooch given to her by Reggie. She lost it somewhere on the Dingle peninsula, when she was researching her travel book about Ireland, *The Dreaming Shore*.

Olivia in her Baker Street flat. Conscious of her receding chin, she would often tilt up her head when posing for a photograph.

Olivia with her close friend, the author Kay Dick, whose interviews with writers remain an important source of information.

FACING PAGE:
(*Above left*) At the publication party for *The Great Fortune*, 1960; Olivia, and (*above right*) Ivy Compton-Burnett, the only woman writer whom Olivia admired without reservations. (*Below*) Christmas 1968: Jerry Slattery holding forth to Olivia and June and Neville Braybrooke. A well-liked and respected GP, Jerry was Olivia's lover for many years.

Olivia and Reggie – their marriage endured because it was founded on mutual respect.

small and skinny, and her nose is too long and her chin too short. When Laura explodes to one of the mistresses, she says, 'Oh, Miss Lamb, I'm so ugly . . .' She hopes, naturally, to be reassured that this is not so. But Miss Lamb tells her crisply that beauty is not everything – and Laura feels even more of a freak.

She is a clever girl – clever and very literary. One morning when she turns up at school with a copy of the *Times Literary Supplement* tucked under her arm, she is jumped on by a girl in her form: 'Men don't like girls who read papers like that.' It was Olivia's mother who had first warned her daughter of the dire consequences of being seen reading the *TLS*.

When *The Play Room* was published in spring 1960, Olivia Manning told Auriol Stevens, who had come to interview her for the *Observer*, that in it she had for the first time examined at length the relationship between herself and her brother when they were children. In the novel Laura says to Tom, 'I tried to murder you once.' He is good-natured and disbelieving – but nonetheless curious. Laura then proceeds to tell the story of how, when he was a baby, she had planted a thermos on the stairs so as to trip her mother as she came down carrying him in her arms. This was, of course, precisely what Olivia herself, aged six, had attempted to do.

To Olivia and her brother the Isle of Wight always represented another world – 'a paradise'. This is what Part 1 of the novel explains. When they were children they would be taken there on day trips on the paddle steamers that plied back and forth across the Solent. Money was tight at home and raising the fare was a strain. Disembarking at Ryde, they would walk along the coast to Seaview, then take a bus to Bembridge and have a picnic on the beach. Often their father accompanied them, sometimes their mother, but not both parents together. There was never enough time to explore the interior of the island or the West Wight. The famous coloured sands at Alum Bay had to be taken on trust. Part 1 is entitled 'The Island' and is largely given over to describing it.

Laura, in an attempt to assert her independence, sets up a week's holiday. Without telling her parents, she has followed up an invitation to go to stay with Mrs Button, a cleaner who once worked for them but has now retired to the Isle of Wight. Mrs Button has kept up with the Fletcher family, each year writing in her Christmas card:

> Best of cheer from Mrs B.
> Won't you come and stay with me?

When Laura's mother finds out what her daughter has been up to behind her back, she is furious: 'You are as deceitful as your father.' In the end she only agrees to Laura going if her brother goes as well. She smoothes the children's path by sending two five-pound notes to Mrs Button.

It is almost dark when Laura and Tom arrive at Mrs Button's cottage. She is all dressed up to go out and greets them rather casually; then she plonks down before them a plate of ham and tomatoes, and pushes off to meet 'a friend'. Laura is dazzled by the glamour of the spare bedroom, with its pink plastic shelves over the handbasin and its neon-lit mirror. Tom is quite happy to double up on the sofa in the living room.

The next morning Mrs Button makes it clear that she does not expect them home until the evening. They are entirely free to go wherever they will. On the last day of the holiday they are cut off by the incoming tide and so have to scramble up the steep and crumbling cliff-face. Unexpectedly, they arrive on the edge of a private garden that surrounds a large house. A peculiarly dressed woman sees them from the french windows and beckons. 'Come a little closer,' she calls. 'I won't hurt you.'

She is certainly weird, but shows a great interest in the children and offers to show them her play room. It is in an outbuilding in the garden, with a heavy padlock on the door. At the door Tom, anticipating model cars and trains, grows excited. But when the door is opened and he peers into the room in the fading afternoon light, he is so disturbed that he instinctively wants to run away. Laura is braver and more cautious. She too peers into the room, trying to pick out what is happening among the group of huge dolls with no clothes on. Mrs Toplady watches the children carefully for their reactions and offers to wind up the dolls to make them move. In a panic, Tom begins to yell and throw himself about, for which he receives a slap on the head from Mrs Toplady. He runs screaming down the drive with Laura on his heels. She says, 'I don't think she was a lady. I think she was a man.'

Part 2 of the novel is entitled 'The Play Room'. Mrs Toplady's life-sized naked dolls, both male and female, have left a mark on Laura, and she comes to see her school friend Vicky, on whom she has a growing crush, becoming 'a doll' in the hands of a local factory boy, Clarrie Piper. But her experience at Mrs Toplady's house has given her a chance to make herself interesting both to Vicky and to Vicky's Best Friend, Gilda – a half-Maltese girl. Clarrie Piper has little in his mind except thoughts of violence and sex. Those who watch him twisting and jiving become mesmerised. Only Laura understands the destructive force within him – but she recognises it too late. He is a psychopath, who has smashed up a Honda and has a history behind him of wrecked cars. When Vicky is dancing with Clarrie, it seems to Laura that the dead are dancing with the dead.

At home Vicky nearly always gets her own way with her fond, foolish mother, even to the point of riding the BSA motorcycle on which her brother had been killed some years past. She is now sixteen. Her father is ineffective, though not beyond making the occasional lecherous swoop on young girls. Laura's father is equally ineffective. It is her mother who, holding the reins, insists, not always with success, that on dance nights she should be home by midnight at the latest. Before the summer term ends, Gilda has bedded Vicky. It is only her absence in Valletta with her parents during the long summer holiday that makes it possible for Laura to step in briefly and by proxy to become Vicky's new Best Friend.

The novel, a not always successful morality about sex and adolescence, is set in the late Swinging Sixties, with period words and phrases sometimes skilfully and sometimes clumsily woven into the teenage dialogue – phrases such as 'doing a ton' and 'she's a real tomato'. Only once is a four-letter word used – and then by Clarrie in reference to the local factory's 'fucking foreman'.

Although *The Play Room* did not attract either as many reviews as the Balkan Trilogy, or such extensive ones, the general tone was approving and encouraging.

Francis King placed Olivia's new novel top of his column in the *Sunday Telegraph*. In the same week Norman Mailer's novel *Why Are We in Vietnam?* appeared. Anthony Curtis, the literary editor, eager to find out which would be first, and hopefully anticipating that it must be Mailer, rang King: 'I expect you will lead with the Mailer. It's a good book.'

'Yes,' replied King, 'it's a good book, but Olivia Manning's is better.' Subsequently, he felt guilty at having told a lie.

Nor did Olivia reward his loyalty to her. She was disappointed because she had hoped for 'a solo'. She wrote to Francis, 'The *Sunday Telegraph* devoted practically a page to Iris Murdoch's last.' Later she said to him, 'I have to be grateful for small mercies.'

'Don't worry! Your day will come,' he replied.

'I suppose you mean when I'm dead?' He left the question unanswered. He – and others close to her – had been through all this many times before.

In July the novel was published in the States, retitled *The Camperlea Girls*. The publishers asked Olivia Manning to provide a word of explanation for the American public. This is what she wrote:

> There is a feeling these days that the young are not simply undeveloped adults, but they are a new kind of creature. Older people are under the impression that the young have been born knowing something the rest of us do not know.
>
> *The Camperlea Girls* is a study of what we may call the New Young, but it is also a study of middle age. The middle-aged have power and money and yet they cannot deal with their own children. They are self-defeated because they are afraid. They are afraid of being old. They cannot belong to the new autonomous world of the young and they suffer from a sense of exclusion. They have no confidence in the status of middle age and the wisdom that should go with it. Because they cannot exert, they are despised. The middle-aged make the mistake of thinking the young will thank them for their over permissive society. The young, in fact, want something against which they can revolt. They need a fixed morality behind them to which they can refer. Without this morality, they are revolting in a vacuum, and they are bewildered.
>
> If the aged cannot exert authority, they have no function. Their job is to govern, they are merely trotting downhill to the grave. The young whatever they think of themselves, are merely undeveloped adults. They are not born knowing something the rest of us do not know. They are innocent, inexperienced and vulnerable. If the middle-aged fail, as they do in *The Camperlea Girls*, the young are the ones that suffer.

Olivia's point about a fixed morality should be noted, because for her morality meant an acceptance of original sin. Of all religious concepts, she thought it best explained a world of suffering, violence and sex. She also thought that original sin explained why there could be happy, but not perfect, marriages. The phrase about 'marriages being made in heaven' she dismissed as 'eye-wash'.

The Play Room is not one of Olivia Manning's best novels, since it ends too abruptly and her knowledge and understanding of a world of troubled adolescents is always erratic. But the note that she provided for the American publishers is as clear a statement as any that she ever wrote concerning her feelings about youth and the generation gap.

Chapter 30

Pursuing the Media

When Olivia first held a finished copy of *The Play Room* in her hands, she turned to Reggie and said that she had hopes that one day it would make a film, a play and a television serial. She was to be wrong on all counts. In the previous year, in August 1968, Heinemann had sent out proof copies, including one marked 'personal' to Francis King's brother-in-law, John Rosenberg, at Romulus Films. Olivia was to have many literary agents, but to David Machin, who was then her agent at A. P. Watt, Rosenberg confided that he had found the novel different from anything else of hers which he had read – and added, 'It gets the atmosphere of youth most touchingly.' All the same he had doubts about it making a successful film, for the story was 'very slight'.

In the following year the same agent sent a copy of the novel to the theatrical impresario Hugh Beaumont at H. M. Tennent to see if it might be considered as material for the stage. 'Binkie' Beaumont's first reactions were favourable but cautious. 'It might be possible to turn the novel into a compact stage play,' he said. But after several discussions with close advisers, he decided it was too difficult to convert from one medium to another. There was, above all, the problem of the scenes on the motorbike.

Yet Olivia remained hopeful that a film would be made. At one point John Brabourne sent in a script to her – but she and Reggie thought that it 'never quite took off'. 'Have a go yourself,' Reggie now urged.

For some time she wavered, but when Ken Annakin bought a six-month option for £500 she immediately began work. He was keen that authors of novels should write their own scripts. Annakin, in his fifties, had scored a considerable success with his film *Those Magnificent Men in their Flying Machines*. Reggie also discovered that he had been responsible for launching Petula Clark, Diana Dors and Julie Christie in films. Early in 1970 news broke that he was holding casting sessions for *The Play Room* and the *Sun* ran a feature about the project on Friday, 13 February 1970. Only Reggie noticed the ominous date.

Olivia had worked hard on the script, revising it several times. On its first page she suggested that the title of the film should be 'superimposed over a dream-like picture of the Isle of Wight coast somewhere near Alum Bay and Totland Bay'. The script was more explicit than the novel. In the novel, when Laura calls early one afternoon at Vicky's home, she hears through a door Vicky's abandoned cries of passion as she lies in bed with Gilda. In the script the moans are not merely heard but are also followed by a scene of Gilda coming to the door in a bathrobe.

This version, of which over two-thirds was shot, ran out of money before it was completed. 'It still had ten minutes to go,' Olivia would say sadly. Capri had been used for the background. Later another island, Malta, was chosen and a new script called for. To prepare this second script Olivia went to Valletta for a week's recce in March 1970 and returned with a tape in which she recorded her feelings about the island. At Sliema she saw discotheques that she thought might be used, but should be renamed. For one she came up with the name of 'Siege'. For another she toyed with the name 'Knights'.

This script differed markedly – and sometimes ludicrously – from her first. On the opening page Olivia suggested that the title of the film should be 'imposed on a figure dressed like a Pantomime Dame, whom we will come to know later as Mrs Toplady'. Mrs Toplady beckons in the opening sequence and 'we float down some steps . . . through an iron door and suddenly find ourselves surrounded by life-sized dolls, kinkily clothed and posed in the attitude of Erotica 70'. Vicky Logan is transformed into a Swedish girl – Vicky Lindfelt – and now possesses a Honda, not a BSA, motorcycle. Buckland House School at Portsmouth becomes a convent school at Medina with an international set of girls – 'many dark and clearly Maltese, a few with Nordic features, one a Persian, two Chinese, another black, several Americans and three British types of the hockey-stick variety'. In the privacy of her home Laura dances topless in her bedroom and sings, 'I'm the cleverest, sexiest doll that ever hit Blighty, Tahiti and Afrodite [*sic*].' Her mother comes in, picks up the discarded pyjama top and throws it at her.

In March 1971 Olivia wrote to Anthony Powell,

Yes, the film is being made after a long delay. It bears little

resemblance to my book as it has become a very sexy story
about girls in Malta . . . All that remains is the title and MGM
want that changed as they bought the film rights for a play
called 'The Play Room', that is never likely to be made into a
film. I don't know what will happen.

Nothing much happened. Some preliminary discussions had taken place,
some names of possible American actresses had been mentioned, and there
had been inserted into the script a scene in which Laura and her brother
are shown arriving at Mrs Toplady's in a kayak.

'Everything fizzled out,' Olivia later told friends. To June she wrote,
'Nothing came of the film. I wasted a lot of time and that is something
which you cannot afford to do when you are sixty . . . [She was in fact
sixty-two.] My true calling is that of a novelist and I must return to it.
Goodbye to the media.'

Chapter 31

England at the Equator

Olivia Manning's tenth novel was to prove her most ambitious, her most imaginative and the most unexpected. It took three years to complete – longer than any other single novel of hers.

The Rain Forest is set on an imaginary island called Al-Bustan, in the Indian Ocean. The year, 1953, is that in which Queen Elizabeth II was crowned at Westminster Abbey on 2 June. The central characters, Hugh and Kristy Foster, have reached the mid-seasonal age of thirty-five and been married for a decade. Theirs is a choppy, uneven relationship. At times he can be bloody-minded, especially when she discovers that she is pregnant. She raps him on the knuckles: 'Anyone might think you'd nothing to do with this. Good God, you've always had my cunt when you wanted it.'

Kristy has published a series of successful novels, under the name of Christine Middleton, in which she has recorded the often uncertain progress of her marriage. Her work, as with Olivia, is of paramount importance to her and she refuses to be distracted from it. On one occasion Hugh asks her if she would care to meet Mr Murodi, the Minister of Culture on the island:

'Not at the moment.'
    'If you don't want to see people when they are there, you'll
find when you want to see them that they are not there.'
    'Yes, that's the artist's dilemma.'

This dilemma has been with her since she married – in London as well as on the equator, where her husband now has a new job bringing out a news-sheet. 'I'm to monitor the Indian satellite,' he explains to a doctor whom he meets on the five-hour boat crossing from Africa.

Hugh Foster himself has published a novel, then turned to adapting other people's fiction into film scripts. In the early 1950s, when the bottom fell out of the English film industry, he dropped behind on his tax returns and so became desperate for money. Providentially, a friend at the Foreign Office then came up with the suggestion that he might apply for the job on Al-Bustan. Soon after his arrival there he meets Mr Murodi, to whom he complains about the way in which he was forced to change storylines to suit the whims of producers. When Olivia wrote these passages she may have had in mind her own experiences with MGM and *The Play Room*. Hugh's comment to Murodi, 'You see, I had no joy in my work,' was something Olivia had felt in the late 1960s.

The creation of the island of Al-Bustan is undeniably a literary feat of the first order. Details of its flora, fauna, geography, history and wildlife are woven into the text with extreme skill. Al-Bustan is some sixty miles from south to north. North is where the rainforest is; at the centre is the walled city of Medina; below the city are the grasslands and plantations; and in the area known as the Dobo, close to the harbour, live the mainly Indian community and its traders. The population is made up chiefly of Arabs, Africans and Indians, and the British raj.

The Daisy Pension is described by its owner, Mrs Gunner, as 'a little bit of England on the equator'. She is a silly old soul, who in her youth did a song and dance act with her sister on the pier at Southsea. Now she is eighty-three. Her son Ambrose is an intellectual whale washed up on a philistine shore. The *pension*, which flies the Union Jack above its turreted front, is a guest house for colonial employees – all of them elderly, except for the Fosters, and all anxiously waiting for the island to be granted self-rule.

The novel has symbolic intentions – but none of these is allowed to slow down its narrative pace. When Hugh sees a black mark on the cornice of the bedroom ceiling, it flies away as soon as the door is opened wide. It is a bat. Light banishes darkness would seem the simple message. But if Al-Bustan is a Garden of Eden, it is an Eden in which there are snakes of both a jungle and a human variety. There are also vultures of both kinds. At Gurgur's sleazy brothel, where the girls wear narrow diamante strips that only half hide their pubic hair, Kristy learns that 'gurgur' means 'vulture'. Everyone is out to exploit the island in some way or other. Speculators and businessmen, with no thought for ecology, wait for the British to release their hold on Al-Bustan. Profit is the only concern.

Reggie used to say, 'My Olivia often needs years, decades, to get everything into perspective. She never forgets a detail. Even twenty years after we were in Cairo, she could remember every sepia photograph hanging on the walls of the first *pension* in which we stayed.'

This was part of her talent as a novelist. But in presenting Al-Bustan she was working from her imagination, not using conscious memory. 'I am working in a new way,' she told Neville. 'More and more my subconscious is taking over.' Thus it was that a dream, not a memory or even something read, inspired her to write of the twin peaks on Al-Bustan, called 'The Guardians' by the Africans and 'The Hills that Disappear' by the Arabs. 'The names came to me out of nowhere,' she confessed.

It is against this background, filled with superstition and religious feeling, that the Fosters spend the eleventh year of their marriage. They have some affinities with the Pringles in the Balkan Trilogy. When they disembark at Al-Bustan the taxi which they hire takes them on a tour all over the island before it drops them off at the Daisy. At one moment, as it careers drunkenly along a road, swinging from side to side, the headlights suddenly reveal a deep chasm on the left:

> Hugh, glancing to see if Kristy was aware of their danger, saw she had closed her eyes. He thought she was asleep and he was alone. But he was not alone and Kristy was not asleep. When he glanced again at her, she had opened her eyes and turned towards him as he turned towards her. Realising she shared his fear, he caught her hand and held to it, and so they sat: feeling united and thankful, in this threatening situation, that each had the other.

The passage is a reminder of the first *trasura* ride that the Pringles take in Bucharest on their arrival there in September 1939:

> The Pringles sitting hand-in-hand in the old four-wheeler that smelt of horse, were more aware of each other than anything else. Here they were, a long way from home, alone together, in a warring world.

Despite the enforcement of British law and order, everything in Al-Bustan is on the verge of disintegration. One evening a group of Arab conspirators rush in and bomb the government offices. When this happens, Kristy is in hospital recuperating from a disaster similar to that suffered by Olivia in Jerusalem in 1943. The child in her womb has died in the seventh month.

When the foetus is painfully removed, Hugh has spent much of that day with Kristy. Then, at sunset, he sets out for the government offices. On the way he notices that there are no lights burning in any of the five storeys of the building. Suddenly, just before the bomb goes off, he feels as if someone had mysteriously seized his wrist. Then the blast propels him up the road towards the residency and hurls him against its wall. Unwilling to move, he finds himself sinking into the earth beneath him. Simultaneously, in the hospital, Kristy hears the explosion.

In Part 3 of the novel another English resident, Simon Hobhouse, finds Hugh lying in the road and heaves him across to his Land-Rover. There could be no better time to take him to the rainforest, Hobhouse decides. No one will be bothering about permits. Hobhouse is a doctor, a little older than Hugh, with a keen interest in science and botany. 'I am making a study of Pteridophyta,' he has previously told Hugh on running into him at the government offices, at which he has been applying for a permit to visit the rainforest. He spells out the word but does not explain that it means the study of ferns. Hugh has been constantly searching for a father figure, or hero, to replace his own father. Kristy thinks that in Simon he has found such 'an ideal friend. A hero.' Others in Al-Bustan see Simon Hobhouse in a different light – as a fanatic who believes that the world is overpopulated and that it is growing more polluted every day – a view which Kristy shares.

Simon in his Land-Rover, with Hugh at the back with a badly bruised forehead, is flagged down by Culbertson, Chief of Police. He barks out, 'Our chaps are under the rubble . . . You're a doctor . . . We'll need all the help we can get.' Simon's reaction – surprising and reprehensible in such an emergency – is merely to press his foot on the accelerator and speed away. No less surprising and reprehensible is Hugh's acquiescence in abandoning Kristy in hospital.

On his previous excursions to the forest Simon brought tents and coffee – and fed himself on manioc: 'I lived as the blacks did on cassava and plantain.' As the vehicle proceeds into the forest, ants, bees, mosquitoes and tiny flies seem everywhere. The darkness is 'like an eternity, like space . . . without a goal'. It was here that African slaves who escaped from their

Arab owners were accustomed to take refuge and to make their last stand – not against those owners, who feared to follow them into the forest, but against death. Deep under the overhanging trees, they cleared away the undergrowth and built themselves conical huts – ten to twenty feet above the ground. Access was by ladders which, once climbed, they dragged up behind them like drawbridges. For two reasons only did they venture out – the search for food and worship. As protection, they erected crude stone images with monstrous, staring eyes. In each hut, just about five feet wide, there was little space for movement. Whole families clung there until they became patterns of crumbling bones.

Hugh's reaction is one of horror: 'I hate this place.' Simon speaks of the village, recently travelled through, in which ex-slaves tried to re-create their former life in Africa, even to the point of communicating by drum with each other. 'Think what it proves,' says Simon. 'Fear can confine you to a place so small you might as well be in a grave.'

The last sentences of the book describe Hugh taking the key of the Land-Rover out of Simon's stiff hand. Simon has missed his footing climbing out of a hut and Hugh has dragged him to a small clearing where, using Simon's rucksack as a pillow, he has laid the head of his friend, while he goes to forage for food. The fall proves fatal. When Hugh returns, Simon's last words are, 'You'll have to find your own way back.' So Hugh lies protectively close to him, falls asleep and when he wakes finds Simon has already died. As he prepares to leave he notices that

> the remarkable blue of Simon's eyes glinted between the half-closed eye-lids. Already the ants were moving through the black-beard and into the delicate nostrils and over the fine pale lips. Hugh dropped the last branch to hide the spectacle of this spoliation. Then, putting the key into his pocket, he set out to find his own way back.

The Rain Forest remains among Olivia Manning's least-known novels. It is not mentioned in the entries about her in the *Oxford Companion to English Literature* (1985), *Chambers Biographical Dictionary* (1992) or *The Reader's Companion to the Twentieth-Century Novel* (1994). At the time she published it she had hopes that it might win the Booker Prize, or at least be shortlisted. Neither happened.

Simon Hobhouse insists that a deadly virus is about to sweep the world.

When *The Rain Forest* came out in 1974, AIDS was unknown and was not to become generally known until the 1980s, by which time Olivia had died. Olivia Manning was a novelist who believed in pursuing 'hunches'. During a lecture in the 1970s she said, '"Hunches" play an important part in a literary career. Always follow them is my advice. I do!'

A virus as deadly as AIDS suits Simon Hobhouse's vision, which is full of destructive elements. He expresses no sympathy when he learns that Kristy has lost her baby. His view of history is one of disasters and plagues. Al-Bustan he sees as an island once populated with dodos, followed by pirate invasions and ending with an Arab takeover. Finally there is a century and more of British rule. He believes the British period to be the best.

This was also Olivia's view and that of her father. Nonetheless she believed with E. M. Forster that history is a 'series of muddles', in which political order constantly gives way to political disorder. For her, only works of art endured, surviving, by virtue of the eternal values that they represented, in 'a permanently disarranged planet'. That last phrase comes from Forster and tied up with her acceptance of a world marked by original sin. Any new order imposed on Al-Bustan would eventually lead to disorder, for that was the pattern of history.

Chapter 32

Reviewing the Situation

'I feel, having given my life to writing, that I do not exist . . .' What a sense of desolation is conjured up in those few words, written by Olivia Manning in a letter in September 1973. The reason was that she had been left out of Martin Seymour-Smith's *Guide to Modern World Literature*, published earlier in the year. Nor, three years later, was the same critic to include her in his *Who's Who in Twentieth-Century Literature*, despite the fact that in 1974 he had placed her novel *The Rain Forest* top of his fiction column in the *Financial Times* and had declared it hard to praise temperately. What Olivia found particularly galling about his 'guides' was that, whereas there had been entries for Doris Lessing, Iris Murdoch, Muriel Spark and her friend Francis King, there had been none for her. She even told King indignantly, 'I can't think why Martin has included you in his *Guide* and not included me.'

In one of her many moans to Anthony Powell she told him that it must be difficult for someone of his 'upbringing, education and great success' to realise how neglected she felt: 'I have never received the sort of encouragement given to writers like Iris Murdoch, Muriel Spark and Edna O'Brien.'

Olivia did not have a contented nature. When *The Rain Forest* came out in 1974, she grumbled a great deal about the fact that there were admirers of her work who did not know she had produced another novel. For this she blamed Heinemann, as so often in the past. Olivia's grudge against Heinemann grew during the twenty-six years that she was with them: 'They are mean, damned mean and getting meaner.' She suggested to Alison Lurie, whose publishers they also were, that Heinemann forwarded letters to America by surface mail. This was absolute fantasy; but where Heinemann (or publishers in general or even literary editors) were concerned Olivia all too often indulged in fantasy.

Sometimes, however, she had hard evidence for her accusations about Heinemann's meanness. At a party given by the firm to celebrate the publication of *The Play Room* Dwye Evans, the managing director, thought that he had caught Jerry helping himself to a second glass of whisky and at once made his disapproval clear. In reality Jerry – always eager to help others – was merely fetching a drink for a friend who had just arrived. Later in the evening, at exactly eight, Evans started ostentatiously pulling back the curtains and opening the windows. He claimed that he wanted to get rid of the cigarette smoke. But Olivia was convinced that he wanted to get rid of the guests. Going up to him she asked, 'Why don't you serve coffee as Longmans do at the end of their parties?' Dwye did not react. Either he had not heard this or decided to pretend that he had not done so. Olivia steadfastly maintained that the latter was the case.

Olivia had no sympathy with meanness. She kept a strict eye on her spending, but the stubs in her chequebooks reveal that she was constantly giving donations to animal charities, even selling her oil shares in 1971 to preserve wildlife at sea. Quietly and secretly she performed many kind acts. When Francis King was involved in an expensive libel action over his book *A Domestic Animal*, she told him that he could always call on her for funds. When he did not do so she upbraided him.

Somebody in whom Olivia had detected meanness was Rose Macaulay, whose novels she categorised as being 'at the smart end of the best-seller list'. The two women had met a number of times, including once before the war, and in 1955 they had run across each other in a grocer's in Marylebone High Street. Dame Rose confided that she had visitors from abroad coming to tea that afternoon. 'What shall I offer them?' she asked. Olivia modestly suggested biscuits. 'How much are biscuits?' Dame Rose enquired of the girl behind the counter. The girl produced a packet priced at one shilling and sixpence. 'One and six!' Dame Rose trumpeted to the shop. 'I wouldn't dream of paying that. They'll have to go without.' Less than a year afterwards she died, leaving over £90,000 – a considerable sum at the time.

Olivia recalled this incident in 1964, when she came to review for the *Spectator* Rose Macaulay's *Letters to a Sister*. She headed her piece 'Oodles and Doodles'. Robert Liddell rebuked her from Greece. 'How dare you', he wrote, 'make sport of so distinguished an author!'

Olivia was furious. 'Robert has these pets,' she informed those around her. 'Who the hell does he think he is?' She admired his novels and gave them good reviews – but there were some sides to Robert that needed censuring. Without so much 'as a by your leave', she would complain, he had burned her letters and those of Francis King. Many of these had concerned Ivy Compton-Burnett, of whom she and King had faithfully sent regular accounts to Liddell, after he had settled first in Egypt, then in Greece, with the resolve never to return to England. Although Liddell had met Compton-Burnett less than a dozen times, he was to bring out a pioneering book about her in 1955. What chiefly infuriated Olivia about the burning of the letters was that he might forget the derivation of the information provided by herself and King, and use it as his own. When she told him this he wrote to assure her, with feline malice, that he perfectly remembered everything that was hers – including her reiterated complaints that she was bored at Ivy's and that going there so regularly had become 'an appalling chore'. Liddell then went on to say that he had deliberated for a long time about whether he should keep Francis King's letters or not, but had decided that they were so indiscreet that it was probably wiser and kinder to destroy them.

Olivia had begun her reviewing career in the Middle East. Back in England in 1945, she looked for a permanent literary base from which to work. Eventually, as already recorded, she was taken on by E. C. Hodgkin, who was acting literary editor of the *Spectator* while James Pope-Hennessy finished his acclaimed biography of Queen Mary. Hodgkin held Olivia in high esteem – 'a definite acquisition to the weekly'.

In 1947 he started her off on the reviewing of fiction. By 1979, not merely in the *Spectator* but also in the *Observer*, the *Sunday Times* and the *Sunday Telegraph*, she had covered a remarkable total of some 400 novels. In her final review for the *Sunday Times*, of Naomi Jacob's *Great Black Oxen*, she offered a distinction between the romantic novelist and a novelist like herself: the romantic novelist chooses subjects, whereas a novelist like herself has 'to await the impulse of significant experience'. No one need be surprised, she concluded, that 'while Miss Jacob has written forty-eight novels, Mr E. M. Forster has managed to produce no more than five'.

In 1963 Olivia returned to the *Spectator* book pages, from which she was then seldom to be absent for the rest of her life. Occasionally she could be persuaded to write for the *New Statesman* by its literary editors (Claire Tomalin and David Caute) and for the *Times Literary Supplement* (by

John Willett and John Gross). At the *Spectator* she was encouraged to branch out and to cover autobiographies, biographies and belles lettres – and now and again a batch of children's books for Christmas.

When Peter Ackroyd took over the literary editorship in the 1970s, he instructed his team that he wanted lively judgements, no matter how hostile or derisive. Olivia had no quarrel with this aim, as she demonstrated when, in 1976, Raymond Mortimer, once a star reviewer on the *Sunday Times*, brought out a ragbag of past reviews and essays. It was Olivia's view on receiving this collection that posterity would have been better served if it had never appeared. Some of his comments she claimed were suitable for Pseuds Corner – and quoted one, concerning *The Unquiet Grave* by 'Palinurus' (Cyril Connolly). Mortimer had written, 'As he tells us of his vivid lemurs, his blessed journeys to the sun and his departed loves, we bless him for the tears of desiderium set free by his cadences in our too long and resolutely arid eyes.' When Francis King suggested that Mortimer might in this passage have been parodying Connolly's own style, she vehemently retorted, 'Rubbish!' The main essay in the book – on William George Ward, a pillar of the Oxford Movement – she blasted as 'impenetrably dull'. Her review closed with the stricture, 'A critic of the works of others should . . . bring an equally critical judgement to bear on his own. It is not, after all, very much to ask.' Many of Mortimer's friends felt that she had been unnecessarily cruel to a once admired critic now in his eighties. Herman Schrijver guessed that, since Mortimer had never accorded her a solo review, she was paying off a score.

Olivia was a reviewer who never minded adding an autobiographical touch or an anecdote to enliven a page. One of her anecdotes in 1976 she had borrowed straight from Reggie, who had heard it at the BBC some years before. She introduced it into her review of Robert Speaight's biography of François Mauriac:

> Mauriac strongly disapproved of Gide's inversion and, when Gide posed as a martyr like Oscar Wilde, pointed out that the martyrdom which had brought Wilde to Reading Gaol had not kept Gide from Stockholm and the Nobel Prize. Gide whose appetite for sex was matched only by his meanness, took sly revenge. Having picked up a boy in Algiers, he rewarded him with a very small coin. When the boy protested, Gide said, 'Just think, my boy, when you grow up you

will be able to tell your children's children that you slept with the great French writer François Mauriac.'

Olivia had had doubts about including the story, but Reggie had urged her on: 'If you get away with it, it will establish a benchmark at the *Spectator* as to how far you can go.' During the writing of the Levant Trilogy she was several times to consult Reggie as to how far she could go.

Here are some comments from her review columns between 1947 and 1949. Of Richard Dimbleby's one novel she wrote in 1947, 'I enjoyed *Storm at the Hook*, which is as easy to read as it will be to forget.' In 1962 Irving Stone's blockbuster about Michelangelo, *The Agony and the Ecstasy*, sent her to the kitchen scales, where it weighed in at 'one and three-quarter pounds of small print'. A reprint in the same year of Arnold Bennett's *Imperial Palace* from 1930 led her to note that it had 'eighty-two minor characters'.

As, during the Seventies, Olivia tried belatedly to impose some order on her papers, so she came to see the ever-growing pile of reviews as a burial mound. 'Who will dig it over?' she would ask Reggie, knowing that he would volunteer readily enough but never have the time.

Chapter 33

Domestic Matters

Olivia was always shrewd about money. Like other well-known writers, she was frequently sent proofs by publishers in the hopes of a puff. To friends she would then say, 'Why should I read a book and give a quote for nothing?' In 1971, when Raleigh Trevelyan was an editorial director at Michael Joseph, she pointed out that he had paid her a smaller fee than he had paid to Francis King for reading a manuscript. He despatched an extra £2 by return of post.

Following in her mother's footsteps she believed that, once a bank made a mistake, they should never be allowed to forget it. Many of Olivia's letters from 1975 onwards reminded Barclays of this. 'It places the customer in a superior position and the bank managers loathe it,' was her view. 'People sometimes think because Reggie and I are bohemians, we know nothing about money. We were taught when we grew up to be very careful about getting the right change.' Once she submitted two insurance claims for a ceiling brought down in a flood caused by a washing machine in the flat above. She was in the process of changing firms. They each replied with offers of compensation by the same post. She rang Neville Braybrooke jubilantly: 'Does this mean I can accept both?'

'No,' he replied, 'I'm afraid it doesn't. Insurance companies are hand in glove with each other and would soon find out what you had done.'

'In that case', she said, 'I'll take the better offer.'

Olivia had instructed Heinemann early in 1974 that she did not wish them to submit *The Rain Forest* for the Booker Prize. If it was called in, that would be another matter. This then happened, at the behest, it later turned out, of Elizabeth Jane Howard. As August approached, Olivia was both hopeful and wary. Unfortunately, one of the three judges was A. S. Byatt, who had said, when discussing the book on radio in *Kaleidoscope*, that it was 'slow'. Olivia told those about her, 'I wouldn't call La Byatt exactly a sprinter.' *The Rain Forest* failed to make the shortlist.

The books shortlisted were *Ending Up* by Kingsley Amis, *The Bottle Factory Outing* by Beryl Bainbridge, *The Conservationist* by Nadime Gordimer, *Holiday* by Stanley Middleton and *In their Wisdom* by C. P. Snow. Olivia dismissed this list as a 'middling' one. She was suspicious that there were only five books, having persuaded herself that in the past the number had always been six. She suspected a plot, which had resulted in her book being dropped at the last moment. Not for the first time, she was misinformed. There was no statutory number for the shortlist and in the previous years, as Reggie pointed out to her, there had been only four choices.

It had not gone unnoticed in the press that Kingsley Amis, chosen for the shortlist, was then married to one of the judges, Elizabeth Jane Howard. There had been some sport in the broadsheets, with the *Guardian* carrying a headline that warned of 'SOMETHING AMIS.' Then, on 4 November, there appeared in *The Times* this letter from a Dr J. M. Slattery:

> Sir – I have been shocked and astounded to learn from articles in several papers that one of the judges of the Booker Award is the wife of a writer whose name appears on the shortlist for this very substantial prize.
>
> As a shareholder I have been uneasy about this prize and have wondered what good it has done. Last year it seemed there was to be an improvement in the work chosen, but looking back at the list this year, I can only feel a sense of deep despair.

Olivia always maintained – though many were sceptical – that she had not at first known of Jerry's intention to send such a letter, that she had not seen it after he had written it and that, when she asked to be shown a copy, he had told her that it was posted. She said that she feared it would link their names in the public eye and, within a fortnight, she was proved right.

The day after the letter appeared Ion Trewin, chairman of the judges, wrote to the paper to say that 'the shortlist of five novels was arrived at unanimously by the three judges'. Ten days later Elizabeth Jane Howard wrote to say that early on 'it had been noticed that out of the 51 entrants a large proportion were known to one, two or even three of the judges – in some cases all . . . Had I resigned when the shortlist was drawn up, a new third judge would have had to be found within a fortnight in which to read 51 books.'

On 9 November 'Willy Waspe' (Kenneth Hurren) closed his *Spectator* column with a sting:

> I was not surprised to see a letter in *The Times* the other day commenting on the fact that one of the Booker Prize judges is the wife of one of the novelists on the judges' shortlist. I was not surprised, either, that the letter-writer did not think it worth mentioning that he is a close friend of a lady novelist who is not on the shortlist.

Three journalists rang Heinemann to enquire who Jeremiah Slattery was: one even went so far as to check with the Booker people to see if he was a genuine shareholder and discovered that he wasn't.

From Northern Ireland, where Reggie was now teaching at the New University of Ulster, he observed these shenanigans and wrote to Olivia on 18 November:

> As for the nonsense in the *Spectator* etc., again what do you expect? . . . If people have got so low that they will do anything for another crate of whisky, you can't expect normal decent behaviour to interest them. They probably think it's old-fashioned. However I see Iris Murdoch has at last won something which shows someone is being loyal to her.

Iris Murdoch had just been awarded the Whitbread Prize for her novel *The Sacred and Profane Love Machine*.

The friendship between Iris Murdoch and Olivia Manning was not an easy one – at least on Olivia's side, though it was she who had originally suggested that they should meet. Iris was eleven years younger and her first published novel, *Under the Net*, came out in 1954 – by which time Olivia had already brought out six books, four of which were fiction. The final tally between the two writers was Iris Murdoch twenty-seven books of fiction, Olivia Manning fourteen. Iris was six times shortlisted for the

Booker Prize and in 1978 won it with *The Sea, the Sea*. Carmen Callil, the managing director of her publishers Chatto & Windus from 1983 to 1994, christened her the Queen of Chatto.

Although Olivia was charmed by Iris when they first met, she never got over a certain competitive jealousy. Also, she genuinely did not care for Iris's type of fiction – a view shared by her friend Jocelyn Brooke. 'Iris seems to be walking away with all the prizes,' was a regular moan.

Iris and Olivia had many things in common. They were both Anglo-Irish and each had spent long holidays in Ireland during her youth. Olivia's mother came from County Down and so did Iris's father. Both fathers were keen readers, who enjoyed discussing the books they read with their daughters. They were interested, too, in what their children read.

The two girls were ideal listeners – in fact, all their lives they could be observed listening attentively to everything that was said. Each was highly observant, for everything finally went into their books. In the writings of both there are references to the Easter Rising of 1916 and to the 'Troubles' that were to follow. Iris saw the IRA as dominated by a group of crazed Catholic fanatics. Olivia, taking her cue from Reggie, saw them as a few hundred psychopaths living on protection money.

Iris and Olivia both became interested in Flying Saucers. Iris never minded asking people if they believed in God. Her husband John Bayley said after her death, 'Iris was interested in religion but she had no belief.' Similarly, Olivia never minded asking people if they believed in an afterlife.

'How scared people are of facing up to the most important questions,' Olivia commented more than once. Many people, she observed, did not care for the notion of something existing beyond human understanding, since that would show that they were no longer in control of everything. When she first met Ivy Compton-Burnett, she had been instructed by a close friend of Ivy's, Madge Ashton (Garland), that if asked 'Do you believe in God?' it was customary to reply, 'No, Ivy, I do not.' Olivia thought that absurd. The idea of death bringing a total annihilation was one that she both feared and could not accept. In letters to friends she would sometimes interject, 'Pray for me.' When William K. Rose died, she wrote confidently to several friends, 'We will see him again.' She was inclined to think that animals shared in the afterlife: they had souls that survived, even if they were small ones. She was convinced, too, that animals had psychic powers – and she built up 'a restricted psychic library' where passing references could be found to all living creatures and their powers of communication. Some of the books that she had on this shelf were: C. D. Broad's *Lectures on Psychical Research*, Rosalind Haywood's *The Sixth Sense*, Andrew Mackenzie's *The Riddle of the Future*, Mathew Manning's *The Gift* and Cynthia Sandys's and Rosamond Lehmann's *The Awakening Letters*. She would recommend these books and occasionally lend them – but not for long: 'I like to have them back safe under my roof to consult.' They were all well thumbed.

Iris, she was to learn, had dipped into some of these books with curiosity. In an interview with Richard Cohen, during the 1970s, Iris had told him that she had sympathetic feelings towards Buddhism and that she thought God might be coming closer to her – although, like Olivia, she had little interest in organised religion. Both novelists believed that the hope for mankind lay with ecologists and the Green Peace Movement. On 13 January 1967, along with twenty-nine other writers, they had signed a letter to *The Times* about 'Moves to Ban Export of Animals' – a petition to Parliament in which Olivia had played an organising role. Behind the scenes she worked continuously for various animal causes and noticed with pleasure that in the animal world the instinct for survival was strong.

When Iris's *A Severed Head* came out in the summer of 1961, Olivia remarked in a letter to Julian Mitchell that 'no doubt we are in for another Iris Murdoch Benefit Week'. Yet no sooner had she posted the letter than she told Reggie she regretted it. Although she knew that she suffered from spite and should rise above it, she also knew that she all too often gave way to it. About *A Severed Head* she had written to Francis King that it 'was painfully novelettish' – and had gone on to speculate, 'Perhaps this was intended. It is said to be all so much cleverer than one supposes. Or is it? I wonder . . .' The speculation was fair comment. But to complain, as she did in this letter, about its being so rapidly in a fifth edition showed envy. The literary world is frequently a mean-spirited place – far worse, she would often say, than Reggie's world of the theatre, even though she herself regularly contributed to that mean-spiritedness.

Olivia encountered genuine problems with Iris's fiction. To several friends, in letters, she recorded how once they had fallen into a deep discussion about 'the Novel – novels which were post-literature and novels which were post-experience'. Iris had stopped her and asked what was wrong with post-literature novels. Olivia had replied, 'Surely one should go straight to life for one's material, not to other people's books.'

Iris had countered, 'I don't know I agree with you.'

This difference of opinion between Olivia and Iris resulted in a discreet parting of their ways as practising novelists, but not as friends. Olivia would confess to her circle, 'I like Iris very much as a person, but I am in an awkward position having to avoid saying anything about her fiction.'

Iris once told Brigid Brophy, 'At Oxford you learn how to hold your tongue, if not your thoughts.'

Olivia had difficulty with this. Once, in the presence of Jeremy Trafford and Francis King, she blurted out, 'Oh, Iris, I do wish I could churn out novels like you.' That night Olivia questioned Reggie: 'Do you think Iris noticed?'

He replied, 'I don't think she's the kind of woman who bears ill will. She probably thinks life's too short.'

Olivia wrote to June about Iris's novel *The Black Prince*,

> She has been lucky in her reviews this time, they all seem wildly excited by her book: she is the sort of writer one can either read or cannot read, according to whether you want her novels to be intellectual exercises or pieces of life. I am not much interested in intellectual exercises, so I find her books difficult, but her admirers think her extremely good.

In Iris Murdoch's obituary in the *Guardian* Peter Conradi, later to be her biographer, stated that she never claimed to paint from life. Olivia Manning did little else.

Olivia also thought that Iris was often lazy about her looks. In a letter to William Gerhardie she wrote,

> She takes so little trouble . . . She does sometimes get something done to her hair, but this night [in December 1973] it hung lank about her face as though cut with a hack saw. Still, she is very agreeable and everyone who meets her likes her.

Olivia was often critical of women's looks – and sometimes downright unkind. At a PEN dinner at the Café Royal in 1971 she described Rosamond Lehmann as 'looking like Lady Hamilton in decline'.

At the same dinner, when Rebecca West saw Rosamond approaching, she said *sotto voce* to Olivia, 'My God, she thinks she's Danny La Rue.'

Chapter 34

Dramas of All Kinds

At the beginning of the 1970s Olivia and Reggie were still living at 36 Abbey Gardens, an Edwardian terraced house of four storeys. But already she was beginning to feel that the stairs were a strain. By the start of the decade Reggie had decided to put in for early retirement from the BBC and had begun to set his sights on a university career. Several friends, notably Walter Allen, suggested that he should apply to the New University of Ulster. In this he was successful and by 1972 he was in Northern Ireland for a few days to enlist future staff. Olivia dreaded his final departure in the coming January, for it would mean living on her own for part of the year. 'Temperamentally I'm not suited to it,' she told friends.

She had no intention of joining him in provincial (as she saw it) and potentially dangerous exile in Coleraine. (Some of Reggie's colleagues and wives were later to express disapproval of what they regarded as dereliction of her duty to her husband and even as cowardice.) If she were to remain in London, however, the present house was far too large. A smallish flat might offer the solution. So she began to make enquiries.

In the Abbey Gardens house there had been hair-raising moments. The worst was when a lunatic Australian girl lodger in the basement almost set the place ablaze – and would have done so had not Reggie woken up in time to raise the alarm. Evicting her had been a ghastly business and had meant solicitors, a court case and costs. Olivia came to the conclusion that what everyone said was true – the law was on the side of the tenant, emphatically not on that of the landlord. She would cut out reports from the *Marylebone Mercury* that illustrated this and post them off to selected friends.

Eventually the Smiths found a new tenant, a charming young doctor called Clive Adam. But no sooner had he settled in than the roof above his basement kitchen began to leak: if he stood at the sink for any length of time, he became drenched. Getting it repaired provided a story on which Olivia was to dine out for many weeks to come. An odd job man had put them in touch with a builder, who claimed to run a firm known as the Tar MacAdam Company. Olivia was suspicious from the start, for he had said that he only accepted 'cash in the hand'; but as she was anxious to get the job done as quickly and, even more important, as cheaply as possible, she agreed to £55 in fivers. The man told her that the kitchen roof did not need asphalting – plastering would do as well. Olivia accepted his word.

The next day he took down the boards above the sink. When Olivia, always vigilant, noticed that the beams behind them were damp, he assured her that in no time at all they would dry out. On her next descent to the kitchen she realised that he and a wild-looking youth who had joined him later in the day had covered the wet beams with uneven planks of wood. Olivia remembered her father drumming into her that dampness and dry rot went hand in hand. So she rang up some friends and invited them to come round to inspect the first day's work. They were horrified and insisted that the next morning Reggie should face the man and his mate, and order them to take down the planks. Reggie, who never cared to be involved in any sort of domestic drama, agreed with marked reluctance. But when next day he ventured a few words of remonstrance, the man pushed past him and raced up the stairs, demanding to see 'the lady'. Meanwhile his assistant had quickly slipped downstairs to the basement. Reggie dithered, not knowing what to do. Having heard the preliminary rumpus, Olivia was by now composing herself in the bedroom. In her relaying of the story, this was its first high point. 'I said to myself "Courage, Olivia" and sallied forth in a dressing gown like one of the Trojan women.'

Her manner and bearing immediately conveyed to the man that she was not prepared to stand for any nonsense. 'Play fair with me, lady,' he began to whine – but Olivia silenced him: 'Have you played fair with me? It's an offence to board up wet beams.' At this, the man began to demand his money – adding that his wife and kids were starving. On cue, the wild assistant raced up from the basement, screaming that his wife and kids were starving too. The two men demanded £25 for the materials and £20 for the work. They threatened to 'do in' Olivia and Reggie if they did not get it. After this, they both belted down to the kitchen, where they started banging saucepan lids together.

This gave Reggie the impetus to act. He stumbled, panting, down the narrow stairs to the kitchen and locked the two men in. At the same moment Olivia had decided to ring for the police. Within minutes a squad car arrived with three policemen and a plain-clothes man. They calmed the men down, let them out of the kitchen with Reggie's key, and asked them to come upstairs. At first the youth refused to budge. Then, suddenly, he changed his mind and rushed upstairs, screaming once again about his starving family. He told the police that after twenty years in prison he was trying to go straight. 'This is what the bastards do to me,' he yelled.

At this point Olivia's telling of the story reached its second climax. Gazing around at her audience, she would say, 'I wonder how he begot those children during *twenty years* in prison?' In life, as in her books, she could be exceptionally sharp.

On 2 March 1973 Olivia Manning was sixty-five. She had lost, perhaps deliberately, her birth certificate during the war and so had no confirmation of her age. But she knew that certain advantages came with being an old age pensioner and began to make discreet enquiries. At a post office out of London, where she knew that she was not known, it was suggested that she should apply to Somerset House for another birth certificate, explaining the circumstances. However, she remained determined that her real age, though known to the authorities, should never be known to the press or her friends. In consequence, when, on 6 December, Somerset House issued her with a new birth certificate with the true date on it, she at once hid it away in a drawer, where it remained until her death. Only once, when she was to have a hip operation in late 1979, did she confide her true age to Michael Laurence, who was a close friend and was to be the surgeon. He promised to keep the secret. She retained the false age in a succession of passports.

In 1973, she and Reggie moved from 36 Abbey Gardens to their new flat at 10 Marlborough Place. Olivia proudly pronounced, 'It's in St John's Wood and it faces south.' In the move they exchanged eight rooms for three. For lack of space, Olivia was saddened to have to sell a set of Hogarth prints, which had hung up the stairs of their old house. Heywood Hill, the Mayfair bookseller, bought them.

During her last three months at Abbey Gardens she tried to acclimatise herself to Reggie's absence in Ireland. It was difficult and she dreaded returning to the big house where a lodger might be out, or away for the night. She heard boards creaking which had never creaked before. Some mornings when she woke in the deserted house she suspected people of interfering with the mail and pinching her letters. The day for the move to the new flat in mid-March could not come quickly enough. She told herself she must now face the fact that Reggie would be away for half of each year.

Reggie knew about Olivia's fears. He was both a selfish husband and a man of sudden generosities. Guiltily aware of how much his wife missed him when he was away teaching at Derry, he would plan unexpected treats for her when he was at home. Without warning he would say, 'We're off to buy you a leather jacket and skirt' and would whip her off to a shop in the West End where he had seen some. Sometimes he would give her a signed cheque and tell her to go and buy herself a new dress. Often she visited the Oxfam shop in Marylebone High Street and it was here that she bought a Lurex number which, after a hard winter's wear, she passed on to a charity shop for the elderly. Sometimes she would go up to Hampstead for the sales or for a visit to the Oxfam shop in Gayton Road, also frequented by the Braybrookes and Francis King. At the shop she made friends with a nun who helped out regularly and who would put things aside for her. Olivia was delighted to be favoured in this way. She had told Sister Patricia that fuchsia was one of her favourite colours, and soon she had a rail of fuchsia scarves and blouses hanging in her wardrobe.

During these years, Olivia's favourite novelists were William Gerhardie and Henry Green (friends and possibly lovers of hers), Malcolm Lowry, Patrick White and Saul Bellow. 'I watch the progress of Jim Farrell and Francis King with pleasure and applause,' she told June. She herself felt undervalued. Reggie used to say that it was good to see his wife's friendship with Margaret Drabble – but would add, 'I know she's a bit miffed by Maggie's speedy rise to fame.'

Olivia told June in a letter that she felt the same way about Beryl Bainbridge, whom she first met at a Duckworth party in November 1974. 'Much of her success has come from the fact that . . . she is so pleasant and unassuming . . . Colin [Haycraft, her publisher] has done a great deal to put her on the map. She is fortunate to be getting large solo reviews for her third [in fact fourth] novel *The Bottle Factory Outing*. I have never known such a rapid rise.'

*

In 1972 Reggie had volunteered to adapt for radio William Gerhardie's first novel *Futility*. Based on Russian themes, its original publication in 1922 had owed a great deal to Katherine Mansfield's active support. But the months went by and, as so often with Reggie, it became yet another case of promises, promises. Olivia knew how sad her old friend and (perhaps) one-time lover would be if nothing happened, for he kept on pestering her to find out how Reggie was progressing. So she decided to take over and do the adaptation herself. At the end of 1973 Olivia drove Gerhardie down to the flat of his great friend and literary executor Anne Amyes to hear the play. Getting him there on time on a frosty December night was no easy matter. Here is Olivia's description:

> William was very eager for me to go so he would have a chauffeur. He knew where the flat was but was talking so much (about himself, of course) that we drove past the block and I realised that we were back in Hammersmith. I had to turn left to find the way back and William got into a panic and blamed me for everything. He was sure the block was further on – somewhere beyond Chiswick, perhaps – and as I drove round Fulham, quite lost in a maze of unknown streets – he became abominably rude. He said he was hungry and I was causing him to miss his dinner and the programme. I was agitated enough, being lost, without having William nagging all the time. He said after all these years, this was the end of his friendship. I really felt that was something to be thankful for. I stopped and had the good fortune to find a very nice man who directed me back to the Brompton Road and so we arrived with William, I am glad to say, quite amiable. Our friendship survived. We had an excellent meal and William was pleased by the adaptation and became excessively flattering, but it is easy to see how he has upset so many people in his life . . .

Olivia had not long been in her new flat before trouble broke out with one of the tenants below. Mrs Dalli was Maltese and lived with her husband and four children. The younger children Olivia regarded as 'demons', because they would play football on the stairs, so that their ball constantly bounced against the door of her flat. At times she would come out and reprimand them and for the next ten minutes they would slink away and continue their game elsewhere before slinking back. These reprimands did not endear her to Mrs Dalli. Often, as was inevitable, the two women would meet entering the flats and Mrs Dalli would then try to ensure that Olivia did not precede or overtake her on the stairs by skilful manoeuvring with two bags bulging with shopping. Where this adversary was concerned, Olivia gave full rein to her paranoia, imagining more slights than real ones.

Since he liked virtually everyone, Reggie liked Mrs Dalli. He would ask her about her holidays and she would then tell him how the sun always shone on Malta. Olivia, her obsession growing apace, decided that Mrs Dalli was sending coded messages – namely that the Maltese nature was naturally more sunny than that of the English.

When Olivia had first viewed the flat she had realised that there was a roof beside it which could easily be turned into a roof garden with pots of flowers and possibly a summer house. She was an expert gardener, who had introduced Elizabeth Jane Howard – another gardener, cat lover and novelist – to the growing of old-fashioned roses. Mrs Dalli had understood from the agents that the landlords of the flat would never give permission for a roof garden. But Olivia got away with it, for reasons that the indignant Dallis never discovered. It was quite simple, Olivia explained. 'I had . . . a letter which proved the agents knew I intended putting the terrace in, and later, when it was constructed, they condoned its existence by accepting rent . . .' Throughout the squabble, the agents only wanted a quiet life. They regarded Mrs Smith as 'trouble', since she was constantly complaining to them about the maintenance of the block or the behaviour of the other lessors. It was therefore better to have as little to do with her as possible.

It was perhaps inevitable that things should come to a head between Mrs Dalli and Olivia. Here is Olivia's version:

> She was banging madly on my door. When I opened it she
> screamed 'Don't you tell my children where they can play.
> They'll play where they like.' I tried to point out that the lease
> did not permit children playing on the stairs and hall . . . but
> of course she would not listen. She told me I was an old
> something – I forget what – and I mildly said I did not think
> I was all that much older than she was. Howls of derision

from Mrs V. who dyes her hair and thinks that she looks like a mere girl. I said 'If you could see the bags under your eyes at the moment, you would not feel so pleased with yourself.' Whereupon she called me a 'cunt' – a word I have never expected to hear one woman call another . . .

Within a short space of time Olivia had brought a successful case restraining Mrs Dalli's use of abusive language and the children's football games. Unfortunately, such legal victories rarely solve anything. Whenever Olivia took friends on to the terrace late at night, Mrs Dalli could not restrain herself from throwing up the windows and shouting, 'Keep quiet, you fucking bastards! My kids are asleep.' Reggie, if he was there, would say softly, 'End of Act 8' and Olivia would then laugh.

One spring morning before the building of the roof terrace, Olivia looked for her cat Miou and was unable to find him. Usually he came to tap at the roof door when he wanted breakfast. 'Miou, Miou,' she called out repeatedly, but there was no friendly miaow in answer. She went downstairs and asked a neighbour in the next-door garden if he had seen a Burmese cat. He replied that yes, he had seen it fall from the roof and then limp off in the opposite direction. He was kind but vague in his information: he believed that the cat had landed on a concrete path, not on a flower-bed.

All that day, which was Saturday, Olivia kept calling, for she remembered being told that cats could hear their owners' voices from up to six miles away. When no response came, she decided to cancel all her appointments for the following week. The next morning she was up and outside the block by 6.30, when she caught sight of Miou coming slowly towards her. As she coaxed him closer, she saw that his back leg was broken. It was Sunday, but she remembered that there was a vet called Lawson who held Sunday surgeries. She then took her cat down to him, wrapped in a blanket. Miou was X-rayed immediately, but it was agreed that he was in too severe a state of shock to be operated on that day. When the operation took place on Monday, it lasted two and a half hours and the vet insisted that the cat should stay with him for the rest of the week. Three legs had survived unbroken and if all went well the pin that held the fourth might be removed in a month or so. However, this was not a certainty. She was told that, in human terms, she must prepare for the possibility of living with a wheelchair patient. Her reaction was, 'What does that matter if Miou does not die?'

In the weeks that followed she began to regret more than ever her move to the flat. Everyone said how beautiful it was, but now she thought of it as a place of punishment. Her selfishness and fear of living alone in a four-storey house had meant that Miou had been deprived of a garden and, worse, his expectancy of life might have been cut short. 'If he dies, I do not know how I shall bear it, knowing how much I am to blame.' To friend after friend she sent these cries of *mea culpa*. She even began reading advertisements for flats or houses with gardens. She made a resolution: 'I will never have another cat.' But what would happen to the poor creature if she herself died first? In the case of such an eventuality, June promised that she would take Miou.

When Miou came back to the flat from the vet, plans for the roof terrace had been made, but had not yet been realised. This did not ultimately matter, because for several months the cat had become used to living in a box measuring two foot by two, while his leg continued to mend. Each day a few steps were allowed on the floor on a lead. At last the pin was removed.

Once, when bringing Miou home from a cattery, she recalled how Stevie Smith had heard a child say of a Palmers Green pug in the local park, 'Mother, that dog is of good family.' It made Olivia reflect how from his stay in a cattery Miou had acquired, though less than a week away from St John's Wood, 'a low-class growl'. Was this a reality or a fantasy? There was always a degree of fantasy in Olivia's attitude to Miou, as to much else in her life. Early in spring 1973 she had summoned a rope maker, to see if it would be possible to make a rope ladder to be let down from the roof terrace: her idea was that it should be strong enough to bear the weight of a cat but not of a man. 'I see,' said jolly Mr Simpkins, 'you don't mind cat visitors, but you don't want cat burglars.' He laughed a great deal at his joke. She did not. Then he concluded, 'I don't think I can meet your requirements. Sorry and all that.'

Olivia's fantasies about Miou were sometimes frightening. In September 1971, for example, she had left Miou at Dr Francis's cattery near Yeovil, which in 1967 she had praised in her book *Extraordinary Cats* as the perfect holiday home for pets. But when she got home that night she typed a letter to June in which she wrote that she thought

Dr F. was perhaps going mad and would ill-treat Miou, and he (Miou) would be helpless there. . . . I wanted at once to go and take him away.

Dr Francis had looked lean and withered, and had been rather scratchy during her last visit. He had said, 'In three days' time you will have forgotten all about Miou.' But now in her bedroom it was 11.30 p.m. and she had no immediate way of getting down to Yeovil. So she put aside the letter and poured herself an extra-large gin, swallowed two Passiflora tablets and eventually fell asleep. When she woke the next morning she crossed out the sentences about Dr Francis – but not very effectively – and wrote in the margin, 'I have cut this out because . . . crazy.' Later that day she posted the letter.

Why did she not cross out the two sentences more effectively? In her correspondence a number of other sentences are thoroughly crossed out. So did she let these particular sentences, revealing her anguished state of mind, remain just visible as a cry for help to June? Was she suffering from her usual neurotic anxieties? Or had she succumbed to menopausal symptoms? At the age of sixty-three she was long past the menopause, but it could have delayed effects and some medical friends of Jerry, whom Olivia had met, had maintained that these effects could last for up to a decade. Certainly she never wrote to other friends as in this letter. There is also the possibility that a recent visit of Reggie's mother, which she always dreaded, had reduced her to a state of near nervous breakdown. The fact that by letter Olivia had appointed June as Miou's godmother may have meant that she could confide in her about her fears for him as to no one else. *Extraordinary Cats* is dedicated to June and Neville, and the 300 'Olivia' letters that June received is a total far exceeding that of letters written to anyone else.

Chapter 35

Festive Occasions

Theoretically Olivia enjoyed parties, but in practice was often timid before setting out. She needed a strong gin before leaving and nothing more depressed her than parties where only red or white wine was offered. At night before turning in she took a stiff gin to bed with her – what she referred to as a sailor's, or club, measure, by which she meant a treble. As a driver, on the way back from parties, she was often near, or over, the limit. Yet, miraculously, she was never stopped by the police.

'I'm really no good at large parties,' Olivia would complain. 'I like small ones. I can't exploit a party like Edna [O'Brien].' When she first met John Gross, when he was editing the *Times Literary Supplement*, she was virtually tongue-tied. 'That's something that Edna would never let happen.' At Margaret Drabble's she would sometimes meet Terence Kilmartin, the literary editor of the *Observer*, and after a few awkward stumbling words each would fall silent. Ten minutes later she would see him sitting on a sofa, deep in conversation with Alison Lurie. How she wished that she had Alison's ability to talk to everyone.

Olivia had longed to meet Spike Milligan – and what a disaster it proved when it was brought about. He was suffering from depression, which soon spread to her, and there they stood in the middle of Jerry Slattery's sitting room saying nothing. How glad she was when her host rescued her. If only Reggie had been there, but he had stayed at home to finish a piece which he was contributing to a Louis MacNeice symposium.

Then there had been the moment at a Hatchards party when John Gielgud had said that he was going to kneel at her feet and pay homage to her genius: but the noise was so great that he gave up and they drifted apart. Instead, she had a long talk with a man who claimed to have uncovered the spy Anthony Blunt – but failed to catch his name. That was something that would never have happened with Edna or Alison.

During the last decade of her life the actual physical process of writing grew harder for Olivia. The ambition was there, but the arthritis that at first had affected only her upper right arm was now slowly creeping down towards her right hand and thumb. She mentions the date of the start of this disability as early as 1970, but it only became acute when she was working on a readaptation – she had already done an adaptation in 1964 – of Arnold Bennett's *The Card* for BBC radio. By January of 1974 she was typing six pages a day of the script, then revising with a pen and retyping. All the time the pain in her right hand and thumb increased. Constantly she talked it over with Jerry, who diagnosed 'neuritis'. When at last she made up her mind to have an operation, he urged her to go ahead as soon as possible: 'One of the wisest decisions you've ever made, Olivia.'

Yet it would require careful planning, for Reggie would have to be in the flat to look after Miou and the only month, still five months away, when he definitely would be there was August. This would mean going privately. On Jerry's recommendation, therefore, she made a booking with the National Royal Orthopaedic Hospital for the first week of August. BUPA would contribute something towards the fee – a room cost £25 a day – and the BBC cheque for *The Card* would be helpful. The first Heinemann royalty statement for *The Rain Forest* showed that it had not covered its advance.

In the days before the operation Olivia's thoughts turned to death. With modern anaesthetics, she maintained, 'one goes out so simply, it is like death. Or, rather, I hope it is like death.' For she hoped that death would be 'a wonderful drifting away from one's poor old tired creaking body'. She had no problems in thinking of the spirit divorced from the body, since she felt the spirit would survive death – and, possibly, 'be resurrected in a refreshed body for good measure'.

In the operating theatre there was a delay, because the preceding patient's operation had taken longer than was anticipated. Olivia could remember, she told friends in letters, an anaesthetist ('How do you spell that?') bending over with a message of kind thoughts from Lippy Kessell – a doctor friend – and then, immediately it seemed, a nurse's voice saying, 'Wake up! It's all over.' She was now in the post-operation room with her hand held up in a sling. When she looked about her she saw other women in a similar position with their hands in the air 'like those crabs with the big fore-claw'. It was a description that she used in several letters. She believed that, if one found a good phrase, it could bear repetition.

Christmas 1974 was a specially happy occasion for Olivia, for in the Christmas number of the *Listener* Antonia Fraser chose the adaptation of the Balkan Trilogy as the best radio feature of the year. Olivia was doubly delighted because David Wade, the radio critic for *The Times*, though enthusiastic enough, had referred to it as 'a relatively routine event'. Reggie told her that 1974 had been an *annus mirabilis* for her – 'First Maggie chooses *The Rain Forest* as a Book of the Year, and now in the *Listener* Antonia chooses the Balkan Trilogy for radio.'

Antonia Fraser had written,

> When I heard that Olivia Manning's Balkan Trilogy was to be done over, I hesitated as to whether to listen to it at all. I had just finished rereading all the three books in the new paper-back edition and I wondered if radio could really add anything to Olivia Manning's subtle and exciting master-piece. How wrong I was! In Eric Ewens's subtle adaptation, produced by John Tydeman for Radio 4, the Balkan Trilogy was a triumph. There should be a special mention of Anna Massey's delicate skill in playing the heroine.

Olivia at once pounced on the use twice in quick succession of the adjective 'subtle' – for the Trilogy and for the adapter's work. She thought it showed haste in writing and carelessness on the part of the *Listener* sub-editor. When she discussed the matter later with Reggie she asked him, 'Why am I so critical? Why am I never content?'

He replied, 'It is because you are a perfectionist.' Yet she could make mistakes and not correct them. In *The Rain Forest* pork is served at a Muslim restaurant, as Francis King pointed out to her, much to her annoyance, but no change was made in the paperback edition.

Before the broadcast went out officially, Olivia and some friends gathered to listen to a preview at a BBC studio. Afterwards, when she left, there were tears running down her cheeks.

In the last days of 1974 Reggie asked Olivia if she had any New Year wishes. She pondered for a long time, then replied, 'To keep Miou on his four feet – and for many years to come.'

Chapter 36

Return to Cairo

On 25 January 1975 Olivia wrote to June Braybrooke, 'I have written a few pages of a novel but I do not feel any compulsion.' This was to become *The Danger Tree*, the opening volume of the Levant Trilogy, published in August 1977. For some time, in the early stages, she referred to it as 'The Cairo Novel' and 'The Fourth Part of the Balkan Trilogy'.

After Chapter 1 was drafted, the new novel soon began to drag for that lack of compulsion. Then, in the New Year of 1976, things took a change for the better and by the end of the year she was writing to June, 'My novel has come together after a long struggle.'

She had known such struggles before – as have almost all writers. She recalled H. G. Wells's advice: 'Try the element of surprise: attack the book at an hour when it isn't expecting it.' She therefore now decided to begin her writing day at eleven o'clock in the morning, instead of in the afternoon as she had previously been in the habit of doing. What counted above all, she believed, was persistence, for she had seen so many gifted writers eventually fail because of lack of it.

The novel raised one problem above all others. In continuing her story, she was moving from the Balkans to a country in which no area was free from the invasion of the desert. On arrival she and Reggie had described themselves as 'living in oases of activity', surrounded 'by wildernesses of shifting sand'. Mirage and illusion were common experiences. She did not know how effectively she would be able to convey this.

Halfway through 1976 Olivia sent June this progress report:

> So many memories have returned to me, so many things I feel
> I must go into – and perhaps I have been over-ambitious in
> trying to deal with a young officer in action in the desert. I am

not really an inventive person. I only feel safe describing what
I have already experienced.

The last remark was to be repeated many times by Olivia Manning. But it
was not entirely accurate, especially in her final decade. In *The Rain Forest*,
her creation of the imaginary island of Al-Bustan had been a remarkable
feat. A hardly less remarkable feat was the creation of the young officer
Simon Boulderstone, a second lieutenant of twenty, who appears on the
opening page of *The Danger Tree* and plays a leading role throughout the
Trilogy.

When Hugh Herbert, a journalist on the *Guardian* asked her what had
set her going on the second Trilogy, she replied, 'My husband and I some
months before Alamein met a young soldier officer, who was looking for
transport to take him to the desert, while I and Reggie were off to a rather
expensive restaurant.' This incident, she confirmed, had long stayed in her
mind as she had become more and more conscious of the dichotomy 'by
which a small number of privileged people were able to live reasonably
well in Cairo, while these young men were going off to risk their lives'.

Simon disembarks at Suez in June 1942, just after Tobruk has fallen to
the Germans for the second time. Recently married, he has had the briefest
of honeymoons before saying goodbye to his wife, Anne, at Liverpool
Docks and boarding the *Queen Mary*. Previously Simon has never been
abroad, except for a school trip to Paris. Nor has he ever drunk anything
stronger than ale. He eats duck for the first time with two officers from the
Hussars on a desert picnic provided by Shepheard's Hotel. He is, in short,
an innocent. Fresh from OCTU (Officers Corps Training Unit), he
notices on arriving in Cairo how slow Other Ranks, in contrast to those
on Salisbury Plain, are to address him as 'sir'. They regard him as little
more than a schoolboy, and within weeks he is wondering if there is any
creature in the Army more wretched than a subaltern who has no real
contact with his senior officers and is not supposed to consort with his
men.

Until now Harriet, who is twenty-two, has believed that she belongs to
the young generation; after meeting Simon, she recognises that there is an
even younger one.

Family constellations fascinated Olivia, especially the relationship
between brother and sister, and brother and brother. Reggie had three
brothers and from her reading Olivia was aware of the bond between

Virginia Woolf and her younger brother Thoby, who died of typhoid in 1906. As a result of his death, Woolf had suffered a nervous breakdown, during which she thought that she was someone else. Olivia had also noticed the effect on Katherine Mansfield when her brother Leslie had been killed in 1915, after a grenade had exploded in his hand while he was instructing a group of recruits how to lob it. Both Thoby and Leslie were twenty-one, and Virginia and Katherine had each used the word 'shattered' about their deaths. Olivia used the same word about the death of her brother Oliver, who was killed in the Fleet Air Arm at the age of eighteen. She blamed the twelve-year gap between the completion of her first and second novels on the shock caused by his death. Kay Dick was to observe that by drawing attention to such 'a work gap', Olivia was firmly placing herself alongside the other two women writers, who had also suffered similar, albeit rather shorter, 'work gaps' after the death of a beloved brother.

In *The Danger Tree*, Olivia carefully examines the relationship between the two Boulderstone brothers: Hugo, the elder, and Simon. When Harriet first dines with Hugo at the Cecil Hotel in Alexandria, she has a premonition that he is about to die. 'He won't come back,' she informs Guy. Indeed, when Simon finally catches up with Hugo's unit in the desert, it is to learn from Hugo's batman that less than a few hours ago he has bled to death with his legs shot off. The team in a nearby ambulance report back that he was killed by mortars, because the Germans would not stop firing until they had wiped out everyone. Up until then Simon had believed that there was an unwritten code which decreed that no one fired at ambulances, or at those tending the dying. Simon had accepted this code – even if he had been struck by the irony of tying sticks together to form crosses to place over graves in the sand: 'You killed men and marked the spot with a symbol of eternal life.'

Few people today would question the persuasiveness of Olivia's accounts of the months leading up to the Alamein campaign. Yet this was not always the case. When the first volume of the second Trilogy appeared, Auberon Waugh in the *Evening Standard* found the description of the military scenes 'implausible'; Martyn Goff in the *Daily Telegraph* dismissed the battles as 'unconvincing'; and Allan Massie in the *Scotsman* maintained that the accounts of desert fighting were never 'full realised'. Massie also attacked the Pringles, castigating them as 'bores' in Bucharest; 'prize bores' in Athens; and 'self-righteous prigs ever afterwards'. Reggie made up one of his puerile ditties, which he went about their flat singing: 'Massie is an assie' was its refrain.

When Tobruk fell for a second time to the Germans, Olivia, then living in Cairo, was thirty-four. When she began to write about these events in St John's Wood she was sixty-seven. This is what she said about *The Danger Tree* in June 1976, by which time she was more than halfway into it:

> I am finding the book difficult – as though I were digging out of complete darkness. Thank goodness I have finished the passages in the desert – they were the worst of all and I do not know if they are any good. It is better to write out of darkness than ignorance.

Patience was an important feature in the process. So was closing one's eye before picking up a pen. The painter Turner, as she recollected, used to lock himself away in a black cellar so as to conjure up in his mind 'flowers of brilliant hue and dazzling rough seas'. It was one of the paradoxes of art. Olivia as a girl in Portsmouth used to shut herself away in her bedroom, close the curtains and not switch on the light. This behaviour worried her parents and, though they usually said nothing, there were times when her mother could not refrain from delivering a rebuke: 'What you're doing, Ollov, isn't natural.' Olivia knew otherwise and many years later, when she was living in Baker Street, she came across this comment in an 1893 short story by Henry James: 'We work in the dark . . . The rest is the madness of art.' She herself used to say, 'Every child gestates in the darkness of the womb before it sees the light.' She thought all forms of art underwent a similar process.

So it was that, when she was sitting in her flat with her eyes closed, the idea first came to her that Simon Boulderstone should have a brother, who would be a year older. The name Hugo 'dawned' at the same time. The other details about their parents, Hugo's view of Edwina as 'the most gorgeous popsie in Cairo' and his rapid rise to being a captain in the Eighth Army were worked out later when her eyes were open and she had a pen in her hand. By a similar process Olivia would imagine the scene in which a Messerschmitt swoops down to blow up his Ronson, just a few seconds after he has left it to answer a call of nature – 'You know, with a spade.'

*

The Danger Tree is the only one of Olivia Manning's novels that does not keep to a strict chronological order. Chapter 1 is set in the summer of 1942, while Chapter 2 reverts to April 1941, which is the month when the Pringles escaped on the last ship from Athens. The cause of the change was because Olivia wished to open her Trilogy 'with a story that would not easily be forgotten'. This is the account, to which reference has already been made, of the death of the son of Sir Desmond Hooper Tree and his wife (characters based on the real-life people Sir Walter and Lady Smart) when the child inadvertently picks up an unexploded bomb when out playing in the desert.

She also made use of another tragic real-life incident. This involved the suicide of the actor and poet Stephen Haggard, whom she had known in Jerusalem. Haggard, who had left behind in England a wife and three sons, suddenly fell in love with a beautiful Egyptian married woman. After some months she decided to end the relationship and, on the train from Cairo to Palestine he shot himself. His death was hushed up and there is no mention of it in Christopher Hassall's biography.

Aidan Sheridan, in the novel, shoots himself during an identical train journey. He had previously been emotionally drawn to Guy. But Guy, benevolent though he is by nature, fails to respond – 'What can be more tiring than being the object of a hopeless illusion?' Aiden, it is clear, is a suppressed homosexual.

Olivia admitted that she had Stephen Haggard in mind when she began creating this character but added that, as she continued, so another real-life actor took over – a homosexual, who thought that Mars, the God of War, had treated him harshly. As she said on another occasion, 'Your characters have the last word. Never argue with them.'

Chapter 37

Before and After Alamein

The second volume of the Levant Trilogy was called *The Battle Lost and Won*. On 26 July 1977, Olivia had written to June to say that she was beginning to find the battle scenes more interesting than the civilian ones.

When Rommel's Afrika Korps are within fifty miles of Alexandria, the streets and pavements reverberate to the boom of distant artillery. Here Guy continues to teach a class which has shrunk to less than half a dozen. It is on commercial English rather than English prosody that he now concentrates. He has plans for a summer school at which he will lecture on *Finnegans Wake* but, as his wife understands only too well, this is no more than a dream. He is far from being the realist that she is.

Promiscuity is so much the rule among Cairo's British residents that Harriet sees the place as a bureau of sexual exchange. When drafting such scenes in her London flat, Olivia had been disturbed by the sexual shenanigans of the couple upstairs. She would hear him shout, 'Come on, you little bitch! Roll over.' In the novel Peter Lisdoonvarna, whose chief preoccupations are girls, fast cars and a transfer to the front line, gives Edwina Little precisely the same order.

After he has bought King Farouk's second-best Bentley, Peter takes Edwina and Harriet out for a spin. He demonstrates how the canvas roof springs back at the touch of a button – an innovation in those days. On the way home they break the journey at Memphis, where Harriet leaves the couple alone to explore the ruins. When eventually she catches up with them, she sees their bodies pressed closely together and for a few fleeting moments experiences the intense solitude of exclusion.

Olivia had remarkable powers of recall, which she backed up with the aid of maps. Pencil marks can still be seen on those that she used. Poring over them, she would relive the past strategies and troop movements.

Montgomery's *Memoirs*, published in 1958, were to become her bible. In reporting a scene, she often deploys a cool irony. An example is the one in which, before a portable altar set in the desert, a padre leads the men in the hymn 'Now Praise We All Our God . . .' Yet the battle preparations do not cease and the singing is drowned out as Wellingtons, wave on wave, fly past towards their targets.

In the autumn of 1942 Simon Boulderstone is promoted to liaison officer. This is one of the most coveted jobs in the British Army, for it means that he is able to survey the whole panorama of battle on foot or by jeep. Later, he discovers that he owed his promotion to a passing conversation with Peter Lisdoonvarna.

'Dissatisfaction' is the word with which Chapter 3 opens, for it was this more than anything else that Harriet believed was eroding her marriage. This dissatisfaction is chiefly on her side, she admits – and it grows in the course of the book. She is constantly amazed by Guy's changes of moods. When they arrived in Egypt, not even wild camels would have drawn him to the City of the Dead at the bottom of the cinderous Mokattam cliffs, since he regarded all rituals of death as morbid. Yet when one of his Egyptian students is killed in a car crash, he becomes consumed with a desire to meet the parents during the traditional forty days of mourning. Harriet asks if she might accompany him to the Qarafa, as the City of the Dead is known. Guy at first says 'No', adding that the occasion is probably reserved for men. But suddenly he backtracks. 'Why not?' he asks rhetorically. 'It won't hurt them to be reminded that women exist. Yes, come if you like.'

At times, in common with his prototype Reggie, Guy is like a musical spinning top, the tunes of which are continually changing. He may not believe in another world, but he believes that his student lately dead is now a spirit. Deficient in logic, he is ruled more often by his heart than by his head. He acknowledges the presence of apparitions and ghosts – even if their existence cannot be proved.

In the second Trilogy only mutual tolerance prevents the Pringle marriage from ending. Mutual tolerance also prevented the Smiths' from doing so. Olivia knew about Reggie's affairs, but never gave them undue attention. 'You know what Reggie's like,' was her usual response. So their marriage survived, even taking on board Jerry and Johnny as part of their joint life. Olivia knew more about Reggie and his long affair with his eventual second wife Diana – whom Reggie never allowed her to meet –

than she let on to Reggie himself or to all but her closest friends. Reggie had first confessed this relationship to her in 1964. Like Jerry, Reggie had found himself in the situation of loving two women simultaneously. The vital importance for Olivia of her relationship with Reggie was that he was, as she put it, her 'other literary half'. She prophesied, 'If I die and he ever remarries, I'm certain he'll put me in the "In Memoriam" column in *The Times*.' Reggie both remarried and commemorated her death each year in *The Times*.

As with the first volume, it took Olivia some time to get the second one moving. She confided in June that the problem had been not that she had not known what to say, but where to begin. When the opening volume had appeared, reviewers had singled out the story of the death of the young boy while playing with a live hand grenade. Where would the author find a story to equal this? Then one day, as she closed her eyes, a picture came into her mind: it was of Simon Boulderstone as still an innocent. She was jubilant: 'I rejoiced for I had found a starting point. But where would it lead or how it would develop, I had no idea.'

So she has Simon boarding a lorry, travelling east on the Alamein road and asking to be dropped off at a cheap hotel in the capital. Having reached his destination, he throws down his kitbag at the entrance to the International. The driver asks his passenger, who seems to be in a trance, 'You all right, sir?' Simon nods and enters the scruffy hotel. Once in his room, he weeps for his dead brother Hugo, until there are no more tears to shed. This is still the day on which Hugo died in no man's land. Next Simon has a bath and slowly plans the hours ahead. First, he decides that he must break the news to Edwina, the woman whom he has mistakenly believed to be his brother's loyal girlfriend. When she hears the news, Edwina does not disillusion him.

In this Trilogy, Harriet's own marriage comes under the magnifying glass. At one point she asks herself whether all married couples spend their evenings apart. At another she comes up with the trenchant maxim, 'Marriage is knowing too much about each other.' Harriet thinks that she is in need of a one-to-one relationship, exclusive of any others, whereas Guy is content with a marriage that also includes a variety of often conflicting friendships. Much of his energy, like Reggie's at that period, is absorbed by endless, aimless conversations; by producing shows for the troops; and by planning summer schools that never materialise. Any activity that will provide him with a sense of purpose is to be seized on.

When Angela Hooper Tree, whose young son has been killed by a grenade, meets Simon, whose brother has been killed in no man's land, both are in need of distractions. 'Let's take this beautiful young man into the world,' she suggests. 'Let's flaunt him.' He complains that he has been nowhere exciting in Cairo – not even to the Berka. 'Oh, oh, oh!' replies Angela, pulling him down on the sofa beside her. 'You dreadful creature wanting to visit the Berka!'

Pleading his innocence, he defends his choice: 'It's the only street name I know.'

Angela decides to take him to the Berka with Harriet and anyone else willing to join in the adventure. First they stop off at the Anglo-Egyptian Club, where she orders a bottle of whisky and six glasses to be brought to her table. The party grows. They then all move on to the Extase, from which her group are ejected for singing a bawdy song about King Farouk, Queen Farida and 'how the boys would like to ride her'.

They next hire a couple of taxis to take them past the Esbekiya to Clot Bey and the narrow streets beyond. This is the Berka, where women ply their trade in the oldest profession in the world. There is a sliding scale of prices – and exhibitions with animals are sometimes offered.

The group is led downstairs. The union between the performers is so brief that Angela feels she has been defrauded. She rewards the student with a 1000-piastre note and her party shakes hands with the young man as they slope off. They feel ashamed for the humiliation which they have inflicted upon him. They are glad to be out of a basement room smelling of carbolic and ancient sweat.

No reviewer failed to mention this scene, with which the first chapter closed. Based on her own visit to the Berka, it was another example of the dichotomy between the rich and poor, between a woman with money to burn and an impoverished student hired for a louche entertainment. The chapters that followed, Olivia wrote with an ease, certainty and speed never before experienced by her. Within seven months the manuscript was completed. She informed the people at Weidenfeld, 'It's a record for me.'

'A great shambles' was Olivia Manning's verdict on the Second World War. What a simple matter military strategy seemed on paper – but what a blind confusion it was in reality, as Simon learns when puzzling over maps with a number of arrows and being obliged to choose which to follow. Peter Luke, who served in the Rifle Brigade and was later to adapt for the stage Frederick Rolfe's *Hadrian VII*, sent her this line of congratulation on *The Battle Lost and Won*: 'If I did not know this was impossible, I could imagine you were beside me in the battle for Himeimat . . .'

At moments in her depiction of the fighting Olivia reveals something of her father's romanticism. In post-war years father and daughter were to hear the story of the young Highlander who had played the pipes to give his comrades heart at the beginning of the battle. 'His CO should have known better,' was the criticism of one seasoned veteran, since within minutes a bullet had killed the piper. Into her account of modern warfare Olivia introduced the collective noun 'a pride of tanks'. Obviously it is derived from 'a pride of lions'. In her Portsmouth home the phrase 'brave as a lion' had often been used by the family to denote heroism.

In Egypt, during the first part of the 1940s, death lurked everywhere – even in the mangoes, despite their sweetness, which could poison fatally. Among Cairenes the tree on which they grew was known as 'The Danger Tree'. In the Trilogy one of the characters, Dobbie Dobson, compares mangoes with duck eggs, which can also sometimes prove fatal. Everywhere in the desert mines lay buried in the sand; booby-traps were attached to innocent-looking palm trees.

Chapter 38

Wonders of the Levant

As Olivia came to work on the final volume of the Levant Trilogy, she told Reggie that her task was mainly tying up loose ends.

In the closing pages of the Trilogy Guy suggests to Harriet that, because of her amoebic dysentery, she should return home to England without him. She is unwilling to do so but, after some argument, agrees to his booking her a passage home at Christmas 1942, via Cape Town. Exact dates of sailing are kept secret for security reasons. The journey is generally estimated at two months.

All along Harriet has been subject to forebodings about the voyage. After she has said goodbye to Guy at Cairo station, these forebodings come back and haunt her on the train to Suez. On the quay, she is still hoping for a last-minute reprieve – and miraculously has one when she recognises Mortimer and Phillips, two women drivers from a paramilitary service, which make regular trips to Iraq with supplies of ammunition. Mort and Phil, as they are known to their colleagues, agree to let Harriet hitch a lift with them as far as Damascus. Now, as she clambers aboard their lorry, all the wonders of the Levant lie ahead.

Eventually she finds herself in Baalbek, on her way to Beirut. Harriet spends less than an afternoon there, although on arrival she has booked into a cheap Arab café for the night, since there is no train to Beirut until the following morning. At the café she is offered freshly made kebabs and says, 'Yes, but later. I must see the temples first.' They are, after all, her reason for being there.

Wandering among the temples, the thought occurs to her that, so far as friends know, she might as well be dead – which is what Guy thinks some few hundred miles away. How surprised he would be if he knew that among these ancient remains she was calling out aloud to him, 'Guy, why don't you come and look for me?' But this is something to which only the reader is party. The sustaining of Harriet's and Guy's two worlds apart shows, technically, what an accomplished novelist Olivia had become.

It is only in Jerusalem, when attending the Ceremony of the Holy Fire, that Harriet at last learns that the ship on which she was due to travel has been torpedoed. As she is waiting with the congregation for the ceremony to begin, she becomes aware of a woman whom she has seen before – but cannot remember where. The woman's large crocodile bag and her gestures strike a chord – and conjure up in Harriet an occasion of unhappiness. Yet what the occasion was eludes her.

After the Greek patriarch appears, things begin to clarify, or synchronise, with the appearance of the holy fire as it passes from hand to hand and candles are illuminated all over the church until the light reaches the outlying chapels. Harriet, too, feels inwardly illuminated as she suddenly remembers who the woman is. She is Mrs Rutter, a rich widow, who has a house on one of the islands on the Nile facing Cairo. Together they had travelled on the same train to Suez; the last Harriet had seen of her was when she joined the queue for the *Queen of Sparta* and Harriet had clambered aboard the lorry bound for Damascus. Yet if this was so, why was Mrs Rutter in Jerusalem when she should have been halfway to England? Harriet follows her quickly out of the basilica – and within seconds all is made clear, for Mrs Rutter turns out to have been one of the three survivors to have been rescued from the ship. Harriet bursts into sobs. 'Poor Guy! Oh, poor Guy. He thinks I'm dead.'

At this point in the narrative Olivia had told Reggie that the novel had another thirty pages to run: 'You might say I'm almost there.'

He cautioned her, 'Show the pages to me when they're ready.'

In October she handed them over. They chronicled Aidan Sheridan's suicide, Guy's continued widowerhood and Simon's recovery from serious injury. Back on his feet, Simon declares, 'The Army's my life. All I want now is to get back into the fight.' While he is waiting to do so, Guy invites him to a party. Just in time for this party, Harriet arrives by taxi.

Then follows one of the most touching scenes in the Trilogy:

> Guy put out his arms. She ran to him and he clutched her against his breast and broke into a convulsive sob. Dropping his head down to her head, he wept loudly and wildly while people watched him, amazed. He was known as a good-

humoured fellow, a generous and helpful fellow but no one expected him to show any depths of emotion.

This account of how Guy believes Harriet to be dead, only to have her return to him seemingly miraculously, was not, like so much else in the book, based on an actual happening. Olivia would often start out with something that she herself had experienced or at least observed, and would then ask herself the question, 'What if?' In this case the question was 'What if Guy/Reggie believed that I was dead? How would he react to that and to the eventual news that I was alive after all?'

On 13 October Olivia wrote to June to say that Reggie had read the present manuscript – but was not satisfied. He urged that there should be more about Simon Boulderstone, who had developed into a central character – like Prince Yakimov in the first Trilogy. 'So I have returned to my labours,' she concluded her letter. Also, she said, 'I have to add a summing up – very difficult.'

This, at Reggie's instigation, became another coda to balance the coda with which he had suggested she should end *The Battle Lost and Won*. But this second coda took sixteen attempts, before she felt that it was right. When Reggie read it he applauded her by clapping his hands above his head, as she had seen him do early after their arrival in Bucharest when he took her to see the gypsy singer Florica at a nightclub. 'Bravo,' he cried several times, then added, 'It is perfection, absolute perfection.' Here is that coda:

> Two more years were to pass before the war ended. Then, at last, peace, perfect peace, came down upon the world and the survivors could go home. Like the figures left on the stage at the end of a great tragedy, they had now to tidy up the ruins of war and in their hearts bury the noble dead.

At a joint lecture given by the Braybrookes on 'Olivia Manning' in the autumn of 1988 at the Henry St John Centre in Ryde, David Gascoyne, who attended with his wife, said as they drove home, 'Those last sentences of Olivia's which you quoted were extremely fine. They have a place for ever.'

Chapter 39

William Gerhardie

The year 1977 was to prove 'a sad, sad one' for Olivia. She would say she could constantly hear the rustle of wings flying overhead, for hardly a week passed by when she did not see announced in the papers the death of someone she knew. In mid-July obituaries of the novelist William Gerhardie appeared everywhere.

William Alexander Gerhardie, born in 1895, was the child of English parents living in St Petersburg, who owned a cotton mill on the banks of the Neva. Although he was never to lose his love of Russia, he showed he was a patriotic Englishman during the First World War by enlisting in the Scots Grays. Later, in 1917, he was transferred to the British Military Mission in St Petersburg, where he witnessed the Bolshevik Revolution at first hand. In 1971, when there was a national census in Britain, he filled in his place of birth as Peterborough, thinking that a fair translation of St Petersburg. A true eccentric, he devised a method of heating an armchair with two electric hotplates, which the London Electricity Board instantly condemned. Penelope Fitzgerald, long before she became a writer, remembered one day finding him during the 1939 war wearing a saucepan on his head to protect himself against shrapnel or flying glass. In 1977 when Neville Braybrooke visited him in a Highgate hospital a few weeks before his death, he saw on his bedside locker a volume of short stories. 'Chekhov's my bible,' he remarked as he tapped the book. Significantly, the volume was in Russian.

Olivia's admiration for Gerhardie's work dated back to her teens, when she belonged to Portsmouth Public Library. In a 1000-word article on him and his work, which she had persuaded *The Times* to commission in 1961, she chose the title 'Buried Alive'. That was how she thought of him, immured in a flat with the curtains always pulled. Yet what genius and talent those curtains hid from the outside world. The article's conclusion was, 'He is one of the immortals. He is our Gogol's "Overcoat". We all come out of him.'

Gerhardie, briefly a protégé of Lord Beaverbrook, was much in demand at private dinner parties. His *tour de force* was generally reckoned to be an account of the massacre of the Czar Nicholas's family at Ekaterinburg in 1917, which he would close with the words,

> One can imagine them, indeed, as they stood there, risen in the astral light over their mangled bodies, bewildered, huddling together. For an awful instant, Anastasia was pulled back into the brutal moment, but they killed her, and she was back in the fold.

If anyone asked if the Grand Duchess might have escaped, his reply was brief – 'an impossible fantasy'.

The more Olivia read and reread Gerhardie, the more she realised what a debt she owed him. Many passages she could recite. The two of them had almost daily telephone calls, often lasting for an hour or more. The novelist Antonia White claimed that Olivia held the record for such calls – over eight hours, with only one ten-minute break for coffee. Sometimes Olivia would say to Reggie, 'He makes sixty minutes seem nothing. There's not a subject about which he is not prepared to talk. Sometimes I suspect he has notes beside him for he repeats himself word for word.'

At the end of the First World War Gerhardie had retired with the rank of captain and an OBE. Now in the 1960s he became greedy for further honours – and began to drop hints. The implication was that an OM was long overdue. Olivia consequently began to make enquiries about this highest of orders and found that the numbers were restricted. She raised the subject with C. P. Snow, Anthony Powell, Evelyn Waugh and Graham Greene – all more worthy of it – to see if they could help. Evelyn Waugh, who had long been an admirer of Gerhardie's work – 'I learned a great deal of my trade from your novels' – wrote to A. J. P. Taylor on 28 October 1965, 'Lord Beaverbrook was much disappointed by his failure to promote the success of William Gerhardie (who deserved it) . . . Incidentally he is old, ill, and poor and longs for a knighthood. Perhaps you can help him?' Sadly, no one whom Olivia approached was able to do more than express sympathy. She then had to endure William's displeasure at her failed attempts. She said crossly one day, 'He always wants one thing too many.'

Over the years Gerhardie had been anxious that she should dedicate a novel to him and in 1955 she had eventually done so with *The Doves of Venus*. Six years later, when she published her piece on him in *The Times*, that inevitably was not enough for him. 'What about the little reviews?' he asked. 'Not everyone reads *The Times* or wants to. Couldn't you also write something for one of them?' Similarly, after she had adapted *Futility* and *The Polyglots* for radio, he reminded her that he had written other novels – *Of Mortal Love* and *My Wife's the Least of it*. She replied firmly that she was now into her second Trilogy and must not be deflected. By 1975 the requests began to fade as he himself faded.

Gerhardie's death was to make Olivia contemplate her own. She knew she had been born with poor health and added to this was her amoebic dysentery, which never left her. In her final three years there were to be unpleasant stays in hospital – and medical examinations: 'Nothing can be more awful than a barium enema.' A hip operation that had failed had to be 'redone' in December 1979 at the Wellington Hospital. Yet none of these events compared with the shattering blow of Jerry's death in November 1977. He had been to a rugger match and on his return his wife had brought up to their sitting room a high tea, which included a steak. At first it was thought that he had choked on it, but the coroner's verdict was that he had died of a massive heart attack. The next night Michael Laurence broke the news to Olivia – and it called for the greatest tact on both sides.

Olivia was aware that at the funeral there might be a lurking journalist, who might question her about her relationship with Jerry. None appeared and she was greatly relieved. Yet when her two Trilogies were shown on television in 1987 under the joint title of *Fortunes of War* several journalists began to probe into her friendship with this doctor friend. Johnny resolutely refused to give credence to any of the stories that were circulating in the late 1980s and the 1990s. In 1994 she made an attempt to have certain references cut from a radio programme about Reggie on Radio 4. Learning that some references to the relationship had been made by Francis King two years earlier in his autobiography *Yesterday Came Suddenly*, she made similar attempts to have them cut. In his book he had written,

Jerry would visit Olivia every afternoon, however busy she might be on a book and however busy he might be in his practice. He was clearly devoted; but no less clearly he was devoted to his quiet, patient, highly intelligent wife. Of the four people involved in this odd situation, none showed any jealousy or hurt. They would entertain each other with unalloyed affection. I found this civilised and sensible.

When Constable brought out a paperback edition of this book no cuts were made.

The Danger Tree was not shortlisted for the Booker, though a number of tipsters in the Sunday papers prophesied that it would be. In compensation, the *Yorkshire Post* selected it as the Best Novel of 1977, which Olivia first thought 'fairly okay' and later changed to 'very okay indeed'. When she went up to receive this award in January 1978 she was hobbling on a stick. The reason for this was that, on the summer's day on which she was present at the scattering of Gerhardie's ashes in the Rose Garden of Regent's Park, she had suffered an accident. Among those present at that scattering were Gerhardie's niece Christina and her husband Hugh Street, Gerhardie's literary executor Anne Amyes, Michael Ivens, Michael Holroyd, Francis King, J. G. Farrell and Jerry Slattery. After the ashes had been scattered, Olivia walked towards a favourite willow tree, which she and William had often admired. Later, she was to refer to the weeping willow, half in irony, as 'The Danger Tree'. As she approached it she mysteriously fell and broke her hip. A columnist from the *Evening Standard* reported her in the 'Londoner's Diary' as saying, 'Some extra power caught my foot.' To Francis King she later remarked, seemingly in all seriousness, 'William was always pulling my leg. That was the last time he did so.'

The *Yorkshire Post* provided a wheelchair, which Reggie showed himself surprisingly adept at manipulating. Olivia had only one criticism: 'I wish his smart suit had been less crumpled.'

At the luncheon itself she found herself sitting next to Joyce Grenfell, who amused those around her by saying, 'At least in your own home you know where the draughts come from.' Olivia thought the food better than at the few Booker Prize gatherings that she had attended and was delighted when she heard that there was a record attendance – 701 guests in all.

On the way back to London she said to Reggie in the train, 'Let me have one moan. Alistair Horne was given a cheque for £350; his account of the Algerian War in the 1950s is an excellent book, but it's non-fiction. I was given £250 and mine was fiction. Literary judges have a habit of discriminating against novels.' Then she sighed. 'Still, one's got to be grateful for small mercies, I suppose.'

For the next two years there were times when Olivia often wished that she did not have to wake up. Jerry's death had been a far greater loss than any other, even her brother's. On occasion she would say, 'I'm still here, so somebody wants me to complete the Trilogy.' But she began to think that the Pringles should take more of a back seat, despite the fact that they kept edging forward. 'Long live Simon Boulderstone. He's the new star! That's my egg.'

Chapter 40

The Sum of Things

Olivia was cheered in her grief about Jerry when she heard on the grapevine that the Balkan Trilogy, already adapted for radio, was beginning to be talked about as a television possibility. Various production companies had expressed an urgency to see the two remaining volumes even in typescript. The names of possible adapters were bandied about and include Adrian Mitchell, Kenneth Martins and Fay Weldon. Nothing came of any of them and by 1980 she was saying, 'It will be just my luck if it's televised after my demise.' Her prediction proved correct.

On the morning of 4 July 1980, Olivia was by herself in her flat feeling bored and lonely. Reggie was away, as he often was, and she did not look forward at all to the weekend on her own. Then the telephone rang.

It was Parvin Laurence who, finding Olivia rather depressed, promptly asked her down to Billingham Manor for the weekend. She and Michael, she said, would pick her up with her cat Miou some time in the late afternoon. Meanwhile Olivia had to clean out Reggie's room in preparation for a new bed that she had ordered from Heal's.

Reggie's room was, as always, a tip. There were old newspapers scattered over the floor – he would never allow Olivia to throw anything away; also, scripts of plays and dozens of books about Irish history, for he had never quite abandoned the idea of writing a history of Ireland, commissioned by Methuen way back in 1962.

In 1975, at a meeting held at PEN in which Francis King interviewed Olivia, she had said in answer to a question from a member of the audience that willpower and the ability to shut oneself away were two essential requirements for a writer. She admitted that her husband lacked the second. 'He cannot bear being on his own,' she said. She recalled, too, how when she had first met Reggie as a young man, he was all set to write a book about D. H. Lawrence. But Reggie's promised book had been lost in talk. Earlier that year he had even gone so far as to promise Olivia that he would at long last get down to his commissioned history of Ireland. She had severe doubts about this. 'It's already thirteen years overdue,' was how she put it to the PEN audience.

The theme of this Irish book was to be 'In Ireland there is no such thing as defeat; it is only that the victory has been delayed'. This statement, which occurs in Olivia's first novel *The Wind Changes*, had greatly impressed Reggie and given him an indication of the profound understanding of history that his future wife possessed. Moreover, unlike the D. H. Lawrence book, he had in fact written the opening chapter, which he had passed round to a few chosen friends. His prose style was self-consciously poetic and much influenced by Dylan Thomas. Reggie had once confided in Parvin, 'I always felt I could have been a poet like Charles Causley. But I'm afraid I had grander ambitions than that.'

All his life Reggie, like Dylan Thomas, had a passion for hyphenated words. Sometimes Olivia would tease him about this weakness. In the Preface that he wrote in 1985, after Olivia's death, for the new edition of her book *The Remarkable Expedition* the hyphens were much in evidence. On the first page he described how he and Olivia in 1939 boarded the Simplon-Express for Bucharest, leaving behind them a London of 'trench-digging', 'sandbag-filling' and 'tree-chopping'.

After Reggie's bed had been delivered by Heal's, Olivia began to sort out his papers and stack them into piles. It was ages since she had had the chance to clean the carpet in his room, which was thick with dust. 'Don't worry,' he used to say to her. 'There's nothing wrong with a bit of dust.' Sometimes he would sing her snatches from a song in *Cymbeline*, adapting the words to suit the occasion: 'Golden lads and lasses must like busy housewives come to dust.'

Reggie, following very much in the steps of Commander Manning, had a fund of such Shakespearean jokes. Another he called 'The Bugger's Creed', which derived from a line in one of the Sonnets (129): 'Before, a joy proposed; behind, a dream.' Reggie claimed that Auden had first come up with this quip; but when in 1976 Reggie met Edward Upward, who had been a close friend of Auden's, Edward told him it was really Christopher Isherwood's. Another friend had entertained Olivia with what he called 'The Gay Concise Shakespeare', consisting of two lines:

'Let those that are chaste stay as they are . . .'
'Pray you, undo this button. Thank you, sir . . .'

She had repeated this to Reggie, who had quickly appropriated it into his own repertoire.

Olivia felt exhausted after she had hoovered and cleaned out his room. She grilled herself a couple of rashers of bacon and a tomato – her staple diet when she was on her own – packed up Miou's food in a plastic box and got his basket out ready for the journey.

The Laurences arrived at exactly four o'clock and the company then just managed to catch the 5.30 ferry from Southampton to East Cowes. Miou, who was well accustomed to travelling by boat, was a model of good behaviour.

On the ferry Michael bought Olivia a stiff gin and tonic, which cheered her up. At Newport, on the way to Billingham Manor, they stopped to buy fish and chips for supper. But on arrival at the house Olivia's first thought was of Miou's supper – turkey breast, which was his favourite. In the scullery she started to cut up the meat with the kitchen scissors, when she suddenly cried out, 'Oh! My God, my head!'

Michael rushed in to see what was up and helped her on to the sofa in the hall. Having a fair idea that she had had a stroke, he rang up a fellow doctor in Southampton to discuss what course of action he should take. Together, they agreed that she had a forty to sixty per cent chance of recovery, but ruled out the idea of any surgery at her age. The best thing, it was decided, would be to get her into Ryde County Hospital and Michael then telephoned for an ambulance.

The following day, which was a Saturday, Michael rang June Braybrooke in Cowes. 'I've got some bad news,' he told her. 'I am afraid Olivia is in hospital in Ryde. She was taken there last night. She'd very much like to see you.'

Later that afternoon he collected the Braybrookes and took them over to Ryde Hospital, where Olivia was in a small side ward. She was wide awake when they arrived and pleased to see her visitors. She was distressed, though, to think that she might have to miss the Foyle's Literary Luncheon, to which she had been invited in the following week as a special guest. 'It's the first time I've been asked to go,' she said. 'Isn't it just my luck to be taken ill? Do you think I'll be able to make the lunch, Michael?'

'There's a very good chance that you will,' he replied reassuringly.

But Olivia's chief concern was for her eighteen-year-old Burmese cat. 'What will happen to my poor Miou?' she asked sadly and June then reminded her of the pact, made between them several years before, to look after each other's cats in the event of illness. 'I'll take care of him until you're better.'

Olivia went into great detail about Miou's diet. He was to have steamed plaice for breakfast. 'Nothing out of a tin,' she emphasised. 'You never know what goes into those tins.'

Then she began to flag and became slightly muddled. 'What will *you* all have for breakfast?' she said. 'Are there any good restaurants round here? What is the name of this place by the way?'

Michael asked her if she wanted him to get in touch with Reggie.

'Yes,' she said. 'But don't worry him about anything.'

'Do you know where he is?' Michael asked.

'Yes, in Ireland. I'm not sure where. You could try his landlady in Derry.'

There was a pause, and when Olivia spoke to them again her voice was as strong and powerful as it had ever been. 'Don't hang about as if you're waiting for a train to go, go *now*!'

Everyone left.

It was not easy to get hold of Reggie – it never was. Eventually he was tracked down and came at once to the Isle of Wight. There, he stayed in Ryde with his old Birmingham school friend Bobby Case. Wanting, as usual, to make out that his friends were also Olivia's, he used to tell people how fond she was of the Cases. In fact, Olivia spoke quite critically of them. 'Well-meaning or not,' she said, 'they are the greatest bores this side of Suez.'

After Reggie had been to see Olivia in hospital, he told friends that he was hopeful about her state. Yet he discouraged them from visiting her. The reason for this, which was only later discovered, was that he knew she would not wish her friends to see her looking a wreck. Her hair was straggly in some places and standing on end in others, whereas in the past she had always been well made-up and meticulously groomed. 'But do send her postcards,' Reggie urged everyone. 'Only for God's sake don't say anything about the stroke.'

David Gascoyne sent her a postcard of a parrot, the facetiously maladroit caption of which read, 'I've just had a stroke of luck.' Reggie did not show Olivia the card, but merely read out Gascoyne's message to her.

At the beginning of that month her publishers Weidenfeld had circulated some advance copies of the last volume of the Levant Trilogy. Auberon Waugh, who had received one of these, sent Olivia a letter in which he said he much looked forward to reading it. Reggie read this out to Olivia and asked if he should write back. 'Certainly not,' she whispered crossly. 'Never on any account suck up to reviewers.'

Michael Laurence had the habit of dropping in on Olivia at the hospital whenever he was on the island and had a free moment, and would read aloud to her from an Arnold Bennett novel. This she much enjoyed. Michael apologised to her for not being able to put on a Staffordshire accent. 'I was never any good at accents myself,' Olivia said consolingly.

Parvin, who was on holiday at Billingham, saw Olivia daily. Quite often she would find her dozing. Once, when she and June visited her together, Olivia was lying on her side, with her knees drawn up, staring at the blank wall. 'Miou sends his love,' June told her, hoping it might comfort her. She did not reply, but instead raised her left hand in a vague kind of salute.

During these last days Olivia began to withdraw more and more into herself. She scarcely uttered a word to anyone, even the nurses. On 23 July Parvin arrived earlier than usual at the hospital, only to be told she could not see Olivia as she was in a terminal state. 'Do you mean that you think that my friend should die alone?' she asked, and walked straight past the nurses into Olivia's room and sat down by the bed. Olivia was now deeply unconscious and breathing heavily. As the hospital clock struck twelve, she died with Parvin next to her holding her hand.

Reggie did not arrive at the hospital until two in the afternoon. After graciously thanking the nurses for their care and kindness to Olivia, he left the hospital and wandered down to the seafront, stopping for a short time at one of the tea shops in Union Street that he and Olivia particularly liked. The idea of going to a pub – so often his solution to a problem or a mood of depression – was out of the question; he needed to be on his own to think things out.

At about six in the evening he got round to ringing the Braybrookes and explained to Neville that he had gone to London the day before* to give himself something to do: 'I simply couldn't bear to sit by my Olivia and

---

* To meet the Church Commissioners, who were the landlords of their flat in Marlborough Place.

watch her fade away inch by inch. It's a nightmare.' Then he said he was going to stay on with the Cases in Ryde, but would definitely keep in touch regularly. His voice sounded full of tears. Before ringing off he asked after Miou.

At exactly twelve noon, on the day of Olivia's death, Miou had settled down on the Braybrookes' bed and fallen fast asleep. Up until then he had spent the morning wandering restlessly about the house. For most of the past three weeks he had chosen to sit on a large oval table, looking out over the Solent in case his mistress should come by sea to fetch him; at other times he would sit on a small writing table, looking out over the road, in case she should be coming by car. However, he adapted himself very well and soon established a routine of visiting the kitchens of the nearby yacht clubs at lunchtime, but always returning home in time for tea. Miou's tea, Olivia had instructed June firmly, should consist of turkey breasts, lightly braised, and nothing else. But Miou also developed a taste for shrimps and doughnuts. He died in the first part of September.

Olivia's funeral was held on 28 July, five days after her death. On the day she died, Michael Laurence had telephoned the BBC and her death was announced on the nine o'clock news. The next day *The Times* ran a long obituary, but omitted to mention her fifth novel, *The Doves of Venus*, which was later to become a set book for schools. At the weekend the *Observer* and the *Sunday Telegraph* carried signed obituaries by Anthony Burgess and Neville Braybrooke. The *Sunday Times*, finding that they had nothing in stock, hastily commissioned Julian Mitchell to write a piece, which appeared on the following Sunday. Paul Binding and Francis King contributed appreciations to the *New Statesman* and the *Spectator* respectively. The *Weekly Press*, an Isle of Wight paper (now defunct), referred to Olivia as 'the Island novelist', which would have pleased her. It was noticeable that no women were commissioned to write pieces about her. Unsurprisingly, there was some uncertainty about her precise age, which was seventy-two. Most of the obituary writers placed her in her sixties, which might also have pleased her. Walter Allen, somewhat ungallantly, protested to *The Times* three days later about this mis-apprehension: 'I never knew Olivia to divulge her age, but I do not believe that she was only twenty-two in 1939.' She was in fact thirty-one.

Anthony Burgess in the *Observer* referred to her Balkan and Levant Trilogies as 'forming a hexateuch'. This term is generally used to describe the first six books of the Old Testament. Olivia had once said, 'How constantly Anthony forces one to consult a dictionary. Still you must hand it to him – his pieces are always lively as well as erudite.'

Julian Mitchell quoted a letter of hers: 'The enemy is the artificial nightingale which is much prettier to look at and does not get tired like the real bird.' He summed up, 'Olivia was the real bird, and she flew higher than most.' He also speculated, 'With proper recognition she might have soared even higher.'

For the last thirty years of her life Olivia was deeply aware of what she described as 'the recognition factor'. When at PEN in 1975 she had been asked about the sales of her books, she had said that naturally she would like to be a best-seller, but that if she had to make a choice between being a best-seller and a writer's writer, she would opt for the latter. Once, when she was yet again complaining that she was not sufficiently well-known, Francis King tried to console her: 'But many years hence you will still be widely read and loved.'

'Yes, yes,' she countered. 'But I want to be really famous now! *Now!*'

To encourage her when she was depressed, June Braybrooke used to say to her, 'Your great talent must be its own reward.'

To this Olivia replied sadly on one occasion, 'But I do wish I could be famous like Peter Sellers.'

By an irony of fate Olivia Manning died on the same day as Peter Sellers. At a booksellers' conference held in Wandsworth the next day, the well-known Hampstead bookseller Ian Norrie said that he had an imaginary picture of her in the next world complaining, 'Wasn't it just my luck to die on the same day as Peter Sellers? He'll get most of the space.'

And so it turned out.

In her will, which Olivia had drawn up two years before her death, she left her flat and possessions to Reggie, and appointed him to be one of her three literary executors: the other two were Neville Braybrooke and Francis King. Her solicitors were Farrer & Co. who, she liked to remind friends, were also the Queen's. Olivia's estate was valued at £167,563, which was almost double the amount left by her friend Ivy Compton-Burnett. Olivia bequeathed nine legacies of £500 each: three to her literary executors, one to Alex Priggle (who had looked after the flat for many years) and five to animal welfare societies. At one stage she had only considered the Cats' Protection League, but on Reggie's advice she included four other animal societies – the Wood Green Animal Shelter, the Blue Cross Animal Welfare Society, the International Fund for Animal Welfare and the Friends' Animals League.

Her last will and testament was dated 29 April 1978. Subsequently Olivia wrote another will, which she discussed with Reggie in detail. In this she increased the legacies for her literary executors and animal charities to £2000 apiece. She also gave Reggie clear instructions that, after his death, she wished her shares and future royalties to be divided between the five animal trusts. He said he thought that two friends, who were both animal lovers, should be added to the list – June Braybrooke and Johnny, the widow of Jerry Slattery. Olivia wholeheartedly agreed. However this second will, which she herself typed out at home and put away in a drawer among her papers, she never actually showed to Reggie or Farrer & Co. and Reggie did not discover it in her desk until after her death. But as soon as he did find it, he immediately got in touch with Kevin Kennedy, who was a friend and partner of Farrer & Co., and together they arranged that Olivia's wishes should be carried out, and on 27 September a deed of variation was executed to this effect.

Reggie was not always as businesslike as this. After he retired from the BBC his dealings with the Inland Revenue were often naïve and eccentric. He did have his own erratic accounting system, and Olivia had eventually persuaded him to go to the tax office and explain it.

In an attempt to make things simpler for the Inland Revenue, he then copied out all the details from his payment slips on to a clean sheet of paper and threw away the slips.

'All shipshape and above board,' he said proudly as he presented his accounts in person to the local tax collector.

'But Mr Smith,' said the tax collector despairingly, 'you have, I'm afraid, destroyed all your most vital evidence.'

'Well,' replied Reggie, 'it's up to you then. Think of a sum and I'll obviously go along with whatever you say.'

The tax collector thought such a suggestion highly irregular and Reggie had to set about writing round for duplicates of the payment slips that he had so methodically thrown away.

During her lifetime Olivia had often expressed the wish that her library and Reggie's collection of books should be kept together: between them they owned many signed and rare editions. Olivia always made a point of asking writers to sign their books for her. In 1972, at a party given by Duckworth to launch Beryl Bainbridge's novel *Harriet Said*, she asked Beryl to autograph a copy for her. 'What shall I write in it?' asked Beryl, rather flustered and self-conscious.

'Oh,' said Olivia. 'Just put – "with admiration and love".'

A few years later at the Aladdin second-hand bookshop in Cowes, Olivia came across a copy of her novel *The Spoilt City*, which she had signed and autographed for a friend in 1962. It was priced at fifty pence.

'I bet Iris Murdoch's signed first editions fetch more than that,' Olivia said tartly as she bought back her own book.

'Well, Iris Murdoch's a famous author, isn't she?' countered the bookseller.

When Francis King and Olivia once visited Glynde Manor together from his Brighton house, a second-hand book sale for charity was taking place. Francis held up a copy of *School for Love* and announced in triumph, 'Look what I've found!' He then added tactlessly, 'Only twenty pee!'

Olivia, far from pleased, complained to the woman in charge, 'You're *giving* that book away! It's a first edition. It's worth *far* more.'

Reggie decided that Olivia should be cremated and this took place at Whippingham Crematorium on the Isle of Wight. It was a Church of England service and was due to begin at eleven o'clock. Just as the clock struck the hour, a large black limousine carrying the chief mourners – Reggie and his brother Roy and Roy's wife Brenda – came racing round the corner and screeched to a halt. 'Reggie will be late even for my funeral,' Olivia had said many times.

Reggie shook hands with the clergyman and then, turning to his brother, whispered, 'He's got egg on his cassock.' Reggie had been uncertain whether there should be flowers. Three days before he had ruled them out completely. Then, on the afternoon before, he changed his mind. 'Tell everyone that they can bring flowers if they want to,' he told June on the phone. Some people were able to order flowers through Interflora; others brought them from their own gardens. A bunch picked by the Laurence children had this message attached to it: 'Dearest Olivia, we will see you in Heaven.' David Gascoyne sent his wife Judy to represent him. He explained that, since both his parents had been cremated at Whippingham, the place held such sad memories for him that he could not bear the thought of returning to it. 'But I'll wear a black tie for Olivia all day,' he promised his wife. This she faithfully relayed to all those present.

The clergyman officiating gave no address and no relatives or friends had been invited to speak about Olivia. The service was over within a quarter of an hour. As the twenty or so mourners filed out of the chapel, Reggie remarked on how he hated the canned music played at such services. Then he came up with a phrase that he was to repeat over and over again in the days that followed: 'That service was a condom against grief.'

Bobby Case and his wife Joan had laid on the baked meats at Pandemonium, their house in Ryde. Bobby, who was head of the Chester Beatty Institute for Cancer Research, was also an expert at making pork pies. 'You'll never taste anything to equal them,' announced Reggie, full of pride at having such a clever friend. In the same way that Olivia regarded Billingham Manor as her second home, so Reggie looked on Pandemonium as his.

Among the friends who came back to the Cases' house after the funeral was a middle-aged Australian about whom nobody seemed to know anything at all. He said that he was called Andrew Smuts, but kept saying to everyone, 'Call me Smuttie for short.' He had travelled down from Waterloo on the same train as Johnny Slattery, with whom he had chanced to get into conversation and had then discovered that they were both bound for the same destination. At Portsmouth Harbour he bought a ticket for the ferry, boasting that so far he had travelled on a platform ticket. On the boat he began to talk about his friendship with Reggie and how he had once had a small part in one of his drama productions. 'Have you heard the story', he asked Johnny, 'about the two blokes on a desert island? Neither had ever met before, but they were both pals of Reggie Smith.' Smuttie said he had vague memories of Olivia sitting in the George, near the BBC, and that he had seen her death announced on television. 'I owe Reggie a lot,' he said.

At about two o'clock in the afternoon, after several of the mourners had left, Reggie took Smuttie off to the pub round the corner. When Reggie returned he was on his own. 'You won't believe this,' he told the Cases, 'but no sooner had Smuttie repaid the hundred quid he'd borrowed off me several years ago than he asked for it back plus an extra fifty.'

Reggie had a number of hangers-on like Smuttie. If he had cash in the bank, he lent money to anyone without question. To a hard-working student* at Coleraine University, who had had a run of bad luck, he ended a postcard, 'Soon more cash to help.'

In the weeks following Olivia's death, Reggie wandered about the country aimlessly. Being perpetually on the move was, he had discovered, one way of assuaging his grief.

Immediately following the funeral, he had two engagements to fulfil at the Edinburgh Festival; then, later in August, there were poetry readings in Cornwall and Aberystwyth. He made attempts to keep in touch with old friends. On the telephone he would talk about Olivia as if she were still alive and writing in the room next door.

He could not bring himself to go back to their flat in London.

It was Michael Laurence, in early September, who finally took him back to the flat. Reggie put his key in the front door, walked ahead of Michael into the sitting room, then slumped down heavily on to the sofa. Staring round at the books and pictures that he and Olivia had collected over the years, and with tears streaming down his cheeks, he said, 'Now I must really accept the fact that my Olivia is dead.'

Throughout this period of mourning, Reggie's abrupt transitions between desolate weeping and almost hysterical joviality showed him behaving precisely as Olivia had had Guy behave in the Levant Trilogy during the time when he thought that Harriet had perished in the torpedoed liner on its voyage to England. Her imagining had been strikingly prophetic.

On 23 July every year, the anniversary of Olivia's death, Reggie would put an announcement in the 'In Memoriam' column of *The Times*. From her last book he always quoted the same phrase: 'The sadness of things passing.'

Diana Robson, the actress whom Reggie married in 1981, was questioned in November 1987 by a reporter from the *Daily Mail* about Reggie's relationship with Olivia. Reggie had already been dead two years. The

---

* This same student, Andrew Waterman, wrote an affectionate poem after Reggie's death, subsequently published in the *London Magazine*, a couplet of which ran,

> The world's a smaller place,
> That can't look up and see your face.

pretext was the first showing on television of Olivia's Balkan and Levant Trilogies, under the overall title of *Fortunes of War*. Diana, with dignity and style, told the reporter, who was obviously looking for a scandalous revelation, that Reggie had certain firm beliefs. 'One of these was that if you were married, you were married for life.' She added, 'He had certain rules – and this was one of them.' It had been a rule with which Olivia totally agreed.

After the cremation at Whippingham, Olivia's ashes were taken to Ryde to await instructions from Reggie as to where their final resting place should be. They remained at the undertakers for nearly four years. Reggie could not bring himself to decide what should be done with them.

When Olivia's brother Oliver had been lost at sea, Reggie was under the impression – as indeed Olivia and her parents had always been – that his plane had crashed into the sea by the Nab Tower, off Portsmouth. So Reggie began to get the feeling that Olivia's ashes should be scattered in the Solent. He also started to think that during the scattering some minister of religion should officiate. Rather tentatively he began to make enquiries. There were a number of clergymen, met at the BBC, who might now help. So, from time to time Neville Braybrooke, Francis King and Michael Laurence met with Reggie to discuss how things were going. Yet, in each instance, Reggie found a reason for another year's delay – either because of work at the university, or because of giving lectures abroad. It seems he could not face so final an act as scattering the ashes. In late 1981 he had married again and in 1984 he was going in and out of hospital for treatment. In May 1985 he died.

The last time that Neville Braybrooke saw Reggie was in April 1985 when he went to visit him at the Royal Free Hospital in Hampstead, where he was being treated for cirrhosis of the liver. This was three weeks before his death. As always, Reggie was bursting with energy and ideas.

He had started work on an autobiography, provisionally entitled 'Party Ticket', which Weidenfeld, on the strength of his synopsis, were anxious to publish. Recently, too, Virago had brought out his edition of *The Writings of Anna Wickham*, which had been widely reviewed. When this book was launched, he and Diana Quick had given a reading from it at the Poetry Society, at which there had been standing room only. 'I was absolutely amazed,' Reggie said afterwards, 'because earlier in the day we had been told that only six people had booked seats.'

In spite of the uncertain state of his health – he had been in and out of hospital for the past few months – Reggie was full of plans for a double bill of one-act plays, which the Falcon Theatre in Camden Town wanted him to direct. The plays were W. H. Auden's early charade *Paid on Both Sides* and T. S. Eliot's unfinished drama *Sweeney Agonistes*. Reggie had designed a simple and practical set, which would serve both plays – a backdrop that could be either the open sky or a high wall. 'Eliot's name will draw the public at large,' Reggie announced enthusiastically, 'and so give them a chance also to see one of Auden's lesser-known pieces. Up till now only university groups have had the nerve to put it on.'

Soon, by now sitting up in his bed, he began to talk excitedly about Kipling's sea poetry – much of which he knew by heart. As often, his enthusiasm carried him away. 'What a wonderful ear Kipling had', he said, 'for the names of ships.' Then he began to recite from 'Mine Sweepers':

> Mines reported in the fairway,
> Warn all traffic and detain.
> 'Sent up *Unity, Claribel, Assyrian, Stormcock* and *Golden Gain.*'

He cleared his throat and took a sip of water. 'Have you ever thought about the amazing word "dazzle"?' he asked Neville. 'Listen to this from "The Golden Vanity":

> The waters came aboard her and did dazzle in their eyes.

Such a line reminds me of Webster's "Cover her face: mine eyes dazzle: she died young". And by the way, do you know Donne's "Mysteries are like the sun, dazzling, yet plain to all eyes"?'

When it was time for Neville to go, Reggie insisted on coming down to the entrance hall and seeing him off. As always, his manners were princely: William Gerhardie had once described him as a natural aristocrat. Going down in the lift, he said a word to everyone in it – whether he knew them or not.

In the entrance hall he said, 'Hang on a minute, I must get my *Evening Standard.*'

While he was buying the paper, Johnny Slattery came through the hospital doors and walked up to Neville. 'How is he?' she asked quietly and before Neville had time to reply, she said, 'He's an immensely brave man, you know – generous to a fault and he never complains.'

When Reggie came back with his paper he greeted Johnny affectionately and said, 'I'll just see Neville off. I won't be a second.'

Walking towards the glass doors he asked, 'What news of David Gascoyne? You won't forget to let me see the poem that he wrote about Mallarmé when he was sixteen, will you? It really is time the BBC did a programme on David. I must think seriously about this.'

These were the last words that Neville heard Reggie speak.

During the forty-one years of her marriage to Reggie, Olivia published twelve novels, three of which were dedicated to him. In some form or other the word 'dazzle' occurs in every book, except for *A Different Face*, where it was cut from the title-page of the manuscript by someone at Heinemann. 'I have never let a manuscript go out of the house without Reggie giving it the okay,' she confided to June Braybrooke.

On the afternoon of 8 May Diana Robson, now Reggie's wife, walked into the hospital, full of news for him about the launch party at the Imperial War Museum for the anthology *Poems of the Second World War*. This was published by Dent and sponsored by the Salamander Oasis Trust of which Reggie, succeeding Dan Davin, had been the chairman for the past eighteen months. One of the primary aims of the Trust was to reprint, or print for the first time, poems written between 1939 and 1945 by members of the Armed Forces.* Reggie, with his phenomenal memory, had been a great help to the publisher in recalling poems, or piecing them together.

The party at the Imperial War Museum had been a huge success and Diana was longing to tell Reggie all about it. As she approached his bed, she thought he must be asleep. She touched him lightly on the hand, which was quite warm – but he did not respond. He had just died.

Reggie Smith's funeral took place at Golders Green Crematorium at 2 p.m. on 18 May. There could not have been a greater contrast between his and Olivia's funeral. At Olivia's, on the Isle of Wight, only about twenty friends had been present, whereas for Reggie's the largest chapel had to be booked and, in spite of this, more than a hundred of the mourners had to

---

* Fifty years on, in 1990, Denis Healey in *The Times* spoke of the power that these poems had to illuminate history.

stand. The congregation came from all walks of life, ranging from commissionaires at Broadcasting House to the Director-General, and included poets, playwrights and actors as well as several ambassadors and diplomats.

The ceremony was a secular one and among those who spoke at it were Reggie's old friends Bobby Case and Wynford Vaughan Thomas. Beryl Bainbridge and T. P. McKenna read poems by Stevie Smith and Louis MacNeice, which Reggie had particularly liked. Maeve McKenna sang an unaccompanied Irish lament, which moved many to tears.

Memorial meetings were held for both Olivia and Reggie. Hers, at PEN on 19 September 1980, was quite modestly attended, while his, at the BBC concert hall on 31 July 1985, was packed out.

The one at PEN was presided over by Francis King, who said he hoped that, rather as at a Quaker meeting, anyone who felt moved to say something would do so. In the event nine people spoke, including Margaret Drabble, Robert Rubens, Jeremy Trafford, Michael Laurence and Ivor Porter. The last of these had been a junior lecturer at the university in Bucharest when Reggie was No. 2 at the British Institute there in the early months of the war. Antonia Fraser compared Olivia's appearance with that of a beautiful bright-eyed bird, and Raleigh Trevelyan was of the opinion that the posthumous publication of the last volume of her Levant Trilogy might well bring about that major success that had so sadly and mysteriously eluded her during the course of her lifetime.

As was to be expected, Reggie was called upon to speak last. It was obviously an ordeal for him. Of Olivia's 'gift' as a writer he had often spoken with great pride when among friends. But to speak of it now at a public gathering was another matter altogether and, up until this very evening, he had never even attempted to do so. The reason for this was probably due to the fact that he considered himself so much a part of Olivia that to proclaim her 'gift' was too near to self-aggrandisement.

He spoke using notes and described how Olivia was basically a shy person – but went on to explain that, in order to cover up this frailty, she had early on in her career adopted 'a complaining act'. Journalists, who should have known better, had latched on to this foible of hers and repeatedly mentioned it because it made good copy. Much the same thing had occurred with two other friends of his – Louis MacNeice and Dylan Thomas. MacNeice had acquired the reputation of being rude and quarrelsome, and Dylan Thomas was always represented in the Press as an alcoholic.

Reggie referred to Olivia's debt both to Edward Garnett and to Hamish Miles, who had launched her as a novelist at Cape. He spoke of her mother and father and the effect on her of being brought up in a Service family. To this way of life he attributed her dislike of cowardice in any form and in particular of 'those people who ratted on a job'. If anything enraged her, it was injustice to human beings plus cruelty to animals. Reggie summed up her character with 'Olivia was totally unafraid – physically, mentally and socially'.

At the memorial meeting held for Reggie at Broadcasting House every seat in the concert hall was taken. Some people even had to sit in the aisles. John Scotney was responsible for arranging this 'Celebration of the Life and Work of Professor R. D. Smith'. Tony Van Den Bergh was the compère. Adrian Mitchell read a poem that he had composed specially for the occasion entitled 'Reggie in Paradise' and John Hurt read a poem by Louis MacNeice about Birmingham in the Thirties. Anna Massey and Brian Pringle read extracts from the Balkan Trilogy, and Maxine Audley from Reggie's book on Anna Wickham. Adam Watson reminisced about Reggie in Romania, where they had first met in 1939, and John Tydeman talked about his work at the BBC after the war. David Hammond, a television producer from Belfast and a collector of folk songs, sang 'The Golden Vanity' – one of Reggie's favourite sea shanties.

The last person to speak was Michael Foot. In the programme Foot's subject was billed as 'Reggie the Socialist'. Being the outstanding orator that he was, he held his audience spellbound as he recalled the shameful causes that Britain had espoused during the 1930s. These causes had fired in Reggie a state of rebellion, which never left him for the rest of his life. Michael Foot then spoke of Olivia, and of how during the years of their long marriage Reggie must continuously have been observed 'by the most perceptive eye since Jane Austen'. Looking directly at his audience, he asked, 'Which of the rest of us could have survived such scrutiny?'

During the period when *Fortunes of War* was first being shown on television, Francis King and Neville Braybrooke received a number of telephone calls from reporters on the lookout for gossip about Reggie's private life. In Bucharest he had acquired something of a reputation as a womaniser. 'Who was the character of Sophie Oreseanu based on?' asked one columnist from the *Evening Standard*. 'Is she still around? Could I get hold of her?'

Neville decided to ignore the question. 'I wonder if you'd care to know on whom Prince Yakimov is based?' he countered.

'Not really,' came the reply. 'My editor is more interested in Guy Pringle and his girls.'

While Reggie was alive, Olivia's ashes remained at Ryde undertakers. Now Parvin went and collected them, and placed them carefully in the grandfather clock in the hall of Billingham Manor. Soon after this the Braybrookes discovered that Olivia's brother's plane had gone down off the Dorset coast, not in the Solent. Taking a boat out in the open sea might prove more hazardous than the protected waters off Cowes – and several of Olivia's old friends, who might want to attend, were getting frail. So a new resting-place had to be found.

Suddenly it occurred to the Braybrookes that a solution might be the garden at Billingham Manor. In its grounds, on the north-west side, was a beautiful old drinking trough for cattle, now filled with earth. It seemed the ideal resting place. So plans were set afoot and it was decided to ask a few friends down for August Bank Holiday weekend in 1987. Three days before the weekend the Braybrookes, who were staying at Billingham with Parvin, began to have doubts about whether they had made the right decision. More important, they wondered would Olivia herself have approved of what they were planning to do?

Parvin now told them of how in her home back in Kerman in Iran, if such a question had arisen, her mother would have taken down a copy of Hafiz's poems and, after saying a short prayer, would have opened it at random to find guidance from the poem in front of her. Parvin went on to explain that the poet need not necessarily be Hafiz: 'An English poet would do just as well.'

On the bookshelves in the drawing room there were collected editions of the poems of Wordsworth and Dylan Thomas. The people present then decided on Wordsworth, simply because it was the fatter volume. Back in the kitchen, they laid it on the table and, after a few moments of silent prayer, Neville opened it at random. There, before them, was Wordsworth's poem 'To the Daisy'.

Only the weekend before, Michael and his elder daughter, Nicola, had started to clear out the drinking trough in the garden, which was full of marguerites or moon daisies as they are sometimes called. After digging them up they had arranged them in neat piles on the grass. The Wordsworth poem now seemed to confirm that the right resting place had been chosen for Olivia.

Bank Holiday Saturday began as a fine, warm day, but by nine o'clock the weather suddenly started to change: storm clouds built up and there was a distant rumble of thunder. It was generally agreed that if the bad weather continued, the ceremony for Olivia would have to be held indoors. Beryl Bainbridge, Moni Cameron and Johnny Slattery had come down from London the night before – Johnny brought with her two decorative ivies to plant in memory of Olivia. By midday, when Francis King arrived with the Miller-Smiths, there was a break in the dark sky.

Other people who later turned up were Alan Clodd, the founder of the Enitharmon Press, who was staying at the time with the Gascoynes; Patrick Massey, who ran the Isle of Wight Model Railway; Edward Upward the novelist and his wife Hilda; and Mark and Jane Patterson from nearby Wolverton Manor.

Until that morning Olivia's ashes had been kept in the grey plastic urn supplied by the Ryde undertakers. Michael now transferred them into a pink silk scarf, which Olivia had given to June in Venice in 1966. This particular shade of geranium-pink was much loved by Olivia.

At exactly half past twelve the ceremony started, with Michael announcing that since this was not a religious service, everyone must consider themselves as individual celebrants. Neville began by reading some passages from Olivia's letters to June. Helen Miller-Smith, who had acted in several of Reggie's BBC productions, then read three scenes from the Balkan Trilogy, ending with the description of Harriet Pringle's arrival in Athens in September 1940: 'She was thankful to come to rest in so beautiful a place.' These words could well be applied to the Isle of Wight garden, which was now to be the last resting place of Harriet's creator.

The next person to read was David Gascoyne. But before he began, Neville read out a letter written by Olivia, dated 1980, in which she spoke of David as 'our most considerable poet alive', whom, she said, she would place above 'that august trio – MacNeice, Auden and Spender'. Quite overcome at hearing such praise, David began nervously to read 'The Gravel-Pit', which Olivia believed to be his finest poem. Judy his wife followed this with Christina Rossetti's 'Remembrance' – a poem that Olivia once told her that she would like to have read at her graveside.

Francis closed the proceedings with a short speech in praise of Olivia's work.

After he had finished speaking, Olivia's friends filed slowly past the granite drinking trough one by one, each stopping to pick up a handful of earth and scatter it over the pink silk scarf. Nicola then began to play on her recorder Olivia's favourite folk song:

> Fare thee well, O honey,
> Fare thee well . . .

Coda

Olivia Manning often alluded to death as a riddle. In 1961, when preparing to write a piece on Highgate Cemetery, she looked up a Dictionary of Quotations and found in it 344 entries on the subject. Six years before her own death, in a letter dated 20 June 1974, her final comment on the subject was, 'I hope death . . . is a wonderful freedom.'

Index